Bee Hill

Jaclyn E. Robinson

For the advocates, born and made.
The world is a better place with you in it.
Keep fighting the good fight.

And for my fellow Romance writers and readers.
You are the bee's knees.
Keep changing the world one love story at a time.

Table of Contents

Prologue 1
Chapter One 7
Chapter Two 18
Chapter Three 28
Chapter Four 40
Chapter Five 52
Chapter Six 64
Chapter Seven 75
Chapter Eight 88
Chapter Nine 99
Chapter Ten 112
Chapter Eleven 124
Chapter Twelve 137
Chapter Thirteen 149
Chapter Fourteen 159
Chapter Fifteen 172
Chapter Sixteen 183
Chapter Seventeen 195
Chapter Eighteen 209
Chapter Nineteen 219
Chapter Twenty 233
Chapter Twenty One 245
Chapter Twenty Two 258
Chapter Twenty Three 271
Chapter Twenty Four 284
Chapter Twenty Five 295
Chapter Twenty Six 305
Chapter Twenty Seven 318
Epilogue 332
Author's Note 349
Acknowledgments 351
Appendix 353
Author's Play List 354
About the Author 355

*"I can be changed by what happens to me.
But I refuse to be reduced by it."*

-Maya Angelou

Prologue

Once upon a time, in a land far, far away, there lived a princess—

Oh, dear reader, how I wish this were a typical fairytale. You see, sometimes a princess marries a REAL toad despite her best efforts to the contrary. And unfortunately for our princess, not even a toad in an expensive suit can hide his warts forever.

Kate Howard-Toliver slowly pushed open the door of the walk-in closet where she'd hidden, breathing a small sigh of relief at the sight of the empty bedroom—as if hiding would have done her any good if her husband had come to look for her, but she'd learned how to buy herself time when he was in a rage. Fortunately for her, it had only been the housekeeper coming upstairs to replace the bathroom linens. No doubt Preston had left for his club and wouldn't be home until late. Hopefully, he'd be too drunk to bother with her, or at the very least, get in another bullseye of a hit.

She moved stiffly toward the phone on the bedside table and quickly telephoned her mother; the long-distance phone bill wouldn't show up until after she was long gone.

"Hello, cow eyes," answered a pleasantly surprised female voice on the other end of the line.

Evidently, her parents had finally upgraded to a phone with caller ID. Kate swallowed the metallic tang of blood in her mouth and gently probed her throbbing cheekbone and eye.

Dammit, Preston—you and your oversized hands.

If they weren't so big, they would cover less real estate on her face. Kate winced. She didn't think he'd broken the bone, but it hurt like a semi-truck had smashed into the entire left side.

"Kate, sweetheart, are you there?" asked Beth Howard, sounding concerned and uncertain.

She didn't blame her mother. Kate had steadily shut her family out over the last two years as the man she'd married manipulated her away from them. In the beginning, it had been subtle.

"You're all I have, the only one I can depend on," Preston had said, using guilt and her own inherent desire to be helpful against her.

"Your family lives out in the middle of nowhere. I need to be in the city where the action is. No one conducts business in Midwell," he'd cajoled, though it was exactly what her family's horse farm did.

When it ceased to be enough to isolate her, he changed tactics, blaming it on her family.

"Let's be honest; they don't think I'm good enough for their precious baby girl," he'd sneered.

Which was true, but only because they had recognized him for the toad he was. Her personal favorite, though, had been the way he'd thrown her own words back at her.

"You promised to leave and cleave...or were your vows just empty promises?" he'd yelled one night after too many cocktails. Even now, she burned with embarrassment, thinking about the looks they'd received from those in the restaurant, and the pity in the server's eyes when he brought the check. But none of them had tried to interfere as she sought to diffuse the situation by capitulating once again.

The credit card bill came to the house on their first anniversary. It was a fluke, the card company said when she called with questions. They were in the process of going paperless, and the system had somehow reverted to a previously listed mailing address for anyone with a connected savings account. Normally, Preston sent anything to do with their finances to his office downtown.

"I have an accountant," he'd explained when she offered to take everything on once they were married. After all, she had an MBA from Stanford she wasn't using, and she'd always envisioned being his partner at home if not at work.

"No need to get your hands dirty, princess." His endearment grated more than soothed. In retrospect, it should have been her first clue as to how things would go between them.

It didn't take her long to realize his travel expenses were for places other than the ones he'd claimed to be going to, places like California and Mexico—though Eastern Europe appeared to be a favorite haunt. Three days in one place, four in another. There were private planes, spas, jewelry, and clothing boutiques, none of which had anything to do with Kate. All she had to do was make a couple of phone calls to confirm her suspicions—Preston was having an affair, and a costly one from the looks of it.

When she'd confronted him, he'd merely laughed and excused it with, "If you were the kind of wife you're supposed to be, I wouldn't feel the need to go elsewhere."

She wanted to vomit. Instead, she pulled a suitcase from the closet and started packing. Moving back home meant admitting she'd been wrong about Preston, and her parents had been right, but at least she'd have her self-respect.

"Why do you have to make me angry," he'd seethed, the smell of bourbon pouring off of his breath and the spittle left behind on her cheek as she turned away, which, as it turned out, had only enraged him further as he applied pressure to her wrist. Yelping in pain, she'd dropped the suitcase from numb fingers, flinching as it hit the carpet with an ominous thud.

In the end, he'd thrown the hard-cased rectangle at the wall and gone off to his club, while she cowered in the bathroom and cried until sleep claimed her in blissful oblivion.

The flowers arrived the next morning. Preston apologized, showering her with gifts and affection. He promised to stop drinking.

Kate forgave him and tried to forget everything as she let him back into their bed. No one was perfect. She could fix this; she could be what he wanted. The mantra became her constant companion, the only voice in her head.

No one ever questioned the large hole in the drywall, not the household staff or the construction workers who came to repair the damage. What they thought happened, she would never know, but none of them met her gaze as Preston made an excuse for the damage.

Over the next year, they established a distinct pattern between the two of them. Kate walked on eggshells and became a husk of the woman she had once been, as though she'd become invisible, as much to herself as everyone else—except for Preston, who always found an excuse, no matter how small she made herself. The apologies and gifts dried up, but the violence continued to escalate, and any predictability on her husband's part vanished into thin air.

"Kate, please talk to me," pleaded Beth Howard on the other end of the line, bringing Kate back to the present.

She gingerly touched her lip and winced again. Her upper lip stung where his ring had split it open an hour ago. Unfortunately, his backhand swing had been spot-on, and her face the ball. It was no doubt swelling and turning a spectacular shade of purple to match the other injuries in various stages of healing in less visible places.

He was usually more careful about where he left his mark, but Kate had gotten reckless lately, speaking when silence would have been the more prudent choice. It was as if she'd developed a death wish. She shook her head and winced again. Maybe she had.

For as much as she resented those who knew but looked away or accepted lies and excuses, she despised herself more—for not accepting the truth sooner, for being afraid to leave, for loving a man who'd hurt her in every way.

She touched her lip once more. Preston would never let her leave, not willingly anyway. A pine box was all her future held if she stayed. Kate slid to the floor, her back against the bed. "Momma," she whispered. "I need help."

The next morning Preston left for work none the wiser, and her parents arrived to take her home. Kate removed the gawdy wedding set Preston had insisted on for his "princess," and tossed it into the bathroom garbage, her hand and heart lighter for the action. Stepping out into the stifling Atlanta heat with nothing but the clothes on her back, she held her head high despite the ugly evidence marking her body for every neighbor to see. Tomorrow looked brighter with each step she took away from the man who had tried and failed to snuff out her light with his words and fists.

Chapter 1

Ben

"Earth to earth, ashes to ashes, and dust to dust," intoned the minister.

Ben Galloway watched as they lowered the casket into the family plot of the small churchyard close to his ancestral estate. Monique Devereaux had been an intern with the British Museum in London when he'd called in a favor to request a curator. He wanted to catalogue the family's more unique artifacts in his quest to move everything into the twenty-first century. She arrived on his doorstep, soaked through, her clothes clinging to the curves of her body and not leaving much to the imagination.

"My car got stuck half a mile down the drive," she explained, her French accent shortening the vowels and giving the words a particular rhythm. The guttural "r" was endearing where it might otherwise have been annoying.

He knew his whole life was going to change the moment she looked at him with those enigmatic hazel eyes of hers, peeking out from beneath a heavy fringe of lashes. However, it was not in the way he'd hoped. Before the year was out, Monique had married his younger brother Felix, the child she carried evident in the whispered speculation amongst the guests and his brother's uncharacteristic reserve.

Ben still cursed the weather and fresh gravel he couldn't afford to lay at the time. Not because his life would be any different, but because the memory would be less dramatic.

He moved out of his family's manor the day after the wedding. "I have plans to renovate the old gamekeeper's cottage," was his murmured excuse to escape the newlyweds. Never mind how living in the dusty, dank, hovel was less than sensical. Henri arrived four months later under a full moon in the spring, and Ben accepted the mantel of uncle, burying his hopes of happiness in place of his brother's.

When Monique found a lump in her breast a year later, the doctor said she was lucky to catch it when she did. They'd all assumed she was in the clear until the severe headaches and tantrums began. Not prepared to lose the wife he'd hardly known or be a single father, Felix had left Henri with Ben, disappearing behind a camera lens and into the world of models and fashion icons he preferred.

"You know how it is, old chap. The world is calling, and a gentleman has to make a living these days," he'd explained without a glance in Henri's direction, who sat quietly with a board book and a stuffed monkey in his lap, as though he were reading.

Felix had always been the more charming of the Galloway brothers, comfortable in situations and amongst crowds of people who caused Ben to tug at his collar and seek a quiet room to hide away in. They were nothing alike, which he'd never resented until the woman he'd fallen for had chosen his brother instead. Still, it was Ben who spent hours beside Monique at a private hospital in London.

Whether he did it out of duty, or because of misplaced feelings, he stopped trying to decipher after the first miserable week. In time, the inoperable brain tumor took her sweet disposition, speech, and eventually her ability to regulate bodily functions or vital organs. It was a less than dignified way to go, and he'd been relieved when oblivion had finally stolen her away.

Ben glanced down as a small hand tucked itself into his large one. The head of dark wavy hair on the child was much like his own, except the eyes looking up at him resembled neither his grey, nor Felix's lighter ones. They were his mother's—hazel and bewitching, like green sea glass peeking from golden sand. It was almost more than he could bear, and the knowledge squeezed his heart painfully. Gently tugging on Henri's hand, he led them through the wrought-iron gate. Taking the worn path, trodden for generations by those who had come before, they made the solemn journey home to Bee Hill.

He snapped back to the present and the boy of seven standing beside him, staring straight ahead at the headstone before them but not attending to the words inscribed. They visited the churchyard every year for Monique's birthday, but this was the first time Henri had neglected to bring up the date. His teacher said he'd become more withdrawn than usual in the past few weeks, avoiding his peers altogether in lieu of his treasured books. It wasn't anything new, per se, but part of a larger pattern. Still, Ben worried it would impede his ability to progress socially if he continued in such a way.

Ben placed his hand on Henri's shoulder, giving it a gentle squeeze and signaling the end of their visit. Pushing open the lopsided gate sheltered beneath trees beginning to exchange their summer green for autumn's yellow, red, and orange hues, he said, "Go on; I'll be right behind you." He took the rare moment of solitude to loosen the tie at his throat. He'd worn the striped nuisance out of respect. The dead may not be keeping score, but he knew, which was enough.

The two-bedroom, stone cottage where they lived came into view as he crested the small rise and watched Henri run to meet the West Highland Terrier scampering across the field to greet them halfway down the path. His checkered accessory was nowhere in sight and had no doubt been discarded somewhere in the garden, where he'd been rolling in the dirt and turning his white coat a dingy beige.

"Sir Percival, you wee scoundrel, where is your bowtie? Don't you know you're supposed to be a dignified knight of the realm?" chided Henri, hands fisted on his hips.

Ben shook his head and chuckled. His amusement turned to concern as he squinted at the clouds above, prompting him to increase his pace at their threat of impending rain. The other two trailed hurriedly behind him.

The cottage was a far cry from the large house situated in the center of his family's estate, but with the rising costs of keeping up the place, Ben had chosen to turn his inheritance into a heritage site after Monique's death, moving Henri in with him instead.

Though it technically remained in the family, it was open to the public daily with the exception of holidays. The house had become a museum, filled with art and furniture, vestiges of the family who'd once occupied its rooms. His mother was certainly rolling over in her grave, but his father, a man of the common folk and one with a great deal of common sense, had accepted his decision. If all went as planned, Clatter Hall would still be standing, and in good repair, for Henri to make his own decision about it someday.

After a dinner of homemade bread and stew—its contents neatly separated for Henri on a large plate—and a quick round of chess, Ben tucked Henri into bed. Brushing back the dark forelock resting on a forehead bunched in thought, he recognized the pensive look on the child's face and tried to intercept whatever question lurked there by reaching for the bedside lamp, plunging the room into darkness. And, as usual, the dark did nothing to deter the precocious boy he loved more than life itself.

"Da?"

Ben smiled tenderly. Henri had begun calling him Da shortly after Monique's death. At first, he had painstakingly corrected him until his own father advised him to enjoy the rewards of fatherhood, since he'd already accepted the responsibilities of it.

Of course, Hamish's tendency to indulge his grandson's inquisitive nature beyond what others might consider appropriate for his age may have had something to do with it, as evidenced by Henri's reference to Felix as his "sperm donator," and refusal to call him by anything other than his given name. Though Ben did nothing to encourage it, he couldn't deny the sense of justice he felt either. His brother wasn't a bad sort, but he was noticeably absent.

"Do you think Mum is in Heaven with Gran?"

"Aye."

"Okay. It's all right for you to believe something different than I do."

"Thank you," Ben replied politely. It wasn't easy for Henri to be gracious when someone else believed something he deemed ambiguous. His acceptance was progress, and Ben hoped the teacher's recent observations didn't mean yet another set of obstacles to overcome. His mother had often said raising children was like dancing—three steps forward and two steps back.

Personally, he felt it more closely resembled driving uphill in heavy traffic and having the car stall because he hadn't released the clutch at exactly the right second. It was an odd combination of instinct and learned skill, all of which backfired from time to time.

"You're welcome," Henri said, keeping with their routine.

"Goodnight, my brave boy. I love you to the moon and back."

"The moon is 238,900 miles from Earth."

"Aye, which is why I used it to express how much I love you."

"The sun is further away at 94.056 million miles."

"Quite right. I love you to the sun and back," he said with a kiss to his son's forehead.

But after pointing out he understood the concept; Henri still didn't return the sentiment. Facts seemed to be more comfortable than emotions for him. Even so, Ben wasn't convinced his son didn't feel deeply, only that he struggled to express himself in the same way others did.

Ben quietly closed the door behind him, leaning against the frame and tugging his hair with frustration until it stood on end. What he'd actually wanted to tell Henri in response to his question was, I don't know. By the end of the day, he barely had the bandwidth to brush his teeth, let alone have a conversation that his child would consider highly illogical.

He'd resigned himself long ago to how complicated the creator of the universe must be since people themselves were complicated—the only difference being God's ability to see the big picture, and humanity's inability to see the forest for the trees. In the Galloway household, life felt like one big test of perspective most days.

Ben pushed away from the wall and made his way downstairs for the bottle of whisky he kept on hand for a day such as this. "Cheers, Monique," he toasted in a single gulp. He plopped into his favorite chair and selected a book from the pile he'd checked out from the library yesterday. "May the devil never dance on your grave or mine," he finished, letting the gold liquid sear away the day.

Kate

Kate glared at the back of the driver's head. She hated being late. If the cab driver had taken her suggestion and gone straight instead of going left, they would already be at the airport. Instead, they were zigging and zagging from Brooklyn to Queens.

Kate breathed in deeply and exhaled slowly. She repeated the action to no avail, the sounds coming from her more of an irritated huff than calm, practiced breaths. It was impossible to have control over everything. Still, a girl could try.

Prayer will solve most problems. And what it can't solve, an hour on a horse will, said her mother's voice in her head. Kate sighed. She hated it when her mother was right, and truthfully, she did miss riding. In fact, she missed the farm altogether, but living in New York made anonymity easier, thanks to its size and distance from her family—all except Uncle Joe, who had made the transition bearable by giving her a home above Walker's Pub.

Preston could find her if he tried, but so far he'd left her alone. Not oversharing, and her ex's determined separation from her family, had turned out to be a boon after the divorce. To her knowledge, he knew nothing about Uncle Joe or her mother's childhood in Brooklyn, which feasibly meant he also didn't know where she'd been hiding unless he went digging for answers.

Kate refrained from giving the cabbie a piece of her mind. The man obviously needed to update his GPS, but being impatient wouldn't get her there any sooner, and being unkind was bad karma. She pulled an emergency box of chocolate-covered almonds from her purse, popping them into her mouth and wishing her temper would fizzle out as quickly as it sparked.

Her sister Laura insisted peanut butter could solve all of life's problems, but Kate knew chocolate was the only practical solution. Crunching in earnest, she searched for a modicum of Zen in the scenery zipping by her window. After months of preparation, she'd have to run for her gate by the time this guy dropped her at the airport.

Kate looked at her feet and cursed her desire to wear heels. Laura was always telling her to buy more practical footwear. Then again, her sister was also the kind of person who arrived at the airport an hour before her flight and still stopped for snacks. They were as different as night and day, which was something she'd always appreciated. Except when it drove her batty.

"Why do you need heels when you're already a sleek five foot nine?" her sister had asked the last time they spoke.

In all fairness, Laura was petite, and Kate could understand why wearing heels at her height might seem a little overkill. The simple truth was that Kate liked the way they made her feel—like a boss. If she also wore them to spite her ex, so be it. She refused to let him take anything more from her. Preston had spent their entire marriage trying to make her feel less than the woman she was.

I don't need to be anyone but myself. I am not in control of how others feel about me. Kate was a self-declared self-help junkie. It didn't matter if it was related to business or personal growth, she had the latest *New York Times* or *Wall Street Journal* recommendation on hand, along with a stack of romance novels, because a happy ever after was good medicine for the soul.

Therapy, she knew from personal experience, was expensive while books were cheaper and less time-consuming. She considered her recent choice to be a more frugal one on all fronts. Besides, she'd rather spend her hard-earned money on a pair of Jimmy Choo red-soled heels—but only during the anniversary sale for twenty-five percent off.

As it turned out, retail therapy was also a strategy that worked well for her, but she was by no means an expert. And for all of her therapy, legitimate or otherwise, any potential romantic relationships had proven to be…complicated. Or rather, nonexistent. Fine; she avoided the possibility at all costs.

Kate didn't believe a woman needed to marry and have a

family to be a whole person. In fact, she knew half a dozen single women with thriving careers and personal lives without significant others. Of course, anyone who knew her history would never judge her for choosing a career over a romantic relationship. She, on the other hand, judged herself constantly because, deep down, she still wanted the fairytale ending. But no potential prince was worth the risk of meeting another slimy toad along the way.

Chapter 2

Kate

Arriving at her gate with tea, a side of chocolate shortbread, and forty minutes to spare before boarding began, Kate tried calling her baby sister again.

"Hi Kate," Laura said expectantly.

"Happy birthday, sweetie!"

"Thanks," Laura replied flatly.

Kate deliberately ignored her sister's tone, and the reason behind it, when she asked, "Any fun plans to celebrate?"

"Nope. I'm packing the last of my things before I leave tomorrow morning."

Kate took the hint and relented. "How was foaling season this year?"

"The same as always," said Laura shuffling around in the

background. "You know, exhausting, messy, and completely miraculous all at the same time. I don't think I'll ever get tired of watching new life come into this world."

"I wish I could've been there," Kate said, feeling guilty she'd missed the chance to see her sister.

"We missed you, but at least you didn't have to witness the group of men Momma paraded in front of me."

"You know, she has your best interest at heart," Kate continued softly, "It's been ten years since Drew."

When her sister grumbled in response, Kate switched topics.

"Anyway, you're going to love Brooklyn in the fall. I'm so glad you're willing to stay with Micky. He's going to adore his Auntie Laura. Uncle Joe has the key to the apartment and, who knows, you might decide to finally settle down."

Laura laughed in disbelief. "I haven't stayed anywhere longer than a few months at a time in a decade; why would I start now?" she asked, rhetorically. "So, are you all set for London?"

"I am. My manager has the shop covered, and if all goes well, I'll be back home for a Christmas visit. We can make the drive to the farm with Uncle Joe together this year."

Her sister laughed under her breath in response. "Why Uncle Joe won't get on a plane is beyond me, but it'll be easier to transport gifts, in any case." Laura paused before asking, "Speaking of Christmas, did you know Lon is planning to be gone? He said something about traveling for work."

"Now that you mention it, he did say he'd be gone for the

holidays, but I'm not sure it has anything to do with work," Kate said hesitantly, trying not to reveal more than she should, or give Laura any extra ammo against Lon. He was hurting and using alcohol and sex to staunch the bleeding. Their brother was only human. "Don't get me wrong, I'd love to see him, but he spirals into a pit every time he sees Abby."

"I know," said Laura with a scrunch of her nose. "I gave her the stink eye the last time I saw her in town. Of course, Momma caught me and gave me a good scolding," Laura complained.

"Don't worry, Momma hasn't forgiven her either. She's trying to kill her with kindness. Besides, Lon's moved on, even if it's only with any woman who looks at him twice."

"I'm not sure hooking up with someone in every bar he walks into qualifies as moving on. It's more of a cry for help," muttered Laura under her breath.

Kate agreed silently. Lon was in a dark place these days. She'd check in with him once she'd settled in. Trying to keep up with her siblings' life decisions was exhausting.

The boarding announcement for Kate's flight sounded in the background. "I've got to go, but I'll call you once things settle down across the pond. Oh, and you'll need to pick Micky up from the vet. I'll text you the address. Love you, moon pie!"

"Love you more, cow eyes," Laura recited right before Kate hung up.

If it all went according to plan, Micky would finally be with his forever home—aka, her baby sister—and Laura would find hers in Brooklyn. Kate had a good feeling about the whole situation and her intuition was never wrong, with the exception of Preston. But asking "what if" would leave her feeling morose and fabulous London was calling. The last thing she wanted to feel was sad and uncertain.

Kate pushed the Coach purse she'd scored from an upscale thrift store two seasons ago under the seat in front of her and sat back in her first-class seat. She'd been collecting miles and points for the last three years and had splurged on the upgrade to celebrate the new expansion of Lavender Honey & Co.

"Can I get you anything to drink? Champagne, perhaps?" asked the flight attendant.

Kate grinned in response. "Please," she said as she opened her laptop, bringing up the most recent email from one of her new suppliers in London. Like their earlier correspondence, it was short and to the point.

Subject: Lavender Honey & Co.

Dear Ms. Howard,

Please find the attached signed contract as requested. Per our agreement, Bee Hill will provide the specified products for sale in your London shop.

Regards,

Bennett A.K. Galloway, Proprietor

Bee Hill Lavender Farm

A mutual friend had introduced Kate, via email, to the proprietor of Bee Hill. She and Eliza Cabot had become fast friends during undergraduate studies, and roommates during their respective graduate programs at Stanford University. Now her friend was living out her wildest music dreams in Britain.

Following an interminable wait in line at customs with the rest of the masses entering the United Kingdom through London's Heathrow Airport, Kate powdered her nose and made her way to baggage claim, visually sorting through the piles of luggage. She was nothing if not practical, which made spotting her vintage Louis Vuitton suitcases with red hair scarves tied to the handles easy to find amongst the chaos of international travelers. Following Eliza's instructions, Kate walked quickly toward the exit of Terminal 3, excited to catch up and get a bite to eat with her friend.

Ben

Ben watched the tall blonde pause outside the sliding doors of the terminal. She was striking by any standard, but the whisky eyes he couldn't see from where he stood were no doubt the icing on the proverbial cake. Her sheath dress was the perfect shade of cherry and a lovely complement to her sun-kissed features, the accompanying jacket designed to accent her waist and curves, while a pair of black heels added to her already statuesque appearance. If clothing and accessories were any indication, this woman had a confidence he found more than a bit unnerving. Or attractive. He couldn't decide which and shook his head in annoyance.

Ben unbuttoned his collar to loosen the tie he'd worn for a meeting with Henri's teacher earlier in the day. When Eliza had rung an hour ago to say she was stuck north with the rain, and asked if he could "Please, please, pretty please," pick up her friend, he'd been annoyed. The American had merely laughed in her obnoxious way. "Ben, trust me when I say, you'll thank me someday."

"I highly doubt it," he'd complained at the time. He heard his best friend, Sam MacGregor, guffaw in the background. "Traitor," he yelled over speaker. "Is the weather so bad, or did you just talk Eli into staying another night?" Neither of them had given him a straightforward answer, and he'd eventually capitulated.

He was supposed to be in town for a visit with his sister Althea and her family. Letting Henri spend time with cousins was an effortless way to help him engage with peers—in as much as he ever did. Ben was also hopeful his sister might have insight into how to help his son re-engage at school. As a mother of three, she often had loads of advice to offer, and was more than eager to share it, solicited or otherwise. He figured the least he could do was ask when, he in fact, needed it.

With another glance at the photo Eliza had texted him, he quickly jumped out of the car and walked toward the woman to introduce himself. As he approached, Ben couldn't deny he felt a certain instinctual awareness, one he frankly had no idea what to do with. The freckles smattered across her cheeks and the bridge of her pert nose weren't helping either. His earlier annoyance resurged making his introduction come out tersely. "Eli sent me to pick you up."

"Oh?" she asked, looking confused and miffed over the change in plans.

He agreed with her assessment of the situation entirely. It would seem Eliza had forgotten to text her friend with the update. No doubt too busy snogging Sam. "Aye," he answered.

Brilliant response, he berated himself. *Absolutely brilliant.*

"And you are?" Kate asked expectantly.

"Ben Galloway." At least he'd remembered his name. He shouldn't expect anything better under the current circumstances. He tugged on his collar again.

"Bennett A.K. Galloway of Bee Hill?" she asked, arching a single delicate brow.

"Aye." Yet again, another brilliant response on his behalf. He sighed, irritated.

"Well, this certainly explains a few things."

He wasn't exactly sure what to make of her statement, but she appeared willing to go with him. Eliza owed him big, like free tickets to her next concert, big. And Ben would be all too happy to let her fiancé know exactly how things stood. He was man enough to admit Eliza scared him, but only because she could wordsmith him into agreeing to anything. Hence, his current situation. He was afraid she'd outsmart him into saying yes to something else if he negotiated directly on his own behalf. Of course, watching Sam grovel would be a bonus.

Ben placed Kate's luggage into the boot of his Range Rover, altogether forgetting to open her door. He quietly berated himself while sneaking a side glance at the attractive woman who slid into the passenger seat. He cringed over his abominable manners. If Lady Anne Bennett-Galloway were alive, she'd be more than a bit peeved with her namesake and eldest child. Still, he couldn't find it within himself to put forth an empty pleasantry.

He briefly wondered if this was how his son felt, except Ben didn't have the same kinds of challenges Henri did. Gripping the steering wheel tightly, he stayed silent and brooded. He was totally off his game if he'd ever had one to begin with. Monique's choice in his brother suggested otherwise.

Kate let out another sigh in the otherwise silent car as he parked on a side street a short distance from the hubbub of Portobello Road. Ben waited impatiently while she dug through her purse for the key.

"Aha!" she exclaimed in victory. Against his better judgment, the corner of his lips tugged upward. Ignoring the moment of weakness, he grabbed her luggage, one of which felt heavy enough to be bricks, and trudged up the narrow stairs to the fourth floor. The least he could do was carry them up, and this way he'd be able to meet his reflection in the mirror when he shaved tomorrow morning.

He placed her bags in the entry and turned to leave, but Kate surprised him by stepping into his space, her light floral scent assaulting his senses and sending his heart into a wild gallop. It was then he noticed her lips moving, a look of concern taking up residence between her brows. She was speaking, and like an absolute dolt he had missed what she'd said.

"I'm sorry, you were saying?"

"I was asking if we could arrange a time to meet."

Ben's brain shut down again. The whiff of perfume he inhaled every time she moved was extremely inconvenient.

"I like to get to know my vendors and familiarize myself with the product," explained Kate.

When he continued to stare blankly in response, hoping his brain would function again sometime before the end of the century, she further clarified. "For the purpose of quality control and advertising." Her tone belied a calm her expression thwarted.

He finally found his voice, only to say, "Can I ring you Monday morning with a few options?" How was it he'd let Eliza talk him into going into business with this woman? It was most definitely a bad idea, but he'd given his word. To back out now would be caddish, especially in light of his reasoning.

"Sure." She seemed to hesitate, then said, "Thanks again for the ride."

When he failed to produce a polite response, Ben reprimanded himself with a mumbled, "Plonker." Fortunately, she didn't appear to have heard him.

"Do you have any pub or restaurant recommendations for dinner?" Kate asked slowly, as though he were a small child who didn't understand.

I suppose I deserve it, he conceded.

"I was thinking maybe something in the neighborhood, within walking distance."

If Eliza had been the one to pick her up, they would have stopped for dinner, but Ben had been so eager to get as far away from her as possible he'd acted like a complete nitwit instead of the gentleman he normally was. It would have saved her looking for an expensive place nearby or the cost of a cab somewhere out of the way.

The problem was, she wasn't the kind of woman he could take to dinner once. Inevitably, he would want more. More dinners. More flowers in the air around her. More freckles across her nose and wondering if they were the only place she had them. More of a lengthy list of activities, which would be harmless enough until they led to something he'd longed for before death stole it all away. For the sake of his business, not to mention Henri, he couldn't take the enticing woman he was now partners with to dinner.

Chapter 3

Kate

Splendid. Just splendid. But also...workable.

Kate tapped her toe against the geometric tiled entry and tried to decide if she should laugh or pout about her new business partner. When she asked him for a dinner recommendation, he looked pained by the request. Ben had finally managed to push the answer past his firm lips, but not without a great deal of patience on her part.

"The restaurants on Portobello are decent, if a bit pricey. You can find the basics from the grocery store on the corner, but only if you hurry. They close early on Sundays."

It hadn't been anything she didn't know. She had done her research into the area during her previous trips to London for the shop and finding a place to live. If she'd hoped for something more, like an invitation to join him for dinner, it was his loss. The man was insufferable.

Kate had been genuinely surprised that Eliza had sent Ben to pick her up without notice, not to mention the recommendation as a business partner. Her friend must be doing him a favor. Perhaps the proprietor of Bee Hill was in dire need of the contract and money. Either way, it would seem her main supplier lacked manners or charm of any kind. It didn't bode well to be in business with a man so taciturn.

Though she would be lying if she didn't admit the sound of his voice, all English aristocracy—rich and clipped—hadn't conjured up girlish fantasies tied to a certain one of Miss Austen's books. Another shiver slid down her spine. Putting aside her romantic notions, though, he was officially the rudest man she'd ever met. Kate could forgive him for not getting her car door. After all, she knew how to look out for herself, even if she did appreciate the occasional gesture by a gentleman. When he'd started the car before she could tuck her legs in or reach for the door handle, however, she changed her mind.

The drive to her sublet flat in the Notting Hill district, a handful of blocks from her new shop, had been awkwardly quiet. She considered herself fairly determined, if not downright stubborn, but her efforts to draw the cranky, yet undeniably attractive, man into any semblance of small talk had proved fruitless. She'd tried to start a conversation multiple times only to receive minimal responses in return.

"What do the A. and K. stand for?" Kate asked. In retrospect, it may have been a tad nosy, but his silence made her all the more desperate to converse, like when she tried to give up chocolate on a particularly difficult day and ate two pints of Ben and Jerry's instead. Restraint rarely made the situation better in her experience. Besides, she justified, if he didn't want people to ask then he shouldn't sign his name with the initials to begin with.

"Pardon?"

"In your name," she said, exasperated.

"Alexander Keats," he replied in the smooth, cultured voice Kate couldn't quite dismiss.

While everything else about him was…annoying, the accent rubbed her in exactly the right way.

Of course, he'd barely spared a glance in her direction.

She wished he were less Darcy and more like Austen's Mr. Knightly. At least Knightly could be affable when he wasn't reprimanding Emma—who, by the way, deserved a good reprimanding. The girl seriously needed to learn to stay out of other people's business.

She tapped her toe again. The sooner she moved past her ridiculous notions, the better off they'd both be. No man could live up to her book boyfriend infatuations anyway, no matter how delicious the accent. *Bennett Alexander Keats Galloway*, she repeated to herself, rolling the sound of his name around in her head and enjoying the ebb and flow of syllables.

"Your name is like the count of a dance," she stated into the once again silent car.

"Pardon?"

"You know; two, three, one, three. It isn't exactly the waltz, but a steady rhythm nonetheless," Kate blurted out before thinking, the heat creeping into her cheeks as she pictured dancing around a ballroom in his arms. It was a girlhood fantasy, which he promptly deflated with his response.

He tugged at his collar and swallowed hard before merely giving her a look suggesting his tolerance for her presence was now at an all-time low, as if it had been higher a fraction ago.

So much for small talk or dancing.

If only Mister Tall, Dark, and Handsome were not her type, it would be easier to brush the guy off. Unfortunately, she'd always had a thing for the Cary Grants of the world. In fact, her ex-husband had only come to her attention because he'd pursued her with the single-mindedness of a predator with prey in sight. At the time she'd found it flattering. Preston was older and well connected.

In hindsight she'd come to realize he was more interested in owning and controlling her than having a relationship. She refused to pretend that love, or a protective nature, had been his motivation. He didn't know the meaning of either of those concepts.

One thing was for certain, though; she'd had enough falsehood to fill this lifetime and the next. On second thought, quiet and taciturn wasn't so bad. At least she knew what she was getting into. *Besides, who pretends to be a grump instead of sunshine?* she asked herself. *No one. Everyone knows you get more bees with blooms in the garden.*

Kate shut down her rambling long enough to finally take stock of her surroundings. After the Blitz of World War II, the neighborhood needed substantial rebuilding, but she'd chosen her building for its Victorian elegance. The apartment was inside a recently converted townhouse. She imagined hers, located as it was on the top floor, may have once been a children's nursery and sleeping quarters for their nurse.

Original crown molding graced the ceilings, and the hardwood floors creaked with age but shone with recent refinishing. There were new lighting fixtures throughout the open living space, accented with a couple of Tiffany side lamps bought at an antique store on her last visit. Wood block counters and stainless-steel appliances brought warmth and modern efficiency to the small kitchen, and while she didn't plan to spend any quality time in there, Kate liked the possibility it presented.

A single bedroom and bath formed the only walls in the space where a delicate chandelier held court and made up for the miniscule wardrobe. She sighed, eyeing the baggage by the door, slightly disheartened by the sight until she remembered Ben had brought them up for her. Kate smirked—there was hope for the grumpy Englishman yet. With a renewed pep in her step, she opened the single suitcase of books she'd allowed herself to bring, lifting the treasure to her nose and taking solace in the familiar smell of paper and ink.

....

Having become accustomed to driving on the left side of the road during her most recent visit, the narrow lanes through certain areas of the countryside and smaller villages still made her hold her breath when another car shared the road. It was akin to playing Russian roulette.

As promised, Ben texted on Monday, but was only able to make that day work for a meeting. As she passed the sign for Bee Hill and pulled into the drive, she realized why. Filled with a steady buzz of people coming out of the unpaved parking lot and going into the surrounding stone buildings, Ben obviously ran a successful business, despite his winning personality.

Or I bring out the best in him.

Kate rolled her eyes, since no one was present to see her. Either way, she wanted to kick herself for her earlier assumptions. Bennett A.K. Galloway had been looking to expand his business through her shop, but by no means did he seem desperate for a contract.

Parking the racer-striped Mini Cooper she'd rented, she dabbed a fresh coat of lightly tinted gloss onto her lips, using the rear-view mirror, before starting for the largest building a short distance from the lot. She kept a mental tally of the small improvements she'd make if Bee Hill were her business, starting with a paved parking lot and cobbled walkways between each building. With the constant damp, rain boots were necessary, but while gravel kept the mud puddles manageable, concrete screamed permanence and future growth.

It was a strategy she'd employed during graduate school, turning ideas over and over again in her head, looking for new ways to make any business flourish in an ever-changing economy. In the end, it came down to three simple concepts. First, provide good customer service, regardless of the customer. Second, but just as important, provide high quality goods—make the merchandise worth buying. Third, know your client and care about them. When the economy failed, because it eventually would, relationships and the loyalty they incurred could mean the difference between living in the black or perishing in the red.

Ben

Ben watched Kate pull into the gravel car park and emerge from the car, taking note of her from head to toe. Dressed more casually in trousers, a sweater, and wedge ankle boots today, she wore her thick, blonde locks pulled back into a low ponytail and looked as stunning as he remembered. His breath hitched a tiny fraction when she looked in his direction, as though she could sense him in the window.

"Get a hold of yourself, man," he muttered under his breath. Kate was lovely to look at, but it didn't mean he needed to act like an untried youth who tripped over himself at the sight of a beautiful woman. Ben continued to chide himself as he went out to meet her in front of the main building.

Holding the door open for her to enter his office, he inhaled the scent of freesia wafting in with her, reaching up to tug on the tie he wasn't wearing and dropped his hand. He'd stopped wearing suits and ties to work when he opened Bee Hill. There was no point when he spent as much of his day taking care of the animals and grounds as he did inside the various buildings on site.

Lavender filled the nooks and crannies of the farm, but Kate's scent assaulted him once again in every sense of the word. He knew she would fill the dusty corners of his life too if he gave in to this attraction for her. Ben frowned, but Kate snatched his attention back with her next words.

"The drive in was picturesque. I noticed a sign for a house museum of sorts down the road from here. If we finish early enough, I might check it out. Do you know anything about the place?"

Ben coughed discreetly before replying, "Actually, quite a bit. The home belongs to my family, as it turns out."

Kate's eyes lit up with excitement and a pale shade of pink

highlighted her cheeks. Before she could bombard him with questions, though, Ben did the unthinkable.

"I'd be happy to give you a personal tour when we're done today if you'd like. That way you don't feel rushed here and can forego the entry fee," he said by way of explanation.

"Really? I love the secrets old homes seem to harbor in their hallowed walls. It's like treasure ferreted out of the past," Kate gushed. "Sorry, I tend to get carried away about old houses," she finished, looking slightly bashful.

The bloom in her cheeks only made her more attractive as far as Ben was concerned. "You need never apologize for being passionate. Better than going through life apathetically," he said, surprising himself. "I find being in your company rather refreshing, truth be told."

Ben watched the shock slide over Kate's face. He blamed himself entirely for her disbelief. He'd been out of sorts—worried about Henri and thrown for a loop over the attractive woman Eliza had thrust upon him when he least expected it. The impression he'd left her with at their first meeting had been less than impressive. He ignored his motives for wanting to change her perception, except to tell himself working together would be easier if she liked him.

Kate followed Ben through the warehouse, picking out several types of honey and taking a few of the lavender bunches drying in one of the side buildings used for the harvested sprigs. She brought one to her nose, pulling in the aroma he spent his life steeped in.

"I believe in selling only what I'm willing to use on myself, in my body, or in my home."

"Makes sense."

"So, tell me about Bee Hill's honey and lavender."

"We have two hives, which produce an average of sixty to a hundred pounds of honey per hive each year. As I'm sure you already know, honey is a natural anti-bacterial. I use it, along with organic oats and goat milk, for the soaps I sell out of the gift shop. I've also had some traction with homemade beeswax candles recently."

"Are there any additives, sulfates, or parabens in them?

"No, completely non-toxic. I developed the soap for my son, and the candles are technically edible, or so my dog has proven," Ben said dryly. Percival's penchant for candles, in general, had been the reason behind making his own natural ones.

"And what about the lavender hand lotion I saw in the shop?"

"It's relatively new, but so far it's selling well."

"How much do you think you can provide on a quarterly basis?"

"It'll depend on the weather this year. Last year's rain wiped out the younger plants and we had to replant. Fortunately, lavender grows quickly. The fields should produce a full crop next summer."

"Which will also keep the bees happy."

"Precisely. If I stick with three-ounce bottles, I should be able to produce enough for your shop as well as the one on site. Ideally, next year's crop will produce enough to increase the size of the bottles and sales volume in both locations."

"Perfect. Let's talk wholesale discount."

"We already agreed to the terms in the contract—"

"Before I agreed to take on three quarters of Bee Hill's products."

"How many other vendors do you have?"

"A few," Kate said with a dainty shrug, not giving anything away.

"Fifteen percent," he deliberately low balled. Being canny came with his Scottish heritage and, on most occasions, had been a boon for the business.

"Fifty," she countered, wisely.

"Highway robbery. Twenty-five."

"Forty, and I'll take the Lavender-Earl Grey tea blend off your hands too."

"Thirty-five and my final offer."

"Throw in a dozen of the single-serve honey jars with the first shipment and we have a deal."

"Agreed," he said, feeling thrown by her ability to negotiate so adeptly. Then there was her direct gaze and charming smile. Thirty to fifty percent was standard wholesale practice. Still, he had a feeling she'd gotten exactly what she wanted from the start—a fair price, leaving neither of them feeling gauged. It was a promising start to their partnership.

"Done," Kate proclaimed, reaching out to shake his hand.

Chapter 4

Ben

It was a mistake. He knew it the moment her hand slipped into his and a heady chemical reaction coursed through him. Ben inhaled sharply, the scent of her perfume adding to the sensation of falling—there and gone as her hand left his, causing him to blink.

He put as much physical space between them as he could on the walking path. His business relationship with the woman was becoming more complicated by the second. Ben pulled the zipper up on his wool jumper and tucked his traitorous hands into his trouser pockets.

They arrived at Ben's ancestral home as the docent from the heritage society was locking up for the day. The elderly woman barely reached the bottom of Kate's shoulder, even without heels. He liked his new partner's height and commanding presence. Anyone would be hard pressed to ignore her, whether she was in the boardroom or the local pub.

"Looks like rain," remarked the petite, elderly woman who was gathering her things in the entrance to Clatter Hall in a gentle but authoritative voice. Kate smiled and nodded in agreement, doing her best to be polite, but Ben could sense her disbelief.

"She's not wrong," said Ben as he closed the door behind Agnes.

Kate laughed under her breath. "I didn't say she was, but you have to admit the sun would disagree—there isn't a cloud in the sky."

"Trust me; Agnes Winthrop is never wrong about the weather. Or any other pronouncement she makes."

"Such as?" inquired Kate, those eyes of hers making him think of cold nights and Lagavulin 16—notes of smoke, toffee, and cinnamon swirling inside.

"The gift she bequeathed me for my eighteenth birthday was a finished cup of afternoon tea, leaves left in bottom, and a note which read, 'Take your time. True love has a long way to travel before she finds you.'" Ben hadn't remembered the wacky prediction in years and wasn't sure why it had come to mind with Kate. What was it about this woman that made him tell her things better left alone?

"I'm sorry; Eli mentioned your wife passed away a few years ago."

He didn't correct her assumption but wondered what Eliza had told her about Monique. It was likely she'd simply told Kate that Henri's mum had died. He knew from experience how easily the details of a story could get lost, especially with the passage of time.

"Thank you." The last thing he wanted to talk about was Monique or how the loss, though difficult, wasn't what she perceived it to be. "Shall we get started?"

"By all means, lead the way."

Kate and Ben went through each room; she asking questions about the smallest details, and he answering with whatever knowledge he had to offer. There were items in his family's possession he knew nothing about, and others he knew intimately— mostly those collected by his parents on their travels with enough personal anecdotes to fill several journals.

As they transitioned to the surrounding grounds and gardens, Kate asked, "Why a house museum and not an inn or boutique hotel?"

He admired her forthrightness. It was very American, but also very much a part of who she was, if Ben had to guess. His mother would have called her impertinent, but he quite liked it.

"Sorry. It isn't any of my business," she said, pulling him out of the rabbit hole his mind had tumbled down.

"No, you just caught me off guard." The truth was, he'd been so concerned with making sure Henri was all right after everything, he'd made the easy call in order to keep the estate for future generations. Instead, he said, "The cost of upkeep on an old and crumbling estate didn't seem feasible and renovations for converting the house into a hotel required an upfront investment which, at the time, I didn't have."

"And now?" she inquired.

Like the drawing room's Georgian grandfather clock, he could see the cogs of her mind turning as she considered potential options. It was no wonder her business had grown over such an abbreviated period of time. Lavender Honey & Co., Brooklyn, was only three years old.

Ben was a careful man and careful with what was his, given or earned. He'd done his research before cementing their business arrangement. Planning to establish Bee Hill for the future, he'd intentionally hooked his wagon onto Kate's for her successful record and desire to sell quality local products. Eliza's recommendation of her both, personally and professionally, along with an MBA from Stanford, had sealed the deal.

"My small holding and subsequent business have become lucrative enough that the possibility holds some merit." Bee Hill had come to his rescue repeatedly. Initially, it had been a much-needed escape from his foolish feelings for Monique and, later, a home and new beginning for Henri upon her death. And then there was the livelihood he had discovered through the farm that he had never envisioned before the renovation of the cottage.

"Are you hoping your son will want to keep it in the family?"

He was once again grateful Eliza had used enough discretion

to leave out certain details of his personal life, namely those about how he'd thrown himself at a woman who had zero interest in him, yet he'd somehow still managed to inherit the child she'd had with his brother.

"I'm not sure if I want to place the burden on future generations, and at the same time I want them to have the choice."

She nodded in understanding.

"He'll inherit Bee Hill as a small holding, in any case, so at least a portion of the estate's lands won't be lost should it be sold or relinquished entirely to the heritage trust."

It was while they were meandering through the garden's hedge maze when the first drops of rain began falling. Engrossed in their conversation, Ben hadn't noticed the dark clouds crowding in until the earlier sunshine seemed like a conjured-up memory. Fat raindrops fell with a split-splat until they became the roar of a torrential downpour.

They were thoroughly soaked by the time they reached the large French doors at the back of the house. Ben quickly opened the door for Kate and forced himself to avert his eyes from the sweater which had looked soft as cashmere prior to the deluge but was now hugging her figure like a second skin. He grabbed the tartan blankets resting over the sofa and chairs in the room, shoving one blindly in her direction.

Kate blanched and fussed over the idea of using it to dry off with. "How old are these? I refuse to ruin a family heirloom, no matter how drenched I am."

He chuckled. "For all of her insistence on tradition and decorum, my mother always made sure the library was a place of ease. No doubt, the moths have already been at them by now."

Kate smiled in reply, taking in the overstuffed chairs upholstered in a damask, floral print and the chaise lounge covered in a soft, emerald velvet. Ben did a double take at the appearance of dimples and cursed his luck.

Drat! God must be punishing him, for what he wasn't sure, but dimples on an already attractive woman only spelled trouble. Ben forced himself to look away while she dried her hair with the worn wool.

"I spent a good portion of my childhood in this room. It was my favorite place to escape," he blurted and flushed, having said more than he'd intended. He blamed her dimples for his unfettered words.

"Books are the best kind of escape, in my experience."

"Truthfully, I think my mum knew she could either make the room into a place where she was as much at home with her poetry books as my father was with his studies, or she could go days without seeing him," he explained, but rushed to say, lest he paint his father in a poor light, "Please don't misunderstand the affection he had for her, but he's a scholar and his studies owned his attention as much as she did. She simply refused to make him choose between the two."

"Your mother sounds like a wise woman."

"She was. When my siblings and I asked her why she put up with it, she said she was happy to share him with his books, so long as no other woman shared his heart. To my knowledge, another never has."

Kate

Kate waited for him to ask about her parents. When he didn't, she decided he was simply being polite by not prying. She nearly answered the unspoken question, except he'd inherited the estate and spoke about his mother in the past tense, which meant… "How old were you when your mother passed away?"

"Nineteen. It was during my first year at university."

"I'm sorry." Kate couldn't imagine losing her mother as well as a spouse. Well, a spouse who wasn't toxic anyway, she reasoned.

"I miss her most of all when I have to make decisions about the estate or see grandmothers out with their grandchildren."

Ben smiled fondly, and Kate's breath hitched as his handsome countenance transformed into a work of art. She couldn't bring herself to look away, and wished she had paper and a pencil to sketch, which she hadn't done in years. Preston had, in his typical way, persuaded her to set aside her "childish" hobby after they married.

What had been fascinating before then had become one more thing for him to be condescending about. She subconsciously hid her hands in her pockets, momentarily forgetting she didn't have graphite smeared on them, or an ex who encouraged her to scrub her hands raw with his words. Ben brought her attention back to the present and she told herself to relax.

"He probably would have driven her insane with his constant questions," he continued, oblivious to her appraisal and momentary lapse. "God knows, I don't always know what to do with him myself," he finished with self-deprecating humor, causing a corner of his mouth to hitch upward.

Kate took a deep breath at the sight, inhaling the dust released from the blankets, and causing an abrupt series of sneezes to issue forth. "Excuse me," she said at the same time he pronounced, "Bless you."

She felt the heat creep into her cheeks and cursed her skin's tendency to filter her feelings. It wasn't as though he'd complimented her. Nope, he'd blessed her, like anyone with good manners would.

You can't suppress us forever, mocked her long dormant hormones as another flush swept over her.

Fortunately, Ben had his back toward her, having moved to the wood stacked inside the fireplace. He lit a match on the stone at the base and touched the kindling sticking out at odd angles from the larger pieces. If circumstances were different, the scene might have been romantic, but hopeless as she was, Kate wasn't delusional. He was simply being practical under the circumstances.

"Henri and I camp out in here on occasion, since it's one of the few rooms still closed off from the tour," he said by way of an explanation. "If we're lucky, there will be tea and biscuits in the kitchen. Agnes usually keeps a stash on hand for breaks."

They pilfered the kitchen and laid their stash out on the ottoman in front of the fire. Kate let loose a delighted laugh and Ben turned in her direction. Their eyes met, causing a snap of electricity to run through her. She swallowed hard and hoped her cheeks would behave.

"What is so amusing?" Ben asked, looking pleased with himself despite the question.

"You have all the makings for s'mores here. I didn't know s'mores were a thing in Britain."

"Of course they are. Who doesn't like a good s'more?"

He sounded so stern that, if she hadn't been looking directly at Ben, she would have worried she'd insulted him. However, it did make Kate wonder if the man had simply been hangry when he picked her up at the airport. She wilted like a flower without water when her blood sugar dropped below a certain point, after all. Deciding to give him the benefit of the doubt and a second chance, she watched as he arranged everything on a silver tea tray.

He dipped his head, a piece of dark hair falling over his forehead. She itched to smooth it back. Meeting her gaze again, she noticed his eyes were grey, shifting from a storm at the edge of the iris to an overcast sky around the pupil in the light of the fire, much like English weather, and potentially his temperament.

Ben's lips mischievously curled up at the corners in direct defiance of his obstinate cleft chin. And, for a split-second, Kate glimpsed the man beneath the reserved veneer. Her heart stuttered and she forced herself to banter back.

"Well, I've never had them with digestive biscuits, but I guess they'll make a passable substitute."

"Passable? I'll have you know I happen to be an expert s'more maker and Cadbury chocolate will change your life," he said as though he were truly offended.

"No doubt," Kate said, grinning in the face of his serious countenance. And so it was; they spent a late afternoon and early evening sitting on the library floor in front of the fire, eating s'mores and continuing the easy rapport they'd fallen into when neither of them was looking.

"What about your family, Kate? Brothers, sisters, parents still together?"

"Yes, to all of it. My parents own a horse farm close to Midwell, Virginia; it's been in the family for generations. And I have an older brother and a younger sister, which makes me the poor, neglected middle child," she said without a trace of seriousness, a slight smile pulling at her full lips.

"Something tells me you were as impossible to ignore as a child as you are as a grown woman."

"Thank you...I think."

"It was meant as a compliment," he said sincerely. "However, I should warn you I'm rather an odd duck. Sam is my best mate after all."

"Ah, the infamous Sam. Eli is head over heels for him. I'm glad she's finally found her person." And she was, but it also reminded her of how very single she was.

"I can assure you he's a great bloke, best mate a guy could have."

"How did the two of you meet?"

"Uni. We both rowed for Oxford. When my mum died, Sam's family made it a point to include me in all of their holidays."

"What about your father."

"Da loves us in his own way, but without Mum to temper his ways, he's buried himself in his studies and only begun to re-engage with us since my sister Alethea had children."

"Grief has a funny way of dealing with everyone on an individual level," she said, thinking about how her sister had tried to outrun hers. Kate, on the other hand, had mourned the loss of her marriage with a proverbial middle finger, doing everything in her power to move another step forward every day. Her brother's situation felt more like a battle for his soul. Only God knew if Lon would come out whole after everything. "I imagine grandchildren are more fun than parenting anyway." She definitely did not envy her parents, in light of everything.

"True."

"Do you see Eli and Sam often?"

"We try to catch up with each other about once a month. In fact, we're meeting up at the end of September for a regatta in Oxford. Would you like to join us?"

"I'd love to, so long as I'm not required to row," Kate replied, moving her arms like a clucking chicken.

He grinned at the sight of her flapping. "Leave the rowing to me and Sam. We could use a cheering squad though."

Chapter 5

Ben

Ben woke up to the early morning light shining through the skylight windows of his bedroom. He didn't hear Henri stirring in the next room over yet, so instead of making his way downstairs to start breakfast, he indulged in the luxury of nestling down into the warm down comforter to nurse his regrets from the night before. Once the sudden deluge had passed, he and Kate cleared the library of any campsite evidence before trekking back to her car in the lot at Bee Hill, the night sky showing off a patchwork of stars between the holes in the cloud cover and lighting the way.

"Are you sure you're all right to make the drive back?" he asked, concerned. Ben knew he was worse than a hen with her chicks. He blamed the loss of his mother and Monique on his tendency to be overprotective. Although Monique had never been his to lose in the first place, he'd always felt to blame for Felix abandoning her and Henri in their hour of need. If he had done less, maybe his brother would have done more.

Kate interrupted his guilt-ridden inner dialogue with, "I'll be fine, so long as no one else wants me to share the road with them."

He chuckled and bid her goodnight, closing her inside the rental care she'd driven and watching until the headlights disappeared onto the main road outside of the stone hedge. As he did, he found himself thinking about her earlier laughter and the pleasure she exuded over something as basic as s'mores. Ben wished it hadn't been so easy to picture himself seeking out her laugh every moment of the day, if given the chance.

His walls toward the American were crumbling fast, like the plaster in the attic walls of Clatter Hall. It's why he'd invited her to Oxford for the rowing competition.

Water under the bridge now, as his father was fond of saying. *Might as well row with the current, old chap.* And the current was flowing in the direction of a shop owner from Brooklyn.

Hearing the floorboards give with squeaks and croaks as Henri jumped down the stairs, Ben roused himself, pulling on a henley and slipping his feet into lambswool slippers as he tied the string of his flannel pajama bottoms. The cottage had new radiators, but the wood floors creaked in all the right places while the pipes shuddered appropriately when the hot water kicked in, providing the proper sounds every home should have to make it feel well lived in.

He had removed any non-load bearing walls in order for the downstairs to be an open floor plan with the exception of the small room he used as a home office, tucked into the back left corner. The cottage opened into a rectangular entryway filled with Macintoshes, Anoraks, and winter puffers hung on hooks, wellies and a basket of trainers stashed below. Directly in front of it sat a living room with a large stone fireplace along the back wall, the kitchen to the left of the entry itself.

Made of English oak, the stairs leading to the two bedrooms and a single lavatory between them were sturdy, if slightly on the narrow side. The plan had always been to add on to the back as time and money allowed, or as a potential family grew, whichever came first. With only he and Henri occupying the space, all other plans for the cottage had withered away in the last couple of years.

Henri sat in one of the stools pulled up to the counter overlooking the kitchen. Ben ruffled his hair as he walked by and asked, "The usual, my brave boy?"

"Aye, but try not to overdo the eggs this time," Henri responded without raising his eyes from the book in front of him.

Ben shook his head in silent humor and smiled. He wanted so badly to give his son what he'd experienced himself as a child—a family and a safe place to land when life wrang a soul through the wringer. Instead, Henri was stuck with him. Ben worried about whether or not he could give his son everything he needed in the end.

"Da, the eggs are done."

Ben narrowed his gaze at his son. "How do you know? The lid is on."

"I can smell them. You're going to overdo them like you do every morning."

"The eggs I make are fine, thank you very much," Ben said, obviously offended, but he removed the lid and placed the pan on a cold eye of the stove.

Henri grinned with a glint in his eyes as if to say, *I told you so,* but wisely kept his mouth shut. Ben moved forward with breakfast, slathering jam on toasted bread, and slicing fruit for the yogurt he preferred to a full British breakfast. As usual, he indulged Henri with a heaping spoonful of honey in his tea and added milk to his own.

Finished, he started for the tiny office at the back while Henri entertained himself with his books and Percival until it was time for school.

"Da, Percy's bowtie is missing again," Henri said, sounding more exasperated than a seven-year-old ought to over such a trivial occurrence.

"Check the kitchen garden beneath the lettuce leaves."

"Percy," said Henri in his most disappointed tone. "We've talked about this. It doesn't matter what Merlin thinks."

And as if he knew his name had entered the conversation,

the British Blue hopped through the small cutout in the front door and began licking a paw. Henri picked the cat up and deposited him onto one of the stools at the kitchen counter, where his feline eyes caught the weak sunlight coming through one of the square windows set into stone and mortar.

Henri continued his peptalk, shaking an index finger at the wee dog. "The bow tie is dapper and sets you apart."

Well, what a telling bit of information. Henri was obviously referring to himself as much as he was their wee dog. It would seem he'd be sending off an email to request a meeting with the teacher in addition to the usual weekly tallies and balances.

While Ben had employees to help run the business of the farm, he made sure to spend time every day tending to the different duties required as a small holder himself. Bee Hill consisted mostly of the lavender fields it was known for, along with a colony of bees used for pollination and the production of honey, but there were also chickens and sheep to tend, three unruly goats, the horses, and of course, a border collie—Bedivere or Betty for short. She was young, but quite possibly the best herding dog he would ever have. And, as an added bonus, she helped corral Henri.

The boy was part scholar, part boundless energy, and Ben never knew which side would take precedence at the moment. Percival would no doubt join him, once he'd found a mudpuddle in which to splash and managed to rid himself of the infernal bowtie Henri insisted he wear. Ben noted it was more likely a metaphor for his son's interaction with his peers rather than having anything to do with the spirited dog.

Ben set the pen next to the stack of receipts he'd added up a moment ago and stabbed them into a pile on the spindle in the corner of his desk. There was an app he could put on his mobile for keeping track, but he liked doing business the traditional way, with old-fashioned tools requiring extra space and actual thinking. New-fangled ideas weren't always better; sometimes they were merely different. He side-eyed the PC in a box taking up useless space in the corner, collecting dust and spider webs, instead of producing electronic spreadsheets to help with the growth of Bee Hill.

This was precisely why Felix referred to him as "old chap." He sighed, resigned to the truth, and called his brother. After leaving the obligatory voice mail, knowing Felix wouldn't return it for at least a week, he called Sam.

"It's about time," said a disgruntled voice on the other end of the line.

Sam's familiar brogue never failed to make Ben smile. "Hiya to you too, mate. Everything is obviously Jelly Tots and lollies on your end."

"Eli and I got into it this morning."

"About?"

"The usual," said Sam letting out an exaggerated sigh.

"Ahh. Well, I think we both know she's right."

"Aye, she usually is."

"So, talking to me is buying yourself time?"

"Pretty much. Besides, I want details."

"About?"

"How it went with Kit-Kat."

"You mean Kate?" Ben asked.

"I swear, sometimes talking to you is worse than nails on a chalkboard."

"A gentleman knows discretion is the better part of valor. You should try it sometime."

"Bollocks. A true Scotsman puts everything out in the open."

"We aren't talking about what you do or do not wear under your kilt."

"Very funny. You do realize you're half Scottish, right?"

"My father is rather fond of reminding me. Please tell Eli she owes me for the favor when you're done putting everything out in the open for her."

"Git," Sam insulted, then pleaded, "Pray for me. I'm off to do battle."

"Right. Godspeed, then." Ben chuckled and hung up, deliberately ignoring the voice in his head poking fun over his own dilemma. Sam might be off to do battle, but Ben had already lost the war as soon as he invited Kate to join them in Oxford.

Kate

Two weeks later, Kate stood at the white marble countertop the construction crew had recently installed in what would soon be Lavender Honey & Co., London, going through inventory and cost projections. Moments later, she received a text from the new store manager letting her know she needed to cancel their scheduled meeting, and to please read the email she had sent earlier this morning. Rereading the perfunctory, yet obligatorily polite, email to be certain she hadn't misunderstood, Kate touched her temple where a headache had started to take root. Nope, she conceded, massaging the spot. It still said the same thing.

This could not be happening to her. Her manager had decided to elope with her Portuguese boyfriend, and would in fact, be living in Lisbon. "Who does something so irresponsible?" Kate wondered aloud again. "And at the last minute, no less." She could admit spontaneity ranked low on her list of personal qualifications for life experience, but this was beyond her ability to comprehend.

So much for an easy transition, and further proof a change in plans never boded well. She slipped her feet out of her heels and hopped onto the counter, swinging her legs back and forth as though she was three instead of thirty-three. Adulting was hard. Picking up the phone, she texted Laura to see if she could talk, instead of trying to solve the problem at hand.

With her sister living in Brooklyn, the four-hour time difference between New York and London should make it easier to stay in touch. Her sister was difficult to track down when she traveled, so this would be a pleasant change of pace. She usually talked with Lon once a week, but he only humored her because she'd threatened to show up in person otherwise.

An hour later, with no reply from Laura, she called Uncle Joe. His only response was to chuckle and tell her, "Yeah, she and Micky are fine. Stop worrying about everyone else so much."

"I'm not worried," she said, tapping a manicured nail against her front teeth.

"Of course, you are. Leave Laura to me. I promise the pub will take good care of her."

She knew he was right on both counts. He would take care of Laura, and Kate was overprotective when it came to her baby sister's happiness. If she were being completely honest with herself, though her fierce concern was genuine, it also allowed her to avoid looking at her own life under a microscope.

One of the fallouts from Kate's marriage was an inability to engage in any potential romantic relationships herself, while over investing in everyone else's. It had been four years since her divorce, and to say her love life was going through a dry spell would be an understatement. Calling it the Sahara Desert was far more accurate. The worst part was knowing part of the problem was her. How could she trust her own judgment anymore?

Fortunately, the door opened with a high-pitched ting from the bell she'd installed above it yesterday, delaying the need to answer the depressing question.

"Hey, Kit-Kat."

"Eli!" Kate exclaimed, hopping off the counter to snatch her friend up in a hug.

Eliza squeezed her back. "You saw me a month ago. What's with all of the hullabaloo?"

"Sam is starting to rub off on you."

"In the most delightful way," sang Eliza with a waggle of her brows and a voice to rival Mary Poppins.

Her friend could be on Broadway but preferred playing the violin and singing to acting. It was doubly unfair, but Eliza had more talent in her pinky finger than Kate contained in her entire body. She brushed off the twinge of jealousy in favor of sisterhood, and reminded herself how hard her friend had worked to get where she was. In her experience, both business and friendship bloomed with more humility.

"Seriously, what is going on? You only sit on the counter and swing your legs when you're trying to solve a problem."

"My manger eloped with her boyfriend." Kate held up a finger to hold off the words waiting to spill from her friend's lips. "To live in Portugal."

Eliza's expression mirrored the one Kate herself had worn when she found out. "Wow, I didn't know people actually eloped to a foreign country on the fly."

"I know, right?! So much for having a life outside of the boutique."

"Yep," Eliza said, the "p" popping at the end for emphasis. "At least The Isis Sculls takes place before the store opens in October."

"True, but I have a feeling I'm going to be so exhausted there's no point in going."

"No problem. Sam will do all of the talking anyway, and Ben is more of a quiet observer than an active participant."

"I bet he can't get in a word edgewise when you and Sam are together. I swear you two finish each other's sentences."

"Except when we're arguing. Then it's a race to be right."

Kate shook her head, baffled. Bickering was foreplay to Eliza, unlike herself who still shied away from most confrontation. Yet another reason for taking a hiatus from dating.

"And besides, I won't let you back out. You'll see, it'll be fun."

"Wait. How do you know Ben asked me to go? And you are totally on my list for ditching me with him at the airport."

"Trust me, you'll thank me someday."

Kate rolled her eyes, to which Eliza laughed.

"Ben showed me around his family's estate when I visited Bee Hill. Have you met Agnes Winthrop?"

"Of course. Sam is a believer in the supernatural, including Agnes' ability to know things other people don't."

"Or she could be using the power of deductive reasoning and observation to sort things out."

"Sam would argue Sir Arthur Conan Doyle was a firm believer in the occult, despite his creation of Sherlock Holmes."

Kate groaned in frustration. "Come on, there's a charity store in the neighborhood I want to check out."

"Shopping therapy for the win!"

Chapter 6

Kate

"It'll be fun, she said," groused Kate as she lugged the picnic hamper and corresponding tartan blanket from the train station at Oxford to Folly Bridge, where she was supposed to meet everyone else. She should have opted for the backpack version and more practical footwear.

The hamper had been too nostalgic to ignore, and the blanket—or "rug" as the British called it—had been practically free at seventy percent off, but only with the purchase of the awkward-to-carry basket. Otherwise, her wedge booties would normally be fine for the twenty-minute walk, she excused. At least there would be tea and baked goods when she arrived at her destination.

"Hey, look who—" started Sam.

"Finally made it," finished Eliza, turning away from the bridge overlooking the Thames River, known by locals as the River Isis.

"The two of you could unsettle the most stalwart of constitutions," said Ben with a frown, reaching for Kate's burden, their fingers lightly brushing and sending a zip through her.

"Thank you," she said. Ignoring the spark between them, she wiped away the perspiration on her brow with the back of her hand. Why did he always seem unhappy to see her? It wasn't as if she'd invited herself to the regatta.

Ben tugged at the collar of his shirt in lieu of a tie today. She shrugged, blaming the warm weather for his discomfort.

"You know you love us," the couple said at the same time, making a Kate sandwich out of her with a hug. She giggled as Sam's copper mop of hair tickled her nose. At least she thought it was his. Eliza's strawberry blonde locks could also be the culprit.

"True, but I think I like it more when you guys are bickering."

"We only bicker so we have an excuse to make up," replied Eliza with a smirk, releasing her.

Kate laughed at the implication, and Ben glanced over to meet her gaze. Why did those stormy eyes make her so nervous, she wondered.

Because girlfriend, we are back in business! exclaimed her hormones, with a rush of warmth to her abdomen.

No, you are not, she sternly forbade her girly parts. Besides, she reasoned, the grumpy Englishman was the last person she should have any kind of feelings for.

First of all, they were business partners. And secondly, he'd worn a button down for rowing. Who wears their Sunday best to an athletic event? And more importantly, why did she keep having to ask herself these ridiculous questions every other day?

To-do list: Get a book about British cultural norms from the library.

At least he was rolling the sleeves up. Never mind. The action only made things worse. Kate staunchly told herself forearms were not attractive. Then why did she wish she had a pencil and paper again in his presence?

"Why don't we find a spot along the river, and the two of you can settle in," suggested Ben.

Oh, she wanted to settle in all right. But chances were, he wasn't referring to the same thing about which she was thinking. Kate blew a wisp of hair out of her eyes. This highly unwanted attraction was already becoming a nuisance. If only the man would stop with his tugging and sleeve rolling, her hormones might relegate themselves to their formerly abandoned state.

Sam led the way, with his wingman bringing up the rear. Kate glanced over her shoulder, sneaking another peek at her new business partner. Once they'd found a suitable spot beneath the trees, the guys laid out the blanket and she began removing items from the hamper.

"This is a veritable feast, Kit-Kat." Sam had taken to calling her by the nickname during her first visit to London last year. He treated her like a brother, which she found endearing, especially in light of her own brother's recent absence and behavior.

She knew Lon's broken engagement had been difficult to swallow, but she had a feeling he was mourning something else other than his former fiancé. If Lon could ever be honest with himself about the situation, Kate believed he would finally move forward with his life. Of course, making his peace with God might be easier said than done.

She, on the other hand, didn't blame anyone for her marriage. Kate alone took credit for the disastrous decision. Blinking back into the moment beneath the sun-dappled leaves of a nearby willow tree, she accepted a cup of tea from Ben and, in exchange, handed him a chocolate marmalade cupcake from the bakery near her apartment.

"This is amazing," complimented Sam, around a mouthful of creamy frosting.

"I can't take credit," said Kate.

"Kate doesn't cook or bake," explained Eliza.

"Ever?" asked Ben, surprised.

Heat infused her cheeks, but Kate owned her choices. "It's not like I can't boil water or make a salad. I'm just more of an insta-mix or take-away kind of gal."

Eliza jumped to Kate's defense. "In all fairness, it's not like you've had time to learn how. Preston didn't exactly support your pursuit of the creative arts and since the divorce, you've been busy building your empire."

If Eliza had been stateside at the time, there would've been no way to hide what was happening with Preston, but after the divorce, Kate had disclosed every sordid detail. And as her friend's fiancé, Sam knew enough about Kate's past to get the gist. This meant Ben was the only one out of the loop regarding her ex. It was a detail she hoped to leave out of their partnership indefinitely.

"True. To Lavender Honey & Co," she said clinking her teacup against Eliza's. "And to new partners."

Ben silently clinked his cup with hers, meeting her gaze steadily, his eyes hypnotic in their intensity.

Fortified by teatime, the men stood up to prepare for their race. Stripping down to shorts and a T-shirt, Kate was relieved to know the collared shirt hid more casual wear beneath, along with a well-honed physique. Ben's quads, broad chest, and arms looked made for rowing. Kate discreetly wiped the drool from the corner of her mouth with one of the cloth napkins from the basket.

Naughty hormones. Now is not the time to come out and play, she chided, cleaning the frosting off her fork with more precision than was strictly necessary.

Ben

In what he was beginning to realize was the usual Kate fashion, she held nothing back, including her appreciative gaze. Ben genuinely enjoyed her boldness and at the same time wished he wasn't the sole focus of it at this moment. He had to admit, though, it was nice to know working the land at Bee Hill had kept him fit enough for an attractive woman—like the one shamelessly eating a second cupcake—to notice him.

Oh, to be the frosting on her lips.

Ben went to tug at his collar, feeling flushed, only to realize he'd discarded his button up. Tugging at one's cotton shirt didn't have quite the same tension releasing effect. Instead, He set about folding his clothes into a neat pile and stuffed his feet back into his trainers, quickly making his way with Sam to the boathouse to pick up the double scull assigned to them.

Scheduled for the next alumni heat, he and Sam set the boat onto the water at the starting dock and settled into position. Rowing with two was different than the eight of university with a coxswain, but as they'd both been a part of the middle four, or engine room, they usually rowed well together. More power, less precision technique, but it got the job done.

"Master's B class," announced someone through a bull horn in the distance, for those ages thirty-six to forty-two. Ben shifted his feet once more before settling in and glanced at their competition to the right.

"Not ready to row with the big guns yet, I see," mocked a deep voice rough with tobacco use.

"Not quite," conceded Ben with good humor.

"Eager for us to show how it's done, are you?" asked Sam.

The older man guffawed, coughed, and spit a wad of thick mucus into the grass in front of him. "Have no fear; it'll take more than cancer to slow me down, boy." He turned on his heel and strode towards the boathouse, where he undoubtedly kept a desk drawer filled with pipes and a tin of tobacco, just like he'd done during their years under his tutelage.

"Good to know the old codger still has a solid pep talk in him," said Sam. "How long's he got?"

"Hilde stopped in last week to buy candles and soap. Five years, if he's lucky," Ben said, the tang of regret bitter on his tongue.

"Or stubborn enough. Well, then, let's win this one. We don't want Coach thinking we've grown soft in his absence."

The sound of a gun went off to start the race and Ben began the sequence he'd learned as a lad, setting the pace for his muscles: half stroke, half stroke, three-quarter stroke, lengthen, full stroke. He pushed first with his feet, keeping his core engaged and his layback short until he and Sam had settled in. As they lengthened their strokes, they moved into a working pace, gaining speed and distance in front of the team to their right.

The cheering around them receded to nothing but white noise as Ben set his focus on the finish line. Unfortunately, the scull to their left had rowers who had either put in more regular time on the water or wanted the win more than they did. In the end, Ben and

Sam lost by a stroke.

"We never hit the swing," accused Sam.

"I know," agreed Ben. The swing was the magical sweet spot for any crew, but it was also elusive; the place where each man in the boat ceased to be an individual and became one fluid unit instead.

"As long as you know," Sam reiterated, as if Ben had missed it the first time.

"C'mon, mate, I'll buy you a pint to dull the sting," Ben said, taking the brunt of his friend's displeasure. He knew Sam was more disappointed in himself than he was with Ben. They pulled the scull from the river and hiked it back to the boathouse, each taking an end and carrying their oars in the other hand, accepting condolences from crews along the way.

By the time Ben and Sam met the girls back at the picnic sight, Kate had packed the remainder of everything back into her old school hamper. At least it would be lighter to carry this time. *Whatever possessed her to bring something so bulky?* he wondered, but it was as much of a mystery as the woman herself at this point.

Besides, as his father would say, "To criticize a woman is to court trouble. Best to let her make her own decisions even if yer the man who has to deal with the consequences." Of course, accepting advice from a man who wore a kilt with nothing beneath his pleats so long as the outside temperature was above freezing was its own kind of trouble.

Eliza kissed Sam in greeting and instantly began to peddle

sympathy, giving Ben a wink over her fiancé's shoulder. Of the two of them, his best friend's pride was by far the more fragile. Sam had always been sensitive to failure and criticism.

He thought it was because Sam was the creative type, and as a composer and former conductor for one of London's most prominent orchestras, he tended to demand perfection from those he worked with, as well as himself. Used to regular bouts of failure, Ben, on the other hand, wasn't afraid to take risks. Raising a child meant failing daily, whether it was disappointment in oneself or said child's disappointment in him. Keeping every creature—great and small—alive at Bee Hill often felt like a huge win all by itself.

They walked to The Bear Inn, off of High Street, leaving the hustle and bustle behind them for the time being. Ben held the door as everyone entered and Kate followed Eliza to a table in a quiet spot, while he and Sam took everyone's drink order to the bar. By the time they returned with three pints of beer and a half pint of cider, the girls were commenting on the sheer number of ties from the various rowing clubs, which covered every inch of the ceiling.

"I'm pretty certain they have one from Ben and Sam somewhere around here. I mean, they're ancient now, but once upon a time they were legends."

"Love, I still am, and I'll be happy to prove it to you later. Forty is only a number," flirted Sam.

"Well, aren't you full of surprises, Mr. Galloway," Kate said, her brows raised.

"I think I had to wrestle it from him," replied Sam. "So don't go thinking too highly of him."

"Don't worry; I won't," bantered Kate. "But maybe you didn't ask him sweetly enough," she continued, looking directly at Ben. "Something tells me he likes it when you say please."

Ben inhaled his beer down the wrong pipe and coughed raggedly as he tried to expel it. Sam pounded between his shoulders harder than necessary, laughing at his expense.

He shrugged forcefully. "Leave off mate," said Ben, hoarsely.

"Are you okay?" Kate asked, having no idea what her saying "please" had conjured up in his mind.

"Fine, fine. Thank you for asking," he replied automatically. This woman was going to be the death of him. *Please and thank you very much.* He cleared his throat again as desire infused his cheeks with heat.

"Well, doesn't every guy like a girl with manners, especially when she's under—"

Ben cut Sam off with a strong elbow to his abdominals and causing him to grunt heavily.

"Never mind," he wheezed. "I'll go get us another round."

"Oh, my poor, poor, baby," crooned Eliza, standing to join him.

"I am rather," Sam replied, still rubbing his abdominal area.

"What have I told you about putting it all out there? What a naughty boy you are," said Eliza sternly, before ruining it with a cackle.

"I think you might have to punish me," Sam said with a waggle of his brows.

"Get a room!" Ben and Kate called out in unison.

"Well, Ms. Howard, it would seem we have at least one thing in common."

Kate arched a single brow in question.

"Our best friends are intolerably rude."

Kate grinned. "Abominably."

"Cheers," said Ben, clinking his glass against hers.

Chapter 7

Kate

October and November came and went in a flash of gilded leaves without the usual holidays of Halloween and Thanksgiving. Kate had considered making the trip north to Scotland with Eliza and Sam to join in his family's celebration of the Celtic Samhain, but in the end, the shop had come first. Part of what she liked about being a small business owner was being her own boss.

In the same vein, she liked how the success or failure of the shop depended on her. But without a manager, she'd become exhausted from being on point at all times.

Kate had hoped to have more time to explore her new home, but—alas—the only thing she saw were the four walls of Lavender Honey & Co. and her tiny apartment. She missed her larger one in Brooklyn but also knew it was exactly what her sister needed to take a fork in the road and reclaim her life. Grief had stolen so much from Laura, but it had also given her something new in the process—if her sister possessed the courage to reach for it. Kate considered it her job to make sure she did, and since the timing worked out perfectly for her own new venture, it had been all the impetus needed to put things into motion on her baby sister's behalf.

A job at Walker's Pub with Uncle Joe—*check.*

A large, remodeled apartment in Brooklyn—*check.*

A dog to aid the healing process—*check.*

A sweet, available firefighter who comes into the pub regularly—*check, check, check!*

Similar to how she'd known Micky was the perfect dog for Laura, she'd realized Nick Kelly was the kind of man she'd pick for her sister. He was the steady, take-it-all-in-stride to Laura's independence and spunk. Austin's Emma had nothing on Kate's matchmaking skills. Of course, she didn't expect everything to go smoothly; true love rarely did, making the ending all the better for the work to get there.

Thanksgiving had been a lonely affair, with only herself, a book, and Chinese take away. She'd spoken with her folks, left an upbeat voicemail for Lon—who was no doubt in a bar—and had a brief convo with Uncle Joe and Laura when she called the pub, where they were hosting a Friendsgiving for those without anywhere else to go. Kate had found being away from home for the holidays more depressing than she'd anticipated.

For one, the UK didn't celebrate Thanksgiving. The closest thing to it was a harvest celebration at school or church, neither of which applied to her—the former for obvious reasons, and the later because the older she became the less she believed in organized religion. It wasn't like Kate didn't believe in God or love Jesus. She did. But for all of the preaching from the pulpit about loving one another, the evidence in the world felt sparse these days.

Secondly, she had a thorough appreciation for the traditional Thanksgiving meal. Unlike Laura, who before now had been half a world away, Kate had gone home to Midwell for the holiday every year since her divorce. Her father knew how to make a mean stuffed turkey. Then there was the green bean casserole, mashed potatoes with gravy, and sweet potato soufflé—a person could never have enough potatoes. And her mother's caramel-apple pie was her favorite dessert, aside from anything chocolate.

If she knew how to cook, Kate could have salvaged the day, but since she had never cooked a meal, let alone a feast, there'd been the very real possibility of burning down her apartment. She didn't think it would be neighborly on her part to force everyone to find a new place to live.

Despite her holiday woes, Lavender Honey & Co. was thriving, thanks to the products from Bee Hill. They were her bestsellers—so much so, Kate wondered if everything Ben touched turned to gold. From what Eliza had said the last time they spent time together over a lunch of gruyere toasties, Bee Hill was the same age as her

Brooklyn shop and had developed into a small business by accident. Ben had stumbled upon its potential in the middle of the rest of his life—or a quarter life crisis—according to Sam, who'd come in at the end of their conversation, kissing his fiancé with a quick smack to the lips.

"Don't get me wrong; Ben is wicked smart, but his success with Bee Hill is the stuff of fairy tales. Before he renovated the gamekeeper's cottage, he had no intention of turning it into a profitable business."

"He has an architecture degree," explained Eliza, noting Kate's surprise. "Have you seen the cottage yet?"

"Nope. Is it as perfect as the one in *The Holiday*?" Kate asked, referencing the movie she watched every Christmas without fail. One of the main characters provided a dose of yearly inspiration to be the "leading lady" of her own life. Of course, the actor was a rock star in and of herself. While there had definitely been room for Jack on the door in Titanic—anyone who believed otherwise was wrong—Kate had rooted for Rose to survive and thrive without him.

"Better," Sam and Eliza agreed simultaneously, pulling Kate back from her revery.

"He took to having a small holding like a duck takes to water," continued Sam. "It's nauseating how good he is at all of it."

"So, he's like a Renaissance man—skilled at a lot of different things and kind of self-taught?"

"Pretty much. Like you, come to think of it, only you're a Renaissance woman. Apartment renovation? No big deal. Successful entrepreneur? Piece of cake. Artist to watch—"

"I haven't sketched in years," interrupted Kate. "Is there anything Ben doesn't do well?" she asked, trying to ignore the missing piece of herself, as if it didn't feel like a missing appendage.

"Relationships," Eliza and Sam said in unison, high fiving each other afterward.

Though her friends hadn't elaborated on the last part, Ben had finished the cottage on the property shortly after Henri was born and steadily added to the small holding until after Monique died. At which point, he took out a small business loan and turned his home into a thriving business. Kate decided genius was born out of necessity.

It certainly had been for her. Truthfully, the shop had been the inspiration Kate needed to help claw her way back after the damage Preston had inflicted mentally and emotionally over the years. The bruises had disappeared within weeks, and the scars he'd left behind on her soul had faded, but sometimes she worried they would never go away entirely.

Black Friday sales for the Brooklyn shop had gone as expected, so with Christmas around the corner, Kate hired extra seasonal help and threw herself into the long hours, counting down to the twenty-third of December and her flight home for a visit.

Ben

He straightened the tie at his neck and took a seat at his son's desk to wait. The school administrator had assured him Mrs. Albright was the most experienced teacher they had when he'd shared his concerns at the beginning of the school year. As it happened, "experienced" had been code for burned out and not long for retirement. The woman wore a permanent grimace, and from their prior meetings, he knew to sit exactly where he was as though she couldn't remember which child was his without a reference point. *Not the least bit disconcerting*, thought Ben, swiveling right then left to take in the entirety of the bland environment. Didn't teachers normally fill a classroom with primary colors, student projects, and the obligatory globe? Organized was one thing, but sterile suggested a lack of creativity and engaging material.

"Ah, Mr. Galloway." Mrs. Albright greeted Ben in a clipped tone as she entered the classroom, her frown firmly in place, and growing deeper if such a thing were possible. She watched him disapprovingly over the top of her reading spectacles.

"Mrs. Albright, good to see you as always," said Ben, letting the trivial lie slip off his tongue as he stood.

"Do sit down, Mr. Galloway," she directed as she sat behind her desk, several rows in front of him.

Ben felt like a student, anxiously awaiting punishment. He wiped his palms on his trousers instead of reaching for his tie.

"I'm afraid we've reached an impasse where Henri's behavior

is concerned."

"Oh?"

"I caught him hiding in the lavatory during break time, yesterday."

"I'm sure he wasn't hiding."

"He was sitting on the sink counter reading a book on Ancient Greece."

"I'm sure—"

"I'm sure we don't have the staff to escort your child from one activity to another simply because he feels overwhelmed and can't follow the rules. He also refused to do the morning's group activity."

"Is there a chance he's being bullied by any of the other children?" Ben asked, thinking of Henri's previous comment to Percival.

Mrs. Albright's features softened minutely, making her look younger and, for a brief moment, allowing Ben to see the woman she might have been, had she taken a different path earlier in life.

"I am many things, Mr. Galloway, but a proponent of bullies is not one of them. I can assure you; any such behavior is delt with swiftly in my classroom" she explained. "If, however, Henri continues to isolate himself, I'll have no choice but to hold him back."

"I understand." But he didn't.

Henri was more than capable of keeping up academically. It was the group-centered activities he was avoiding. Surely, it was better to teach him to navigate the ways in which he was different, instead of pretending as if a repeat in the same year would suddenly change things. Ben sighed deeply as he lowered his forehead to the steering wheel he gripped tightly on either side, his hands becoming a mottled shade of white and purple. He needed help.

⋯⋯⋯⋯⋯⋯⋯⋯⋯⋯⋯⋯⋯⋯⋯⋯⋯⋯⋯

"Bennett, are you listening to me?" asked Althea.

He watched the soppy weather through the office windows, cursing the rain and taking another sip of lukewarm tea. The biscuit in his mouth tasted oddly like blue cheese. He'd spent the morning going over inventory in the warehouse and boxing up a delivery for Kate, whose grand opening had been a tremendous success, but missing lunch in the process.

"Aye, and don't call me by my full name. You know how I hate it."

"Yes, well, it got your attention, didn't it?"

Ben swapped the phone to his other ear and ran a hand through his hair, abandoning the tea and stale Jammie Dodger. At the time, calling his sister had seemed like an excellent idea; now he wasn't so sure. Or he could simply be hungry, he considered with another glare at the offensive food.

"Henri needs more than the public schools can offer. They're shorthanded and bursting at the seams, thanks to budget cuts. It's not the school's fault, but your son will pay the price if you don't do something to help him."

"Private school is expensive and farther away, not to mention how difficult the change will be on Henri." Ben could already picture the ensuing tantrum.

"At least request a change in classrooms. I know we're taught to grin and bear it from the cradle, but this isn't our parents' generation. Henri deserves better support and so do you," she finished gently.

"Fine, but I doubt it will help."

"Hope is as important as endurance."

"Aye, but nothing kills hope faster than reality."

"Don't be such a stick in the mud."

"Yes ma'am, General Ma'am," he teased, his lips quirking into a half smile.

"Goodnight, Bennett."

He chuckled. If nothing else, getting a rise out of his little sister had been worth the call.

Ben watched through the rear-view mirror as his father maneuvered awkwardly into the backseat of the Rover with Henri. He would undoubtedly scorn any suggestion or help. At least he wasn't getting an eyeful of the older man's nether region, since he'd worn his tartan trews instead of a kilt. Like their mother, Althea knew how to bring Hamish Galloway to heel, and, like any good general, she chose her battles wisely. Their father would sell his soul for Christmas turkey and Yorkshire puddings, which meant wearing trousers to dinner, despite the temperature being four degrees above freezing.

"Right then, everyone ready?" asked Ben, waiting to hear the click of his father's seat belt and trying not to be annoyed with his chauffer status or their inevitable tardiness.

"Aye, aye, Captain," they said in unison, eyes glued to a crossword puzzle from the newspaper.

"Da, did you remember the gifts for Althea and the kids?" Ben asked on a sigh.

"I'm old, not senile, son."

"Right. Are they in the bedroom or the study?" he inquired, looking up at the quaint house his father had moved into upon his wife's death, as if he couldn't stand to live at Clatter Hall without her.

"Neither. I left them in the entry for you," said Hamish as if it only made sense.

Ben silently got out of the car, catching himself mid tie-tug. With an effort, he retightened the offending apparel and straightened the sport coat he'd worn over a button down. He was at the door when his father yelled from the car window, "Don't forget my pipe and tobacco."

"Right. In the study?"

"Of course, where else would it be?"

Tonight is going to be a long night. His new business partner being present for the festivities only added to his conviction. When Althea had called to say she'd extended the invitation after speaking with Sam, he'd gotten an earful of choice words.

The first had been, "Bennett, why am hearing about Kate from Sam, and why didn't you invite her to begin with?" Followed by, "The poor woman is alone for Christmas in a foreign country." And ending with, "Where are your manners?"

There was no need to respond with anything other than, "I'm not sure where they've gone missing, but I'll be sure to find them by Christmas Eve."

When they arrived, there was no sign of Kate, and Ben's shoulders relaxed a fraction. He obediently carried the bag of paper-wrapped gifts to be set beneath the tree decorated in family heirlooms and garland. His family had always celebrated the night before rather than the day of, and Althea had continued the tradition since she went to her in-laws for the twenty-fifth. Her husband Douglas was a good man, content to let his wife rule over his life so long as she kept him in relative comfort. Though truthfully, he'd let her even if she didn't.

"Doug," said Ben, extending his hand in greeting.

"Good of you to come," Doug replied, shaking each man's

hand in turn.

"Yes, yes," said Hamish, eager to move past the niceties and get to the fun. Or was it the anticipation of food? Who knew where his father's priorities lay from one moment to the next?

"Henri, the boys are in the living room with Christmas crackers and soldiers. The battle of Waterloo is up next," said Doug conspiratorially.

"Ooh, I'll join you," gushed Hamish, a boyish gleam of excitement in his eyes as he trotted behind his grandson.

When the two disappeared from sight, Doug said, "Althea is in the kitchen, but I wouldn't go in there if I were you."

"The crackers?"

"I'm afraid so. In all fairness though, her temper didn't go off like a sparkler until we opened the second bag. It was something to behold," said Doug, doing his best to keep a straight face and losing spectacularly.

Althea was a perfectly rational Englishwoman until her Scottish temper lit up everything in its path.

"The boys, no doubt, ran for their rooms like the cowards they are."

"Quite right, but in all honesty, I haven't hurdled since uni. I may have pulled a hammy going over the couch," he replied with a noticeable limp down the hall.

Well, at least the night is off to a proper start.

"No bagpipes, I see."

Ben raised a single brow in response to the careless statement. He had deliberately left the infernal instrument in the boot of the car in hopes his father would forget about playing.

"Right," his brother in-law replied. "Best not to bring it up under the circumstances."

Chapter 8

Kate

"It's nothing," said Kate as she tried dislodging her coat at the same time as she handed bottles of brandy and red wine to Althea. "Eli and Sam left for the Highlands yesterday, and I was going to drown my sorrows."

With her flight home cancelled, and train travel shutting down due to the weather, Kate hadn't wanted to travel north in case she wound up stranded somewhere in between. Intending to spend Christmas alone in London, she'd explained the situation to her friend, but Sam had called in reinforcements at the last minute. Surprised to hear from Ben's sister, Althea, she worried it would be rude to turn down the invitation. Besides, she might as well have a happy Christmas instead of a sad, drink-alone one.

She had no idea if her business partner was planning to attend or if he knew about her own invite. Spontaneity was highly overrated in Kate's opinion, yet she had been engaging in it frequently since her arrival. She wondered if this was one of those moments when she was supposed to appreciate how her new home forced her to go beyond her comfort zone.

Kate self-consciously touched her forehead, feeling the small bumps clustered there. To top everything off, she'd woken up with a headache and the offending acne to herald her impending period. *Stupid hormones.*

Her mother would say she needed time on a horse. It was true, which was the main difference between herself and Laura. Kate knew her mother always had their best interest at heart, while her baby sister believed every suggestion from their mother required an automatic rebuttal.

"Come in, come in. Everyone else is through here," said Althea, leading the way. "Don't mind the mess; the boys have already been into the Christmas crackers."

She was clearly annoyed with her brood's antics in the way Kate imagined any tired parent would be. Kate followed Althea through the narrow townhouse entry into a sunken living room with a sunroom attached at the back to extend the space. The walls held framed watercolor scenes of parks and historical buildings above low-lying bookshelves stacked higgledy-piggledy with books of various covers, heights, and gilded spines. It looked like the ideal place to curl up with a cup of tea and stay a while, especially with the fireplace burning brightly in the background.

The men in the room stood from their various roosts as Althea introduced each of them. "And, of course, you know my brother. Here, let me take your bag and put it beneath the tree. It wasn't necessary to bring gifts for the children, but we both know they'll like you more for it."

"A girl's got to have goals," replied Kate, taking a seat in one of the vacant chairs closest to Hamish. She watched Ben from beneath her lashes, the frown she'd become accustomed to whenever he saw her lingering between his brows.

"So, you're the new business partner," said Hamish, his soft burr teasing Kate's ear. "No wonder Ben has been keeping you to himself."

"I haven't been keeping her to myself," Ben said from his other side, shaking his head in the negative.

"Then why haven't you brought her 'round?" Hamish accused, sounding mildly annoyed.

"Because she's my business partner and I didn't want her to change her mind," replied Ben with a smile playing at the corner of his mouth.

Hamish merely harrumphed in response and pulled his pipe from his coat pocket, only to have it snatched away by Althea on her way across the room. "You know the rules. Outside."

"Have a heart, lass; it's cold outside. You don't want yer poor Da catching his death of cold."

"The smoke is more likely to kill you than the weather."

"I bet Ben's new lass doesn't make him smoke outside."

"Da—"

"I know, I know. She's only yer business partner," he conceded, winking at Kate.

She laughed over the way he needled his son.

Ben scootched over to take his father's chair beside her. "I'd apologize on his behalf, but it wouldn't do any good."

"No apology needed. I like him," she said, smiling. "So, do you smoke?"

He gave her a half smile in return. "A cigar here and there, but nothing regular."

Kate nodded in understanding and an awkward pause filled the space, before she jumped in with, "If anyone should apologize, it's me. I'm the one crashing your family holiday."

"As you already stated, no apology needed."

"It's not like I haven't been away from home before." Why did she feel compelled to explain herself to him, she wondered.

"Oh?" he asked, but Kate didn't know if he was simply being polite.

"When I was married, my ex refused to visit my family for the holidays. Don't get me wrong, the ones we had were picture-perfect creations by a professional decorator and chef, but…" she trailed off, catching herself.

"A sterile affair lacking any warmth, huh?"

"Yeah. It was like there wasn't anything real behind the pretty trappings and we were just going through the motions," she said, taking another large swig from the wine glass Althea had placed in her hand—God bless her.

She was oversharing, even by American standards, but she felt inexplicably comfortable with Ben. And if Kate wanted to be honest, she was lonely. Eliza and Sam had their own life as a couple, and she was tired of being a third wheel. Her existence in Brooklyn had been full of family and friends. So far, London was only busy, damp, and cloudy instead of the fun, vivacious adventure she'd expected while expanding her business abroad.

"How long ago were you divorced?"

"Four years, but I've spent every Christmas since then with my family," she said wistfully.

Ben quirked a smile. "My mum was the queen of holidays. She always started with Guy Fawke's Night on the fifth of November and merrily made her way through Burns Night at the end of January. She was never happier than when she had a sparkler in one hand and a cocktail in the other. Of course, nothing compared to the year my father let the dogs into the dining room by accident with the dinner laid out and no one the wiser."

Gasping, Kate barely kept her wine from sloshing out of the glass. "Oh no!"

"Oh yes. And I ate so much trifle and mince pie, I had a stomachache for days. Meanwhile, my brother Felix vomited all over the new rug. Of the three of us, Althea was the only one to show any restraint when Mum told us we could eat dessert instead. I'm not sure she ever forgave my father for the rug."

Kate laughed softly. "Sure, she did. How could she not?" she asked, watching the older gentleman who now smelled of campfire playing with his grandchildren.

"I think she would love seeing him like this, especially with Henri."

"They seem like two peas in a pod."

Ben looked back at her, undecided. "He and Henri share certain similarities, most of which I can appreciate, but…" He halted as if he'd revealed too much.

If she wanted to be polite, she'd refrain from asking anything more, but the more time she spent with the man, the more intrigued she became about what made him tick.

"But?"

"Henri is incredibly intelligent, but he processes the world differently than other children. Relationships are…challenging, and emotions are difficult for him. He spends hours in his books and loves to run amok on the farm but doesn't seek out his peers at school."

"Is it possible he's introverted?" While Kate had always taken her sibling responsibilities seriously, part of why she enjoyed reading and horseback riding so much was because they offered peace and solitude.

"Aye, but his teacher thinks it might be something more. His development has been normal in most regards, aside from talking and reading, which occurred early by most standards. But he appears delayed in other areas."

"What do his pediatrician and teachers have to say?"

"At first, they said he'd catch up in his own time."

"But he hasn't?" she asked tentatively, trying to be sensitive.

"Not entirely. The tantrums occur less with routine and logical explanation or preparation, but life isn't always predictable."

"I prefer planning to spontaneity myself."

"Don't most reasonable people," he said dryly. "But for Henri it's something more. Flexibility and peer relationships are difficult for him."

"Actually, I know someone who might be able to offer some insight if you don't mind my reaching out on your behalf." Kate didn't tell Ben how she'd come to know the school psychologist through a volunteer program where she tutored kids in reading. Or how giving back to her community had been its own lifeline after Preston.

"Any help would be welcome at this point."

"Time for dinner, everyone!" trilled Althea from the dining room, dressed to the nines in a red velvet cocktail dress and matching lipstick. Kate didn't often feel underdressed, but she'd missed the memo tonight with only dark jeans and a Christmas sweater with Fa-la-la-la-la alternating in red and green on a snow-white backdrop.

She took her assigned seat and grinned until her dimples made a show of themselves. There on her plate lay a bright-yellow paper hat. She placed it atop her head and introduced herself to the dinner companion she had yet to meet. "Hi, I'm Kate. I work with your dad."

"I know," he said, looking at his plate instead of meeting her gaze.

So far, so good. "I hear you like to read."

"Mm-hm."

Kate grinned. "Me too."

He peeked up at her through the hair hanging over his left eye. "Cool."

It wasn't much, but it was a place to start. She smiled again and looked around the room, admiring the fresh greenery hung in celebration of the season. Her gaze traveled the length of table filled with platters and bowls, some of which she recognized and others at which she could only guess. When she locked eyes with Ben, he dipped his head in acknowledgement and a slight smile. The simple action shouldn't have meant so much, yet for a reason Kate couldn't fathom, it had.

Half an hour later, she sat back in her chair, her stomach uncomfortably full. "I think I ate too much," Kate said to no one in particular.

"No room for dessert, eh?" asked Hamish on her other side. "What a shame. I'm fond of dessert myself," he said with a twinkle in his eye, and for a split-second Kate wondered if Ben's father had let the dogs inside on purpose.

"If you're going to forgo anything though, it should be the spotted dick."

Kate almost spewed her wine all over the table, catching herself at the last second. "Words to live by," she croaked instead, flushing a bright red despite knowing the man was speaking about a traditional pudding with currents and custard.

Note to self: Remove spicy books with food references to prevent any future national incidents of epic proportions.

A hefty helping of the trifle later, and minus the infamous dessert, Kate said goodbye to her hosts, insisting they open gifts without her. She had a long day ahead of her tomorrow if she was going to throw a last-minute sale together for Boxing Day. She'd given her only employee the day off, thinking she'd be out of town anyway, but since she was here she might as well make the most of it.

"Kate," said Ben as she reached for the door handle. "You're leaving before the children open gifts?"

"Yeah, I've got some stuff to do tomorrow to get ready for Boxing Day."

"Oh."

She dithered for a moment before saying, "I should be going."

"Aye," he said, tugging at his tie.

No Christmas sweater for him like Doug or Hamish. Nope,

Bennett A.K. Galloway wore button downs with starched collars and ties he could tug on.

She'd like to tug on his tie sometime. *Wait, what?!*

"Well go on, kiss, or you'll have bad luck all year long," Althea said as she marched up the stairs with another bag of crackers, mumbling something about overgrown children and war.

"Um," said Kate, unsure of how to respond as she and Ben looked up to find they were standing under a sprig of mistletoe.

"Right," said Ben a second before leaning in to kiss her chastely on the cheek.

The touch of his lips was here and gone in a flash, but it made her wobbly in the knees, his scent of lavender and mint teasing her nose with its herbal scent. Or was it basil? Either way, yummy was what it was.

This is not happening, she firmly told her hormones, taking charge as her body perked up in unwanted ways at his nearness when he reached past her to open the door.

"I'm glad you came," he said quietly on the way to her car.

"Me too."

"Want to come to Bee Hill for Burns' Night?"

Kate paused mid-stride. "Maybe. What is it?"

"All the more reason you should come and find out," Ben replied vaguely.

"Okay," she said, still feeling warm from the brief contact of his lips on her skin.

He smiled fully, and her heart jolted to life at the sight.

This is so happening, cackled her hormones.

"I'll call you next week with the details. Happy Christmas, Kate."

Happy Christmas, indeed. Kate burrowed down beneath a heavy down comforter, the weight of which pushed her deeper into the mattress. Outside, the snow muffled the sounds of the city and goodwill of the season, while she dreamed of Nutcrackers with ties and stilettoed sugar plum fairies who weren't afraid to tug on them until lips met lips.

Chapter 9

Ben

As promised, Ben called Kate the next week with the details for the twenty-fifth of January to include supper, whisky, and poetry.

"My wife loved to celebrate Robert Burns," Hamish explained as they sat down at the dining table. "She was a great fan of the romantic poets. I never understood the fuss, but at least Burns was a Scot, and we get to eat haggis and drink uisge beatha. Or 'the water of life' as we like to refer to it," he said with a wink.

"Slàinte Mhath," said Sam, lifting his glass in a toast, to which everyone responded in kind.

"What does 'slanj-a-va' mean?" Kate asked under her breath, while everyone else dug into supper. "It wasn't in the book I checked out at the library."

He grinned, not surprised she'd done her research. "Good

health," Ben said, watching as she tasted the haggis pie with neeps and tatties.

"Wow, this is amazing," said Kate around a mouthful of turnips and potatoes.

"Aye," agreed Sam. "I don't know why haggis gets such a bad rap."

"Probably because it's made from a sheep's liver, heart, and lungs," interjected Eliza.

Sam pecked her cheek. "It's all right, lass; I love you even if you're a misguided vegetarian."

"You mean pescatarian."

"Aye, that too."

By the end of the night filled with toasts and odes to Scotland's poet, Hamish had loudly declared for everyone to hear, "Kate, yer delightfully charming and a breath of fresh air. Exactly what this stuffy place needs."

Ben heartily agreed but kept the opinion to himself.

Eliza had, of course, whisper-shouted, "I told you so," on her way out the door, slightly tipsy from a dram too many.

Sam clapped him on the shoulder and said, "Good luck, mate," and followed his fiancée and Kate in the direction of the walking path between the cottage and village, where they'd booked rooms at the Pillory Inn. "Stop swinging your torches in every direction," he yelled ahead. "I can't see two feet in front of me." The women merely laughed and swung their lights in a wider arc.

True to her word, Kate had also reached out to her friend on his behalf and brought with her a page of notes filled with strategies he could use at home and talk about with the teacher. It had only been a matter of weeks since then, but Henri's eye contact was improving, and Mrs. Albright had agreed to try a peer-to-peer mentorship in the classroom to help him engage more without feeling overwhelmed.

Kate had also brought Henri a few books from her own shelves and sheepishly confessed to toting a suitcase full across the pond. No wonder the thing had weighed a ton of bricks. She must have paid a pretty pound for the overage.

"I only brought the ones I feel homesick without. A solid romantasy is hard to come by, and who doesn't want to be Arwen and Éowyn from time to time?" she confessed, referring to two of J.R.R. Tolkien's heroes.

He would be the last to ever criticize her assessment, since every tale in which good conquers evil is essentially a love story, but wondered how the author would feel about her designation of his life's work. "Personally, I always thought Aragorn was the most fortunate man in Middle Earth."

Ben was also beginning to think he might feel homesick without her if she ever returned to Brooklyn. Still, as much as he liked Kate and found her attractive, he couldn't bring himself to do something about it. He pattered over to the front door in a pair of wool-lined slippers at the sound of a light rat-a-tat on the windowpane, Henri directly behind him and Percival yapping in excitement at his heels.

"If it isn't my favorite greeting committee," said Kate, smiling with her dimples and setting his heart into overdrive. As usual, she smelled like spring and looked like a summer day despite the winter weather. If he could have hung mistletoe in the cottage and office year-round without it being weird, he would have. The kiss he'd given her on Christmas Eve had been swift, innocent, and not at all the kind of kiss he'd wanted to give her.

Bracing herself against the door frame, he watched as Kate toed off her Chelsea boots onto the entry mat. He noted her switch to practical footwear. Bee Hill in winter was, unfortunately, no place for heels. Ben helped her out of a smart-looking wool blazer and hung it up beside his Mackintosh, wishing it lived there too before setting the notion aside like all of the others he had where she was concerned.

"I brought supplies to make Valentines for next week." She picked up the canvas tote bag she'd set down upon her arrival, stopping to rub Percival's belly when he shamelessly rolled over at her feet.

Returning his attention to the present, Ben scolded Percival without any bite behind it. "You wee scoundrel, always looking for attention."

The small dog cocked his head as if to say, *Aren't we all?*

"Valentine's Day used to be a Christian feast day to honor the martyr. He married couples in secret after Emperor Claudius

II banned marriage for soldiers. Now it's a commercialized day to celebrate love," said Henri in his usual factual manner.

Kate looked at Ben, her brows raised in question.

Ben stuck his hands in his cardigan pockets and shook his head in the negative. "Not my influence, I assure you, especially since St. Valentine is also the patron saint of beekeepers."

"Actually, Henri, my sister agrees with you," said Kate, her cupid lips pursed, drawing Ben's attention.

The little boy nodded in the affirmative as if to say, *Any levelheaded person would.*

"How do you feel about the holiday?" Ben asked, trying hard not to ogle her long, toned legs in the leggings she wore with a man's pinstriped button-down shirt, belted at the waist. As usual, Kate made an outfit look better than he'd normally notice. He switched gears from the idea of undressing her and kissing every potential freckle on her body, trying to pay attention to her words.

"Unfortunately, I'm a hopeless romantic. However, I prefer handmade Valentines with sappy poetry to fancy dinners or gifts," she confessed, picking up her bag and heading for the kitchen table to spread out supplies.

Ben smiled wide, following her with his son and Percival in tow.

An hour later, the trio had finished their homemade Valentine cards, and Percival had found his way into one of the chairs at the table, looking pleased over the inclusion.

"Who are your cards for?" Kate asked Henri.

Ben looked at his son's cards. They were each made from a single piece of folded red construction paper with the words *Happy Valentine's Day* written with black marker across the front. On the inside of the one closest to him was a drawing of the sun in relation to the earth and the words directly below it written in Henri's precise penmanship were, I love you to the sun and back, Grandad.

"One is for Grandad, and one is for Da."

His heart filled with so much love, Ben worried it might explode from his chest and all over the table. *Pull yourself together, old chap,* he admonished.

"Very considerate of you," Kate acknowledged.

She watched their interaction with a gentle smile, and Ben realized this was how Kate treated the people in her life—with tenderness and generosity. She extended herself to others without any consideration for what she might receive in return, and he and his son were simply the newest recipients of it.

Ben gently nudged Henri with his knee to remind him of his manners.

"Who are your Valentines for Kate?" Henri asked, twisting his lips back and forth, before peeking back at his father.

Ben ruffled his dark waves, and murmured, "Well done."

"I made one for my sister and I made one for you," she said, handing Henri what at first glance appeared to be layers of pink and red hearts held together by a brass button pin in the center so it resembled the petals of a flower.

"Um, thank you."

Kate chuckled at his forlorn expression. "Turn the hearts until you solve the word puzzle hidden within."

"Huzzah!" Henri exclaimed running from the kitchen.

Ben and Kate laughed in unison. "It won't take him long to figure it out, but it's more fun than a paper flower."

"One day, he'll understand receiving any flower from a beautiful woman is infinitely better than a puzzle he can solve."

"I guess it's a good thing I have one for you too then," said Kate, blushing a peachy pink he wished he could capture with his palm.

"Thank you," he said, his heart pumping full steam ahead once again.

Kate had a knack for making him feel more seen than he had in the last decade. He could get used to whiling away his afternoons with her. "Stay for tea?" Ben asked before he talked himself out of it.

"I'd love to, if it's not an imposition."

"I wouldn't have asked if it was."

"Of course you would," she said, her dimples playing peekaboo with him. "You're British; you can't help yourself."

"You're right," he said, chuckling. "But in this instance, I mean it—on one condition."

"Oh?"

"You have to take your tea and scone the proper way."

She didn't hesitate. "Milk after water and butter before jam."

"Good girl."

Kate

Kate squeezed her thighs together. The compliment was something her grandmother would have bestowed on her and Laura when they were children, but the luscious warmth winding through her body was anything but childish. How did Ben always know the right thing to say, and more importantly, why did his praise make her think of lying beneath him in a king-sized, four poster bed?

All right, so my to-be-read pile needs more diversity. But could anyone blame her for wanting to live vicariously through characters who took charge of their life in every way possible; they were her favorite kind of role models.

Who am I kidding; it's the only spice I currently have in my life. For every self-help book she read, there were four romance novels next to it on the bedside table. It didn't matter whether they were historical, romantasy, or contemporary. As long as the story had a happily ever after, it was fair game—all except for the ones labeled dark. Kate would never judge another reader's proclivities, but for herself, the violence and trauma could be potentially triggering.

Wiping crumbs and a dab of butter from her mouth, she rose from the dining table to carry her plate to the sink, where Ben was already washing the teacups. Like the rest of Bee Hill, the cottage reflected its owner, Kate noted. Constructed of local limestone and English oak, a bevy of windows let in an abundance of natural light, despite the murky weather that often dominated the skyline. The fireplace along the far wall was nearly tall enough to stand inside of, and the open floor plan held plenty of storage for books and an extensive vinyl collection, while the lived-in furniture upholstered in jewel tones matched the soft fabrics and informal style Ben adopted outside of the office. All of this produced a cozy respite from the world, similar to coming home to a giant hug at the end of a grueling day. In Kate's opinion, it was better than any movie cottage, and as real as the family who occupied it.

"There's been a break in the weather. Fancy a tour of the property? It'll be another couple of months before anything looks presentable but seeing everything at its dreariest will only make it more appealing when you see it in full bloom."

Kate decided a walk couldn't hurt after having eaten several biscuits in addition to the scone she'd slathered with butter and jam. She loved teatime and the British propensity for sweets and baked goods, but her pants were starting to hug her hips uncomfortably. Since turning down the afore mentioned wasn't even a consideration, farm tromping would commence henceforth. Shaking her head over the phrase, at least she could say her vocabulary had grown right along with her curves since moving to London.

"Sounds good."

"Henri," called Ben into the living room, where the boy sat on the couch beneath a bookcase bower. The large window at his back let in the muted light of a cloudy day and his flower valentine lay discarded next to him.

"Kate and I are going for a walk. Want to come with us?"

Without saying anything, Henri bounced up from the couch, Percival at his heels, and headed for the door.

Forty-five minutes later, they had seen the pruned lavender fields and the hibernating apiary that would produce next year's supply for Kate and Ben's shops. Henri had finally stopped running in circles with Bedivere as she returned a small flock of sheep to their pen for the night, except for a black ewe who followed Kate around to the side of the stables. She looked at Ben questioningly.

"I'll deal with her later. In the meantime, meet Calliope, Clio, and Thalia; the Greek muses of Bee Hill." He swept a hand in the direction of the goats munching in an adjacent patch of grass.

Kate snickered with disbelief. "Seriously?"

"Deadly. My father decided it would be vastly amusing to name the animals with Henri."

"And once he did, there was no going back," she said, understanding Henri's propensity to be inflexible.

"Precisely."

Henri grabbed her hand. "Come on, Kate! Let's visit the sultan and his harem."

She looked over her shoulder at Ben. "Do I want to know?"

Ben merely grinned until it reached his eyes, making her stomach do somersaults.

When they reached the hen house, Kate belly laughed. The sultan crowed loudly in response, out of competition or insult, she didn't know. She admired the fluffy feathers covering him from crest to feet and remembered reading about the breed in a random magazine article at her dentist's office. She snapped her fingers in recognition, saying, "Silkies."

"You would think he'd be less overbearing for the designation," said Ben, standing close enough for her to feel the heat of him. Kate barely stopped herself from leaning back into his chest.

Friend, friend, friend, she repeated to herself. *Not your boyfriend,* she reiterated for good measure, and excused the impulse as a result of being cold. The last thing she wanted to do was complicate their working relationship or the friendship blooming between them recently.

"It's never stopped a man before," she said, teasingly. Bouncing on her toes, and blowing into her hands, she tried to warm herself up. Why had she ever thought a blazer would be warm enough for this damp weather, she asked herself.

Ben slid his coat off and without a word put it over her shoulders before pulling a wool cap onto his head. She put her arms through the sleeves and firmly forbade herself from taking a sniff of the spicy, herbal scent trapped within the lining.

"Touché," he said, leaning in further and causing Kate's heart rate to spike. His neck was within nuzzling distance of her cold nose.

Damn this damp English weather.

"And there are the four horses of the apocalypse," Ben said, pointing to a fenced paddock a short distance away, pulling Kate from her silly notions.

"They're magnificent," she remarked, looking back and forth between their distinct coloring and the mischievous gleam in Ben's gaze. "Let me guess, all mares?"

"Every single one."

Kate swatted in his direction as if Ben were one of those pesky midges she'd heard about, though she wouldn't mind if he nipped her so long as it was in the right place. He chuckled as he grabbed her hand, sending a sigh of longing through her whole being. Against her better judgment, she stepped forward into his space.

"Percival, you scoundrel, you've lost your bowtie again," scolded Henri in a perfect imitation of his grandfather's brogue, bringing Kate back to her senses.

The pup rolled back and forth in the dirt between Henri's attempts to grab him.

"I should probably go referee," Ben said with an exaggerated sigh. He released her hand and reached for the tie he wasn't wearing.

Kate could practically hear his frustration over the missing article as he tugged on the collar of his chamois shirt instead. She gave him a quick, reassuring smile. "Parenting is a full-time job, or so I hear."

"Unfortunately. Shall we?" Ben asked, presenting her with his arm to take.

"I thought you'd never ask."

"Cheeky."

"Guilty as charged," she said as they passed a cat with a poof of short, greyish-blue hair all over its body. The animal lay stretched out across the path, a dead rodent before him as he methodically licked a paw. Kate raised a winged brow in expectation.

"Merlin."

"Naturally."

"Naturally," he confirmed, gracing her with a wink.

Her knees turned to Jello. Standing in close proximity wasn't helping her with the *this is only platonic status* either, but anything more would be a risk she wasn't ready to take, no matter how much he made her wobble.

Chapter 10

Kate

Kate dismounted and led Pale back into the stable where an elderly gentleman waited to take the reins. Bee Hill employed people from the local village to keep it running smoothly, but Jonas Dobbs was the only one she saw on a regular basis. Wherever something needed doing, whatever the job entailed, Dobbs made an appearance. From stable hand to carpentry or sheepherding, he was Ben's right-hand man.

"I've got this," she said, taking a brush from one of the metal hooks hanging across the way.

He blinked, his wiry eyebrows dipping so low they virtually connected with his wizened cheeks in the process. Taking a handkerchief from his pocket, he wiped his forehead before placing a tweed driver's cap back on top, hands gnarled and knotted with arthritis. She watched him take short, measured strides toward the paddock outside. Mr. Dobbs was a man of few words, and though she didn't know him well, she liked him for the simple reason the horses did. His patience and gentleness were clear in the way he oversaw them, and they responded similarly to those who rode them.

She led Pale into her stall, removing the saddle, bit, and reins with practiced competence. Brushing long, smooth strokes over the mare's body and murmuring words of praise, Kate watched her white-blonde ears twitch in pleasure. Afterward, she ran her hands over the legs to check for any injuries and cleaned out each hoof.

"If you want a job as a stable hand, you're hired," said Ben from where he leaned, a cap pulled low on his brow. He pushed off the gate and walked into the stall.

"I think Mr. Dobbs might be offended."

"True. He's worked for my family for as long as I can remember."

"No desire to retire, huh?"

"Have you ever met Mrs. Dobbs?"

With a negative shake of her head, she said, "No."

"There were never two people more opposite than Jonas and Eugenia Dobbs. As you may have noticed, he is a man of few words."

"Yeah, so…Oh my. Loquacious, is she?"

"Quite."

Kate laughed. "Well, this explains a few things."

"It does, doesn't it?" he murmured as if deep in thought about something she was unaware of.

His accent wasn't helping her put aside the twitterpated nonsense she'd begun feeling since her tour of Bee Hill. Who was she kidding? She'd had feelings for the man since he picked her up at the airport. They hadn't been overly warm and fuzzy, but every couple had to start somewhere.

First impressions weren't always accurate. Determined to avoid an attraction, Kate could admit to initially overreacting. It would seem she was more like Austen's Elizabeth Bennett than she wanted to acknowledge. Either way, she now knew Ben was the kind of man she could potentially pine after for the rest of her life.

Pine? she asked herself, smacking her forehead with a hand as she followed him out of the stables.

Reminder: remove Regency romances from your weekly bookstore trip to Waterstones this week.

Besides, she reasoned, no one needed a full-sized bookcase in an already tiny apartment, let alone two. Fine—she had enough books for three but who was counting except herself?

March had been surprisingly warm and dry, squelching her doubts about London's capricious weather, until April arrived with enough rain and cooler temperatures to reverse her opinion. Everyone who came through the shop swore it was a fluke. Still, Kate was glad to see May arrive in the expected fashion.

Creating an excuse to visit Bee Hill and its proprietor, as well as taking her mother's advice, she'd started riding the course on the property with Ben regularly. Fortunately, it was like riding a bike and she had yet to embarrass herself beyond how she walked after an hour on a horse.

"I hope you don't mind my taking you up on the offer to ride without you. I checked in at the office, but they said you were in the village. With the break in the weather, I couldn't resist getting outside and the solitude was a breath of fresh air," she rambled.

"Of course not," Ben said, his gaze steady and penetrating as though he could read her every thought. "Sometimes, a person just needs a break from the city."

"You'd think I'd be used to it by now, but I'd forgotten how much I miss this," she said, looking around.

"Oh?"

"Yeah, the space, fresh air and, best of all, the kind of exercise you can feel in your muscles."

"So why do you keep moving to the big city?" he asked, the corner of his mouth twitching with a smile.

"Honestly, when I left for Stanford, the plan was to move back to Midwell and go into the family business with my siblings."

"How come you didn't then?"

"I met Preston," she said on a sigh. It wasn't a good reason for giving up her dream, but it was the truth. "And now, the city offers a certain anonymity from the past. Life went sideways for all of us, but my sister seems to have found her way with Nick. Something tells me I'll be an aunt in no time," she said with a snort."

Ben's lips inched up at the corners in a slow smile. "They sound genuinely happy."

"Yeah, I think they are," she said, wistful. "I leave for the wedding on Wednesday."

"How long will you be gone?"

"A week. This way I'll be there for all the pre-wedding activities and have a couple of days afterward to take care of any outstanding items at the shop in Brooklyn.

"So, no visit anytime soon."

Did he sound as disappointed as she felt? Surely, it was a figment of her imagination caused by the insatiable yearning for something more with her business partner. Or was it time to take a break from Regency romances for real? Seriously, how did writers produce such drivel? Ugh.

If it were possible to kick oneself, she would. Instead, she said, "Nope. You'll have to find a way to carry on without me, I suppose."

"Whatever will we do without you, my darling girl?" he asked, the look on his face unreadable.

Kate's heart jumped into her throat. She was sure he didn't mean anything by the endearment, yet it made her feel bright and shiny, as if he'd sprinkled her in glitter or fairy dust. Finding her voice, she replied lightly, "Pine for me, no doubt."

Ugh. Now she'd said the word aloud.

He extended his arm for her to take, as was his recent habit, watching her steadily. "No doubt."

She'd become so accustomed to his manners, Kate had stopped

asking herself what he meant by it and snuggled in as closely as she dared, enjoying the scent of lavender and herbs wafting from his coat. Ben was the consummate gentlemen, her business partner, and a friend. Surely those were the reasons he acted the way he did, without her reading anything more into it.

They walked in companionable silence until cresting the knoll overlooking the office and parking lot.

"Bloody hell," Ben muttered.

"Is everything all right?" asked Kate, confused, as a tall, lanky man loped up the hill toward them.

"No. My brother Felix is here," he said, right before the offending family member came to an abrupt stop in front of them.

Kate's guard instantly rose up in defense, though for Ben's sake or her own, she didn't know. The man had hair the color of brown sugar, a calculating gleam in his sky-blue eyes, and a solid chin. He looked nothing like his brother, but she could see the resemblance he bore to Althea.

"Hi, you must be Kate, the business partner," said Felix reaching to shake her hand before swiping the bangs out his eyes, as was the most recent trend. She preferred Ben's more refined style turned rake when he was tired or stressed to his brother's forced attempt to look roguish.

She noticed Ben tug at the collar of his shirt where he'd already pulled the tie loose beneath a navy sweater vest. She didn't know why he bothered to wear one when he was in the office, other than a leftover routine from his previous life in London, and it made her think of Henri's bow tie for Percival. Did the tie make the man any more than it did the dog?

The concept made her grin, and Felix grinned back in response, mistakenly thinking it was for his benefit. She looked away in an effort to convey her disinterest. He was certainly an arrogant one, but in the scheme of things, harmless.

"Old chap," the younger Galloway said with a quick dip of his chin in his brother's direction, all the while keeping his eyes glued to Kate.

"Felix," said Ben, sounding strained. "What brings you home? Did the fashion world take a hiatus?" he growled.

Kate found the deep sound strangely titillating.

Okay, so no more books with Alpha males for the time being either, she conceded. At this rate, romance as an entire genre would be nonexistent in her TBR pile by June. Kate forced her attention back to the situation at hand.

"Oh, you know, in between jobs for a minute. Thought I'd stop in before heading back to Paris."

Kate could see the gleam in his eyes, but she didn't know what to make of it, until he asked, "Fancy a ride, Kate? My brother says your horsemanship is excellent. We could get a drink down at the pub afterward."

How Felix managed to turn a compliment from Ben into something resembling an invitation to hook up, Kate wasn't certain, but decided his ego could use knocking down a peg or two.

"Actually, a ride sounds great, as long you don't mind Ben," she said with a glance his way. "I can meet you back at the office when we're done with the course?"

He was normally grumpy when his blood sugar dropped, but this was a whole new level of cranky. Ben was glaring at Felix like he wanted to throat-punch him. Had his brother done something to warrant his reaction or was the man only hangry? Personally, she could use a charcuterie board and large glass of wine herself, especially after this interaction.

But first, she planned to wipe the smug look off Felix's face by winning.

"Fine," Ben growled, pulling so hard on his collar the top button popped free and sailed directly into his brother's temple.

"Ouch," the younger man yelped.

"Apologies," Ben remarked, but the toothy grin on his face said he was anything but sorry as he strode away.

Half an hour later, Kate skipped all the way down to the office with her own wide smile. She'd beat Felix on the course by two jumps. It would seem out of the Galloway brothers, Ben was the better rider. She made a quick combo punch with her fists to celebrate her victory in contrast to the stillness of twilight as it descended over the land surrounding Bee Hill, a quiet guardian of all it surveyed.

Ben

"Not out with Felix, I see," said Ben as he entered the office, trying to sound neutral despite the jealousy eating away at his stomach lining. He'd been watching for Kate from the warehouse, pretending to work on an order for a tea shoppe in the States. "I wondered if he'd talk you into having a drink with him, after all."

"He didn't seem to be in a celebratory mood after I won," she replied with a dainty shrug. "And he suddenly recalled dinner plans with your father. Besides, he kind of reminds me of someone I once knew."

"Felix has never been a gracious loser, I'm afraid." Ben gave her half smile and let out the breath he'd been holding since watching them disappear together over the rise. He might not be ready to tell Kate how he felt, but if she'd gone out with Felix tonight it would have been the first time he'd hated his brother for longer than a minute.

His feelings for her were already well beyond any he'd ever indulged in for Monique. Those had been shallow and shaped by what was surely the warped memory of an initial meeting. "Wait. Are you talking about your ex?" he asked, going back to her last statement.

"Yeah, but I don't want to discuss Preston tonight."

He'd have to be a total plonker not to notice how reticent she was to talk about her marriage whenever the subject came up, but he was beginning to think there was more to it than the usual regrets caused by divorce.

"Why didn't you correct me when I assumed Henri's mother was your wife?"

Ben sighed and plopped down on the leather couch beside her. "I take it Felix tried to garner your sympathies as a widower."

"Something around the vicinity of it," she replied, waving the scenario away.

Leaning his head against the back of the wall, Ben closed his eyes in exhaustion, real or imagined didn't matter at the moment. "The situation was…is complicated."

"I'll try to keep up," she said dryly.

A laugh rumbled from him in response before he caught himself. It hardly seemed appropriate under the circumstance. "Monique first came to Clatter Hall when I called in a favor from the British Museum. She was the intern they sent to identify and catalogue certain artifacts in the gallery." He swallowed hard over his foolishness yet again. "I fell for her at first sight, and in the end she chose Felix. Henri arrived shortly after."

"Wait. Were you and Monique…did she marry your brother after the two of you…" Kate's skin turned a pretty blush with her assumptions, reminding him of the Pashmina roses his father had given his mother every year on their wedding anniversary.

He wanted to reach out and touch her cheek but refrained. Ben feared his heart might not survive if she rejected him, as he expected she would. They were friends, which was too valuable to carelessly cast aside because of a romantic inclination on his part. And then there was their working relationship to consider. Both Bee Hill and the estate were better off for her influence as well. Instead, he told himself to focus on the present conversation.

"No, no. It was nothing of the sort. Regardless of my intentions, Felix won her heart, and before I realized what was going on right under my nose, they were married, and the rest is history as they say."

"Oh, Ben."

"No pity, please. Whatever my circumstance, I brought it on myself."

"How come you're raising Henri then, and why does he call you Da instead of Uncle?"

"The sicker Monique became, the more Felix faded into the background. You might say my brother's constitution for the trials of life is lacking fortitude."

"But yours isn't," she said staunchly, making him crack a genuine smile for the first time since his brother's arrival.

"I blame it on a misplaced sense of duty. You know, onward and upwards, and whatever else we do in the name of family honor."

It was Kate's turn to smile, the lines at the corner of her eyes peeking out to taunt him with something else he couldn't have.

"Or maybe chivalry isn't dead, after all," she said, her dimples on display.

"Regardless, I accepted the responsibility."

"And Henri, as logical as he is, understood the situation perfectly. Felix is his biological father, but you're his Da."

"Still, with no time to prepare Henri for Felix's visit, today could have ended very differently." All the way around, thought Ben, with another longing look at Kate's profile within touching distance. He curled his fist at his side to keep from reaching out. At least she didn't appear enamored with Felix.

"I think your brother, for all his foibles, knew exactly with whom he was leaving Henri and what would happen when he did."

"Oh?" he asked, seeking her approval.

"Mm-hm. Felix may not be a man of his word, but he knows you are." Kate softly kissed his cheek and sprang to her feet, not looking back at him until she reached the doorway. "You are an honorable man, Ben Galloway. The world could use more like you."

Chapter 11

Kate

"Hey Lon, it's me. Again. Checking in—for the THIRD time—to see when your flight arrives."

She had hoped to catch up with her brother before the night's festivities, but it was only one of a dozen things currently in a holding pattern. The redeye flight from London to New York had been turbulent, sleepless, and, to top it all off, her luggage was MIA.

Kate harrumphed in a decidedly un-ladylike fashion, adjusting the neck pillow clipped to her purse and tapping her toe in irritation as she waited to move forward in line at the airline's baggage counter. It would have given her a semblance of satisfaction had she been wearing heels, but alas, she had on white platform tennis shoes with the Ralph Lauren pant suit she'd bought at a TK Maxx on clearance. Laura would be proud, but flying the friendly skies overnight was highly overrated.

Archive the following for future reference: Basic Economy is exactly what it sounds like—cheap.

Kate discreetly sniffed the air. The man in front of her smelled like bacon, eggs, and maple syrup, making her stomach grumble loudly with hunger. Before she could get in another whiff of eau de breakfast, a smartly put together airline representative said, "Next," with more perkiness than five-thirty in the morning called for.

Kate slung her purse onto her other shoulder, coming close to giving the petite woman behind her a black eye in the process. "I'm so sorry," she said with a grimace. "Ooh, I like your scarf. Silk?"

The woman gave her a polite smile and bobbed her head in the affirmative, the material in question staying firmly in place over her hair despite the movement. Kate could barely keep her hair tucked into a ponytail without the wisps at the front finagling their way out. Any woman who could keep her hair fully contained had her admiration, and the shimmering mocha material was to die for.

Ignoring the kink in her neck and pasting a winning smile into place—the one she used with finicky customers—Kate stepped forward. "Good morning. I was on flight BA1527 from Heathrow, but apparently my bag missed the memo," she finished, chuckling lamely.

"Oh dear," said the employee. "Hold on one moment."

"Sure." Kate resumed tapping her toe and tucked her hands into her pockets in lieu of crossing her arms.

"Your ID, please."

Unzipping the side pocket of her purse and pulling out her passport, Kate set it on the narrow ledge of the counter.

Clickety-clack went the keys of the keyboard. "Ah. It would seem your luggage is stuck somewhere in between."

In between?

"I'm sorry, but how does luggage get stuck somewhere in between when the flight was direct?" Kate took a deep breath and refrained from jumping over the desk to check the computer for herself. "It's either still at Heathrow or it's somewhere here, right?"

The employee flashed another placid smile but in the face of Kate's expression dropped the peppy demeanor.

"They overbooked the flight and sent a load of bags on the next one due to weight restrictions. Yours is one of them."

"Okay," said Kate, taking in a deep breath. There was obviously nothing more she could do other than wait. "When should I expect my bag?"

The employee clacked away at the keyboard yet again before saying, "This afternoon. Here, write your address for delivery on this."

Reaching for the notecard and pen, Kate scribbled the address of the hotel she'd booked and slid it back across the counter. "Thanks."

Without sparing Kate a glance, the employee called, "Next!" The overbright smile reappeared for the benefit of everyone else in line.

Fortunately, Laura's bridal shower brunch wasn't until the following morning and Kate's bridesmaid dress was awaiting the final fitting in a schmancy Manhattan boutique their mother had picked.

Fine, everything will be fine. She reached for the box of chocolate-covered blueberries in the bottom of her purse, aggressively tearing it open in her haste and losing half of the contents on the floor. She stopped to survey the damage, then emptied the rest of the box directly into her mouth, feeling cranky and moderately feral. What would Ben think if he could see her now?

He'd wink and say, "Time to put the kettle on. Everything will sort itself out."

Come to think of it, that was the primary reason King George lost the American colonies to begin with, Kate mused. If he'd refrained from taxing tea without representation, the situation may have resolved itself over a strong cuppa. Kate gathered up as many chocolate blueberries from the ground as she could hold and tossed them into the nearest garbage receptacle, then marched off in the direction of a café for further fortification.

According to her mother, the next three days would be a whirlwind of pre-wedding festivities, all of which should be easy-peasy, lemon-squeezy. *Competent is my middle name,* chanted Kate's inner voice. She took sips of the fragrant bergamot tea in between bites of scone, wiping a dab of whipped butter from the corner of her mouth. Laura deserved a perfect day, and Kate had every intention of being the maid of honor her baby sister deserved.

Stepping to the curb, she put her game-face on, brought two fingers to her recently glossed lips, and let out a sharp whistle into the muggy East Coast air. Hopefully, the predicted storm would hold off a while longer.

"Where to, Miss?" asked the cabbie as she slid into the backseat.

"Library Hotel, Midtown, please. The one across from the public library."

Due to the fire at Walker's Pub a couple of months before, she no longer had an apartment to go home to. Thankfully, no one had been hurt. Laura and Micky were living with Uncle Joe until the wedding, and though Kate could've stayed with Chaucey, she and her fiancé Dean were busy planning a double ceremony—Catholic and Hindu—for June, the following year.

She would have felt left out, except it was impossible to around Nick's family. For one, there were a lot of them. But they also had a way of embracing everyone who came into their orbit. As far as they were concerned, the Howards, by proxy of marriage, were now honorary Kellys.

"Here, you look like you could use this," said Nick's oldest sister, Aria, a few hours later.

"Thanks," said Kate, looking up and taking the fluted glass of bubbly. She sounded loud to her own ears with the heavy bass bouncing off the walls of the club. Nick and Laura were on the dance floor slowly dancing, lost in each other's gaze, despite the upbeat tempo of the music.

"They're disgustingly happy, aren't they?"

Kate laughed low. "Yeah."

"Don't get me wrong; I'm happy for them, and God knows they both deserve some love out of this life."

"But?"

"But it also makes me feel pathetically sad for myself."

Kate looked directly at the other woman. "I'm sorry. Laura told me you lost your husband a couple of years ago."

"We would have been married fifteen years next week. But who's counting?" She shrugged as if to say it was what it was.

Kate knew better though. Grieving was a natural part of the healing process, but it could also steal the future away if a person let it. Ben was a prime example. Aside from messing up their partnership, or worse, their friendship with a silly crush, she was afraid to tell him everything about Preston. What would he think of her if she told him how she'd stayed in an abusive relationship?

Kate rolled her eyes. No one ever got what they wanted with self-doubt; it was time to rein in her self-talk with some action. She stood, taking Aria's hand. "Come on, let's show them we still know how to have fun."

Aria smirked, shaking her hips with the rhythm of the music until her mini dress shimmied down her thighs and shimmered under the strobe lights, causing those seated at the bar to watch the brunette appreciatively. Kate laughed, carefree for the moment, and strode after her, earning several head turns of her own.

With a shake of hips and her hands in the air, Kate allowed the attention to assuage her insecurities momentarily before forgetting everyone else and dancing only for herself.

The next morning arrived early with a throbbing headache. "Whoever opened the curtains is hereby banished and cursed," Kate mumbled too loudly for her poor head. "Oo."

"Morning, cow eyes!" yelled Laura. "Goin' to the chapel and we're gonna get married," she crooned directly into Kate's ear.

Kate tossed the nearest pillow in her sister's direction. "Oo," she moaned and grabbed her head with both hands as she sat up. "Aria is a dead woman."

"The last three shots were all you, gorgeous," said Chaucey, handing Kate two acetaminophen and a tall glass of water, which she thirstily gulped down. "Now, drink this. Careful, it's hot."

"I wouldn't have had them without the three glasses of champagne first. Those were definitely Aria's fault." She lifted the steaming cup to her lips. "Hmm, tea. Better. Thank you."

"Like I would give you anything else," Chaucey replied, her dress muffling the response as she slipped it over a fancy lingerie brand Kate recognized from London.

"You sound like him," she grumbled, missing Ben.

"Like whom?" asked Chaucey.

"The grumpy Englishman," piped Laura from the vanity,

where she was trying and failing to apply eyeliner.

"Here," said Kate, forcing herself out of bed. "Let me help you," she continued, placing her teacup on the bedside table. "Oo," she moaned before catching herself. "Serves me right, and what are you talking about?"

"You mean who, and I'm talking about Bennett Alexander Keats Galloway, the guy you couldn't stop blabbing about after one shot in."

Kate felt her jaw drop open as if it were missing a hinge to hold it closed. She snapped it shut with an audible click, which only made her throbbing head ring more. "Oo," she said once again and sat down on the floor, drawing her knees into her chest.

"I told you his whole name?" Kate put her head into her hands. "Oh my—

"You shared more with a club full of people than you have with me in the last nine months," interrupted Laura.

"Please tell me I didn't," begged Kate, mortified.

"Drink," said Laura, getting down on her sister's level and handing her the teacup. "You know, it's okay to let yourself fall for someone again," she finished gently.

"What if I pick another bad apple?" Kate asked in a small voice she despised. It reminded her of the woman she'd been with Preston.

"You won't, because you know better now—love is never manipulative, threatening, or abusive."

"I second the motion," Chaucey said staunchly.

Kate didn't smile, but she nodded her head in understanding—she wasn't alone, and though the lesson had been hard earned, she knew real love looked nothing like Preston's distorted version of it.

"Technically, Ben is both English and Scottish."

"All right then," Chaucey declared, "let's hear all about your grumpy, tie-tugging, sleeve-rolling Brit. He sounds absolutely scrumptious."

"C.J., you're engaged!"

"Yes, but I'm not dead."

Chortles of throaty laughter filled the crowded hotel room and something akin to hope rushed into the black holes Preston had left behind in Kate's heart, birthing something new for the future.

Did you know, dear reader, one theory suggests a new universe is born when a black hole collapses. I wonder what this phenomenon could mean for our princess. It may be nothing but science fiction, but wouldn't it be fun if it weren't?

The wedding was exactly what she would have expected from her sister, if somewhat understated when compared with Beth Howard's expectations. Escorted by Nick's older brother Leo, Kate followed the radiant bride and besotted groom down the aisle to the applause and whistles of family, friends, and colleagues, all the while wishing she could take back the three shots of tequila from the night before. Even smiling hurt.

An hour later, Kate dug through the bag she'd thrown in the corner of the surf-and-turf restaurant her folks had rented for the reception at Laura's insistence, instead of an oversized, and potentially overpriced venue in Manhattan's SoHo or Upper East Side. For someone usually so pragmatic, their mother had a tendency to show off with lavish entertainment.

"Looking for these?" asked Aria, holding out a bottle of ibuprofen.

Kate glanced over her shoulder to see the rest of the Kelly clan getting down on the dance floor to "We Are Family" by Sister Sledge, including Nick and Laura, who had mysteriously disappeared after the first dance. Her new brother in-law's shirt appeared to be buttoned cattywampus and her sister's perfectly steamed dress was suddenly…distressed. Kate shook her head and hoped wherever they'd gone to celebrate privately had been sanitary, if not comfortable.

"Is it that obvious?"

"Nope, but I figured you're as hungover as I am."

"For the first and last time in my life."

"Seriously?"

Kate shrugged. "I don't like being out of control."

"Me either. At least nowadays. Once upon time though, I was

fun."

"How fun?"

"Dance-on-top-of-the-bar fun, and I was completely sober at the time."

"I want to be you when I grow up."

"Actually, it's how I met my husband. Some jerk couldn't keep his hands to himself, and Miles was the bouncer at the club. He kicked the guy out and promptly asked me to dinner."

"When did Miles decide to become a cop?"

"It was always his plan. I was barely twenty and incredibly naïve."

Kate watched Laura as she mingled amongst the other guests.

"Don't worry; Nick and the squad made sure Laura knows what she'd getting into."

"Of the two of us, she was always the brave one."

"I don't know," Aria said, bumping shoulders with her. "Loving yourself enough to leave a bad situation sounds pretty brave to me."

"Did I spill my entire life story last night?"

"Not everything, but enough for me to get the gist. And for the record, your grumpy Englishman sounds like an excellent way to get back in the saddle."

"Oh my gosh, who else did I tell?"

"Only everyone within a city block radius. You were quite animated about him."

"At least Ben wasn't there to witness my fall from grace,"

groaned Kate.

"Whatever makes you feel better," laughed Aria.

"All the single ladies on the dance floor, please," announced the D.J., playing Beyoncé in the background.

Aria grabbed her by the hand. "Come on, let's show them how this is done with dignity."

Kate tried to pull away, but the other woman held steadfastly to her hand. "You don't have to reach for it, but you do have to stand here with me."

Laura had her back to the crowd, the blue satin bow tied lopsided at her waist, droopy from its earlier groping. Kate rolled her eyes and focused on the electrical tape running the length of the makeshift dance floor. At least her sister didn't seem upset by Lon's absence. Apparently, the love bubble was holding steady and made of durable plastic. She, on the other hand, had every intention of giving him what for when he finally returned her phone calls—if he returned them. Her last message may or may not have contained several threats and uncomplimentary truths about his current behavior. Broken heart aside, it was time Lon removed his head from his gluteus maximus.

"One, two, three," Laura counted.

Trying to be a good sport for her sister's sake, Kate beamed and looked up just in time to catch the bouquet of peonies and tulips—with her face. "Eff me."

Aria cackled beside her. "You are officially my new wing

woman. Two pieces of cake coming right up."

"And tea. A ginormous cup of tea," whined Kate, leaving the offending bouquet on the ground for someone else to pick up. She missed London and missed Ben more. Despite the economy flight awaiting her, she was ready to leave Brooklyn in her rearview mirror again.

Chapter 12

Ben

Bees bobbed and droned amongst the tightly closed blooms, eagerly awaiting August and the opportunity to pollinate, as Ben moved up and down the rows of lavender bushes. He longed to run his hands gently across the tops, to feel the flowers before their peak and capture the fragrance with his fingertips, but it would only earn him a sting for the effort. Instead, he contentedly raised his face to the sun and breathed deeply, sorting the smell of hay from the heady aroma of manure tilled into the dirt.

This year's lavender crop and honey production would be as large as he'd hoped if the weather continued to cooperate. Ben crossed the fingers he'd tucked in his pockets to avoid the temptation of touching the plants. Henri soared from field to field in the distance as though he were a bird riding the wind, Bedivere close at his heels and herding him between the gently rolling mounds dotting the property.

If he had to guess, they were the burial grounds for those who'd made Bee Hill their home long before his family, but he had no wish to disturb the dead or his peace with archaeology at present. Someday in the future he would call in another favor, this time from a former classmate turned professor at Oxford, but until then he could hypothesize about them.

"Da," Henri called, interrupting his musings. "When is Kate coming to visit?"

It was an excellent question. He hadn't heard from her since she'd left for her sister's wedding. "I'm not sure," he answered honestly and wondered yet again if something had happened to cause her to pull away from them. When he'd asked Eliza if she was back and well, she'd merely given him a vague answer about settling in and taking stock.

Was it possible he'd done something to make her feel uncomfortable about their time together? They didn't usually discuss relationships aside from their mutual friends or families, which meant it was entirely possible she had a life outside of the one he knew.

Ben frowned. *Like a random bloke she met at the wedding.* Kate might very well be taking stock of her life in London if there was someone new back home.

"We should visit her then," piped Henri with the innocence of a child. "Maybe she thinks it's our turn."

Well, he couldn't very well argue with such reason. "Right, then; we may as well take next week's delivery with us. All hands-on deck tomorrow, but for now, what say you to dinner and an extra chapter at bedtime?"

"Aye, aye, Captain!"

The following day, Agnes arrived early and uninvited, taking charge of the situation. She checked his list twice and suggested he add two extra boxes of soap, a box of lotion, and another case of honey samples. He didn't argue, knowing better than to doubt her intuition or intentions. Henri and Hamish helped him load the smaller boxes into the lorry, while he loaded the larger ones.

Ben closed the back of the truck and dusted off his hands. "I think that's everything."

"I thought I'd go with you," declared Hamish.

A single dark brow rose above Ben's right eye. "Since when do you frequent the shops on Portobello?"

"I don't. I want to see yer sister and the boys."

"You do know Althea lives in Fulham, not Notting Hill?"

"Of course I do. I'm old, not senile."

"You also know the lorry is going to be a tight fit for the three of us?"

His father watched him as though he'd gone daft to ask such a thing.

"Right, then. Let me make a quick phone call before we leave."

By the time Ben returned from calling Althea to make her

aware of the change in plans, Henri and Hamish were engrossed in a book about ancient Egypt. Neither of them acknowledged his return, which suited him just fine. He could use a moment of peace and quiet to gather his thoughts after the hectic morning.

He'd left a message detailing the premature delivery with someone named Zaya yesterday but hadn't heard back from her. Would Kate be excited to see him? He gripped the steering wheel tightly. This was a bad idea.

"Are we going sometime today?" asked Hamish. "And turn up the air conditioning. It's bloody hot in here," he complained as Ben turned the key in the ignition.

The lorry's tires bumped roughly over the graveled car park, causing the three of them to bounce on the bench until they reached the main road.

"You're the one who insisted on going with us. Besides, it's only twenty degrees outside."

"Yes, but you know how Althea feels about my going *au naturel*," he grumbled as he looked down at the utility kilt no doubt concealing shorts beneath it.

"Doubled up, are we?" was all he said in return, cranking up the air as his father rolled down the window. Ben lifted his eyes heavenward.

An hour later they pulled to the curb near Lavender Honey & Co. The traffic into the city had been maddening, his stomach clenching with hunger a half hour into the drive. He frowned and tugged at the collar of his knit shirt, feeling hangry, as Kate referred to it. Hopefully, she had a snack on hand, or better yet, she could go to lunch with them. At least Henri had eaten a proper breakfast and seemed no worse for the journey.

"Althea is going to meet us here after Doug gets home with the car," he told his father.

"Fine, fine," said Hamish. "Anything, so as long as I don't have to take the tube. No one minds the rules anymore."

Ben sighed, knowing it would be futile to argue with his father's perspective of the world. He'd had one encounter five years ago and hadn't taken public transportation since. "I know, Da, everything is going to Hell in a handcart."

"Exactly."

"You did put Althea into a bit of a bind with the last-minute visit though."

"Tosh, your sister doesn't mind. Besides, I wanted to see Kate anyway—top notch, that lass. You'd do well to snatch her up before someone else does."

"Right. Let's keep your unsolicited advice between us for now." Ben held the door open for Hamish and Henri, who had his face pressed to the glass of the pet grooming boutique next door.

Kate's flawless taste instantly enveloped them in cool marble countertops, painted display tables, wide-planked wood floors, and the smells one would expect to encounter based on the shop's name. His shoulders relaxed, the tension between his shoulder blades caused by the drive easing marginally.

Henri was the first to spot her toward the back with a clipboard in hand, the throngs of people milling around not at all a deterrent for his laser focus. "Kate, we brought you a delivery," he said, rushing past the crowd near the cash register and display tables, limbs pulled in tight and lips twisting from side to side as though they were a compass directing the way.

Kate

Turning at the sound and eyes wide with surprise, Kate exclaimed, "Thank goodness you're here!"

She'd come back from her sister's nuptials to a disaster of epic proportions. Okay, epic might be overkill, Kate conceded, but this would never have happened if she'd been there.

Due to inventory errors, three regularly scheduled deliveries hadn't shown up, and now she was scrambling to keep up with demand. Summer tourism was one of her biggest sources of income before the holiday season and the end of the year. Proximity to the seasonal crowds had been the main reason she'd chosen Portobello for the shop's location in the first place, but it was only as good as her products' availability.

Seriously misjudging her manager Zaya's capabilities was something she'd berate herself for later though. It certainly wasn't going to solve her problems right now. Bee Hill's delivery, on the other hand, was a gift straight from Heaven and an answer to the prayer she'd flippantly put out into the universe in a moment of desperation. As her mother often reminded her, God was open for business twenty-four hours, seven days a week. If she didn't take advantage of it, she had no one to blame but herself.

She didn't stop to think as she strode directly for Henri, taking his hand and pulling him along with her before reaching Ben and kissing his cheek with gratitude. "You are my knight in shining armor. How did you know?"

Kate could tell it wasn't what he'd expected, but when he reciprocated with a hug, she leaned into it. Fine, she may have nestled in more than was necessary, but she'd gotten a nose full of lavender and herbs for her efforts—completely worthwhile and a balm for her frantic pace.

"Didn't you get the message I left with Zaya yesterday?"

"Ugh. No, but I'll explain why while we unload the truck."

"No kiss for me?" Hamish asked.

Ben's brows rose, losing themselves beneath the hair waving over his forehead, but Kate merely grinned and leaned in to give the older gentleman a kiss on the cheek he presented.

"Thank you."

The pleased smirk Hamish shot at Ben made him frown, and Kate laughed.

"You look like you need to eat."

"I do," he groused, causing Kate to smile widely.

"Let's put everything inside and then go to lunch."

"Sorry, I'm late," said Althea with a rush as she entered before they could exit. "Doug had to pick the boys up from camp first."

"We only just arrived. Your brother took the long way," supplied Hamish.

Ben and Althea gave each other a beleaguered look of understanding.

"Kate, can I pick up my order since I'm here anyway?" Althea asked, turning towards the main counter.

"Of course," said Kate at the same time Hamish asked, "What order?"

"It's nothing," replied Althea, a vibrant shade of strawberry infusing her cheeks.

Kate discreetly handed her the small, stamped bag with ribboned handles she'd put aside earlier in the day.

"What are you making such a fuss over?" Hamish said. "Ben is more than happy to provide whatever you want from Bee Hill."

"Bee Hill doesn't sell this particular tea blend!" Althea declared, flustered.

It was the first time Kate had seen her in such a state.

"Well, there's no need to yell, lass," said Hamish, disgruntled. "I'm old, not hard of hearing."

"Huh," huffed Althea. "If you must know it's for the hot flashes," she said, scarlet with irritation instead of embarrassment this time.

"Oh. Well, why didn't you say so," said Hamish, looking anywhere but at his daughter.

"Maybe we should go to lunch now," suggested Kate, trying to change the subject for everyone's sake.

"You think?" said Ben, dryly, his stomach concurring with a loud growl.

"Why don't you two go without us," suggested Althea. "I'll take Da and Henri for a few hours."

"If you're sure," Ben replied, looking relieved.

"Swing by on your way out of town." Althea waved him off as if she hadn't been on the verge of a nuclear meltdown seconds before. "Come on, boys. We'll pick up scones from the new place around the corner. I hear they're cheeky," she said, her good humor restored as she took charge of her troops.

Efficiently stacking the boxes in the back of the shop, she and Ben set off for a local Italian restaurant. Kate believed pasta and focaccia could salvage any day, no matter how awful it was. Sitting at a table for two with a red-checkered tablecloth, she listened to the couple behind them speak in hushed tones. It was Slavic in nature, but she couldn't discern from which country. No doubt, Laura would've known due to her extensive travels.

Ben ordered tiramisù, even though she declined. "We'll share," he promised.

Obviously, she wasn't fooling anyone; dessert was her favorite part of the meal.

"You saved the day," she said, taking a sip of tepid water.

"It was Henri's idea," Ben replied, refusing to accept any praise. "Though Agnes knew in the strange way she knows anything. She showed up unannounced and insisted I include certain extras."

"Please tell her thank you for me. Better yet, I'll send her a thank you note." Kate paused as the server delivered their dessert. "I overestimated my new manager's abilities," she confessed quietly as if Ben were her priest.

"It happens."

"Things were such a mess when I got back from Brooklyn I spent days taking stock and trying to sort everything out."

"You don't say," he said.

"The best part though is that Zaya quit yesterday afternoon."

"Oh?"

"Something about how the position was interfering with what she was meant to do. Honestly, what kind of person quits their job to become a full-time influencer?"

He grinned.

"Potentially anyone these days. But you're missing the point. Now I have to hire someone new," she complained, which also meant spending less time at the farm.

I missed you, she confessed to herself.

We missed him too, shouted her hormones. Delectable, tie tugging, sleeve rolling—stop!

Gushing about Ben to Laura and Chaucey—fine, the entire club and a city block—when she was tipsy and hungover was one thing, but Kate was still very aware of the line she couldn't cross. They were friends and business partners—full stop. Never mind her previous relationship baggage.

Ben took two neat bites of the square espresso-and-custard dessert the waiter placed between them. Putting his fork down and leaning back in his chair, he left her with the rest, because he was one of the good guys. To share was one thing, but Kate believed any man who persisted in eating the majority of the dessert was selfish, potentially in more ways than one. Of course, Preston had always eaten more than his fair share.

"So, how was the wedding? Meet any dashing blokes?" Ben asked into the comfortable silence between them at the exact moment Kate took her last bite.

She immediately inhaled the creamy goodness down the wrong pipe. Her chi must be seriously out of whack, she reasoned and tried to cough past the glob of goop stuck in her windpipe, all the while reassuring Ben she'd be fine in a minute. It was the only explanation for the past month's sequence of events.

Giving the man across from her a strained smile, she accepted the glass of water he'd poured.

No one caught a bridal bouquet with their face, had an employee try to fatally screw up their business—but quit—let alone choke on tiramisu. It was practically impossible to choke on custard, yet Kate had managed it. And to top it all off, the crush she'd blabbed about for everyone in New York to hear wanted to know if she'd hooked up with someone at her sister's wedding. What alternate universe was this, and more importantly, how did she get back to her relatively normal life?

Chapter 13

Ben

"Meet any dashing blokes? Seriously, you couldn't have found another way to ask if she was seeing someone?" Sam asked.

"I told you; it wasn't my finest moment."

"How long has it been since you've been on a date?"

"It wasn't a date." And it wasn't, but he must have made her uncomfortable, because they hadn't spoken since he'd left her at the door of the shop afterward. Email had become the only form of communication between them. He shouldn't have gone poking around.

Eejit, as his father would say. *Bloomin' eejit.*

Ben knew what happened at weddings, and if Kate chose to hook up with a groomsman or start a relationship, it wasn't any of his business. They were partners, which meant he couldn't pursue her, no matter how often the idea crossed his mind. To top it all off, she was as much Henri's friend as his. He refused to mess things up for his son, even if wanting Kate had begun to gnaw on him like a dog with a bone.

"Apparently," commented Sam, bringing him back around again. "Answer the question, mate."

"You already know the answer."

Sam sighed loudly, as if his patience had finally reached a pinnacle of mountainous proportions. "Not since the landscape architect."

Ben winced. "No."

"Long in the face maybe, but she seemed quite animated about her work."

"She wouldn't stop touching my leg at dinner."

"Some men might enjoy being latched onto."

"She talked about pollination the entire evening."

"Again, some men might not mind the insinuation."

"I was afraid to leave my drink unattended, lest she take advantage of the stamen she spoke so passionately about."

Sam guffawed. "Stamen, huh?"

"Yes, now you understand why I haven't been out since. It's a bloody zoo out there."

My being attracted to Kate has absolutely nothing to do with choosing to be single for the past eleven months, he tried to convince himself.

"I think it's time to get back on the horse."

Not a chance. "I'm a single parent and, for obvious reasons, I can't bring just anyone around Henri." Ben winced again. Routine was paramount to his son's well-being, and therefore his own. Besides, dating was a delicate dance of getting to know someone and allowing them to know you. The process was complicated enough without the presence of a child, let alone one with his son's needs.

"What happened to the dashing bloke I knew at uni?" asked Sam, poking at Ben's predicament once more.

"He was indiscriminate and, when it counted, overestimated his charm."

"Are we talking about Monique or Kate?"

Both, he answered internally but refused to dignify the inquiry with an audible response. The first person in question had humbled him; the other was simply off limits. He refused to lose what they had and was no longer arrogant enough to think he couldn't screw it up. Point in case, their recent lunch. For Henri's sake, if not his own, he needed to figure out how to fix things between them, no matter how awkward it was.

"Summer is one of Kate's busiest times," said Sam offhandedly to fill the silence.

"Has Eli spoken with her?"

Sam remained silent.

"Exactly. I have a phone call to make."

"Can you wait until tomorrow?" pleaded Sam.

"How much did you bet this time?"

"Ten quid."

"Tell Eli she won," said Ben, hanging up on his best friend's bluster.

Kate

The sign came into view and Kate turned on her blinker, preparing to make a right into the familiar gravel lot filled with parked cars. People came and went, not a boot or raincoat in sight, everyone basking in the sun and light breeze the early August weather had wrought. Originally, she'd assumed the surrounding buildings, which served as office, storage, and production warehouse, were all the property consisted of. Since then, she'd come to realize how a name could encompass so much more.

Bee Hill was a business, but it was also the land, and the cottage Ben had built at its heart. When he'd left a voicemail inviting her to attend the harvest, she'd briefly considered not going. Carefully putting up walls with absence and emails had been her way of protecting herself from disappointment later. After all, why would he ask if she'd met someone at the wedding if he had any feelings for her other than those as her friend and partner, she'd reasoned. Crushing on him had seemed innocent enough when she'd been in Brooklyn, but lunch had been a wake-up call and a good reminder of the facts.

Driving past the outermost building and onto the dirt road to the cottage, Kate replayed in her head the voicemail Ben had left on Wednesday. It had been curt and formal, as if he too had decided they'd become overly familiar with one another. She tried to let go of her irritation. It was hypocritical to blame Ben for behaving in the same manner she had—none of which changed how sore her heart felt over the recent events.

Me. I'm the problem. It's me.

"So, are you going to go?" Eliza had asked bluntly when she called the day before.

Kate could hear Sam yelling at the game on the television in the background. *Manchester United must be losing,* she thought, twirling and untwirling a piece of hair around her finger. "Maybe," she hedged. No sense in handing Eliza an immediate victory. "The shop is pretty busy right now. By the time Sunday rolls around, all I want to do is stay in bed with a book." The electric kettle came to a boil and Kate adjusted the phone between her shoulder and ear as she placed a teabag into the porcelain teapot she'd found at Alice's Antiques on Portobello.

"You do know there are other things to do in bed besides read, right?"

"Yeah, yeah."

"Kate, you've been hiding since you got back from Brooklyn."

"I'm not hiding."

Yes, you are, rebelled her inner voice.

"Did something happen at the wedding?"

"You mean aside from catching the bouquet with my face in front of everyone?"

"At least you don't live there anymore. However, you do seem to be hibernating, when what you should be doing is enjoying a perfectly lovely London summer."

Kate chuckled. "It's not like I haven't seen the sun or am holed up in some den."

Eliza ignored her. "Not long from now, the sky will be perpetually gloomy, and a damp cold will move in the way mold does an old house, no matter how many times you spray it with bleach. It gives me the heebie-jeebies just thinking about it."

"Why do you live here if you can't stand the weather most of the year?"

"For the same reason anyone lives here: the variety of cookies they carry in the supermarket is obscene."

"The term is 'biscuits.' And of course, Sam is here."

"He'd live anywhere so long as it's with me. He's sort of like a golden retriever."

"Loyal and happy to be wherever you are?"

"Yep. Now, why are you acting like a confused groundhog?"

"What is it with you and the animal references today?"

"Stop avoiding the question."

Kate paused, trying to figure out what to say to dissuade her friend from her current line of inquiry. "Um…"

"When was the last time you went out for a meal, instead of takeaway?"

"Maybe I'm tired of getting a table for one," Kate excused. "The last time I put my nose in a book at a pub, the barkeep side eyed me as if I were an afront to society."

"Kit-Kat, we hang out by ourselves and don't care what others think. Your attitude is starting to scare me and every other introvert on the planet. What is going on with you?"

Kate took a deep breath and plunged forward. "Fine. It was hard to see how happy Laura is, but even more so, to realize what I'm missing in my own life," capitulated Kate before finishing with, "And I may have gushed about a certain grumpy Brit while under the influence—for everyone within earshot."

"I'm glad you're finally being honest with yourself."

"Thanks," said Kate flatly.

"Look, whether it was about Ben or only your heart's way of telling you that you're ready for a relationship, wanting to be in one is no more a crime than wanting to stay single. Either is an acceptable desire, so long as it's an active decision on your part."

"You're right."

"I know. Love you—mwah!" smacked Eliza, sending her a kiss over the line.

"Love you too."

"Oh, and Kate?"

"Yes?"

"Go. If only to find out for sure how you feel about Ben."

Kate came back to the present as she put the car in park and reached for the tote in the passenger seat. She'd gone to a quirky, but quaint, bookstore she'd discovered on a barge docked in Regent's Canal to stock up on secondhand editions for Henri.

If she were being honest, she didn't need to see Ben to know how she felt about him. Staying away from the farm had been the only time, aside from those first holidays, she'd felt homesick since moving to London. Kate had found herself weepy and with a stomachache at the oddest times, like watching a Cary Grant movie or eating by herself, neither of which had ever made her sad or lonely before meeting him.

If home was where the heart was, then Bee Hill should be her permanent place of residence.

"Hullo, stranger," he greeted, pulling her from her revery.

Ben would undoubtedly cringe if he had any idea about what she'd been thinking.

He was leaning against the doorjamb, looking like he'd come from a recent shower, and wearing a T-shirt with jeans. Not a starched collar or a tie to tug on in sight. Why then, did he still look as tempting as a Boston cream donut after a workout, Kate asked herself.

Who cares what he's wearing; what you want to see is his birthday suit, yapped her ovaries.

"Hey," said Kate, her brain completely deserting her in

response to the last thought.

"Want to come in?" Ben asked, straightening.

"No need."

In other words: I'd love to, but it will only make this harder.

"Right. Tea afterward then."

"On second thought…" If she were going to stay for tea, now was as good a time as any. At least she could eat her feelings in scones. Speaking of, "Fruit or plain?" Kate asked as she walked past him into the cottage.

"Fruit."

Ben looked so insulted, she nearly laughed. He was right; friends knew each other's scone and biscuit preferences. Was she willing to give up his friendship simply because she found him attractive? Doing so would be petty. All she had to do was focus on being a good friend to Ben and Henri. After all, they had proven to be good friends to her. The least she could do was the same in return.

"I brought books," she said with a lift of the heavy canvas bag. She refused to call it a bribe, but if they greased the wheels between her and the little boy after her absence, so be it. She crossed her fingers.

"Kate, you're here!"

She set the tote on the floor in time to catch a barreling Henri as he collided with her mid-section. Kate chuckled, wrapping him up in a tight hug on instinct and taking note of his clothing. Like all his others, the shirt was a shade of green, and despite the warm weather, he wore his usual khaki pants. The single difference was the absence of long sleeves.

"Whoa! I think you've grown since I last saw you, but it's only been—"

"Four weeks, two days and ten hours," he informed. "Much too long for a visit between friends," he chided honestly, as only a child can.

"Henri," Ben said sternly in warning.

"No, he's right," said Kate apologetically. "I'm sorry Henri. Can you ever forgive me?"

"Percy, can we forgive her?" he asked his sidekick seriously. "Hmmm, I agree."

Kate watched him expectantly.

"Percy says yes, on one condition."

"Oh?"

"You read us a chapter before bed tonight."

Laying a finger to her lips, she pretended to think long and hard on it before exclaiming, "You drive a hard bargain, but we have a deal." Kate extended her hand. After a shake to seal the verbal contract, Henri ran out of the kitchen with Percival on his heels, an excited bark escaping in his wake.

"Tea in ten," called Ben as the two disappeared up the stairs.

Chapter 14

Ben

An hour later they exited the cottage and headed for the fields, Henri tromping in front of them with big steps and a thick tree branch over the uneven terrain.

"Look Kate, I'm *Henry the Explorer*," he proclaimed, in reference to the books she'd found at a library giveaway months ago. They were well below his reading level, but he'd enjoyed the adventures within all the same, asking Ben to read them over and over again in the past couple of weeks as though they were a talisman to bring Kate back into their lives.

"Should we call your companion 'Angus McAngus'?" asked Kate in reference to the book's secondary character, a black Scottish Terrier.

"Percy prefers his own name. Come on, Sir Percival, let's find the fox who keeps trying to get into the henhouse. His den must be around here somewhere," Henri said, dashing away after the pup.

"Should we be worried about him finding the fox?" Kate asked, turning her gaze to Ben's profile.

"No, if they come across ours, he's more likely to run away than engage. Foxes are solitary creatures unless they're mated. Of course, once they do mate, it's for life, and they tend to be fairly protective of their territory."

Hands clasped behind his back, Ben continued to stare at the ground, though he could feel Kate's eyes upon him. Why on earth was he talking about the mating rituals of foxes? It was inane, and he blamed his feelings for her on his inability to make normal small talk, instead of sharing random facts about the males of the animal kingdom.

Today, she wore her hair in a braid, the tendrils at the front blowing away from her face in the breeze. She was paler than she ought to be for the season, her freckles lightly faded as if she hadn't spent enough time out of doors recently. He couldn't help but wonder if she'd been hiding away from more than Bee Hill.

Since Henri was no longer within hearing distance, now was as good a time as any to apologize for his latest mistake. "Kate," he began, pulling himself to his full height of one hundred eighty-six centimeters and looking directly into her fathomless eyes. "Did I say something to make you uncomfortable at lunch the other day?"

"No, no, of course not," she replied but shifted her gaze away from him.

In for a penny, in for a pound, old chap.

"I'm not sure what possessed me to ask about your personal life. It's clearly none of my business."

No doubt it's the same reason you mentioned the mating rituals of a fox.

He cleared his throat and tried to tamp down the heat creeping up the column of his throat. He shouldn't be surprised a few weeks out of her company would once again render him a blathering nitwit in her presence.

"It's okay," she rushed to reassure him. "But to answer your question, I didn't meet anyone who caught my eye."

"Good."

Good? There was no hope for him today. "I meant honey."

"Honey?"

His head whipped in her direction. *Yes, darling,* he very nearly replied, catching himself at the last moment. "Bees." Why couldn't he get more than a single word out at a time?

"Bees?" she smirked and a dimple peeked out to mock him.

He clenched his jaw in frustration. Why was he behaving as if he were a young boy, still wet behind the ears instead a grown man? Ben shook his head to clear it of the nonsense.

"Yes, let's visit the bees." He should count his blessings that he hadn't said birds in the same sentence. Ben stared at the ground, his cheeks a match for his neck. No amount of pulling on the collar of his cotton shirt could save him now.

"Is Henri looking forward to the new school year?" asked Kate, as Henri ran back and forth in wide circles with Percival chasing after him.

"Honestly, I don't know, but at least he's moving up."

Kate bobbed her head in understanding. "Did the school agree to provide an assistant in the classroom?"

"Part time, until he settles in, and they'll continue to use the peer-to-peer model."

"He mentioned a new friend over tea. Hayley?" Kate inquired, glancing at him from beneath long sable lashes.

"Hayley was his peer-to-peer in Mrs. Albright's class, but their friendship is genuine. Fortunately, her parents have agreed to the same arrangement for next year."

"All good things, then?"

Ben wanted to believe the coming school year would be easier, but it was hard to picture.

"Fingers crossed," he said, watching Henri and Percival veer off in the opposite direction toward Dobbs. The man was in the far pasture with Bedivere, herding a flock of sheep through the opening in a stone wall.

Ben and Kate continued on, walking in silence until they could hear the buzzing of the apiary at the edge of the property. Hidden by shrubbery to keep those who visited the lavender fields a smart distance away, they stopped and donned protective clothing from a nearby bothie that had originally served as shelter for a shepherd and his flock in the 1800s. Rarely used for its original purpose these days, it made a good supply shed or shelter from an unexpected downpour with a pot belly stove at one end, a square table with two chairs shoved against a wall, and a single bed along the opposite one.

On the wall nearest the door hung full body suits and accompanying veils from large bronze hooks. Made of layered mesh fabric, the suit would allow for air flow while still providing protection. Ben reached for the first one and gave it to Kate before picking up two sets of gloves from a basket on the table and snagging an EpiPen from the first aid kit.

Kate's eyes went wide. "Should I be worried?"

"Are you allergic?"

"No."

"Then it's only a precaution. Make sure to tuck your hair beneath the veil. We wouldn't want the scent of your shampoo to draw the attention of the bees."

"What about my perfume?"

"Let's hope they don't notice it the same way…" he caught himself and let the rest of the words die as he pulled the veil over his lose tongue. "Here, put your feet in these, and make sure the suit covers them and hugs the ankle," he said, pointing out a pair of army green wellies splashed with dried mud.

Fully garbed in his suit, Ben took a smoker out from the chest beneath the hooks. He filled it with pellets and bay leaves, struck a match, and tossed it inside the contraption.

"This will keep the bees calm while we remove the frames with honeycomb from inside the Supers." Closing the lid, he handed it to Kate. "Squeeze the bellows."

In and out went the miniature accordion, producing smoke as they approached the hives made from polystyrene boxes to keep out the moisture of a wet climate. "After I've removed the finished frames, we'll take them offsite to uncap the wax seal and extract the honey from the comb."

Kate bobbed her head in understanding.

Ben gently lifted the lid off one of the ten-framed Supers, taking five frames out and placing them inside another waterproof Super for the purpose of transportation. He continued this pattern until the last hive had been emptied of its finished frames, the rest left behind for the bees to continue their work.

Kate

She followed Ben to a metal shipping container with a sliding glass door and a line of windows near the roofline. Cooler inside than the small cabin they'd used earlier, the utilitarian building resided within the shaded sanctuary of an apple orchard a short distance from the apiary. Kate assumed it was to keep the honey as close to room temperature as possible during the harvesting process.

Ben moved past her to retrieve a box of glass jars from a tall cabinet on the far side of the building. They reminded Kate of the ones her mother used for canning local fruit before the winter, sealed with a tin lid and corresponding ring to make it airtight.

"Sorry I'm late," said a man as he entered, wearing a protective suit similar to Ben and Kate's.

Kate didn't recognize him, but he appeared to be in his early twenties, with cropped ashy curls atop tightly shaved sides, and a plug in each ear. She could also see an expansive tattoo peeking out of the suit at his collarbone. The dragon's wing was the work of an exceptionally talented artist, in her opinion, and she briefly wondered if she'd ever be good enough to draw something like it with practice.

"Hiya, I'm Liam. I don't think we've met before," he said, putting aside the Super in his hands so he could extend one in her direction.

His twenty-watt grin and the twinkle in his eyes alone could make a nun rethink her vows, but the lilt was pure magic. Kate shook his hand, amused to see a wedding ring boldly tattooed around his finger. He might not appear mainstream, but he believed in a traditional institution like marriage. As the saying went, it was a reminder not to judge a book by its cover. The only way to truly know someone was to spend time reading their chapters.

"The fellas aren't far behind me."

"Everything okay?" Ben asked.

"Yup. The baby's colicky, and Meg needed a break. Ivaan's got car trouble, so he and Krish caught a ride with me."

"What about Jack?"

"No idea," he said with a shake of his head. "The boy's a right bellend." Liam turned to Kate. "Sorry. Jack is my younger brother. One of four, in fact, but he's the only one who's a lizard brain."

Kate chuckled and looked at Ben in time to catch his smile.

"Well, seventeen is the height of idiocy for most of us."

"Don't get me wrong, I was no saint, but he's making Mam's life harder than he should." Liam pulled out his cell phone, texting furiously.

She could only assume he was trying to contact his tardy sibling. Two more men came in, tossing apologies and flashing Kate identical smiles set in full lips against their golden skin. They set their Supers down and quietly got to work slicing off the wax seals on the honeycomb with hot knives to expose the honey inside. Next, they placed the uncapped honeycomb frames into an extractor, which would spin the frames and displace the honey for collection in the glass jars.

"Once the extraction is complete, we'll strain the honey through a mesh sieve to remove any debris or other particles," explained Ben. "For small batches we could use a method called crushing, but it's not ideal for a full harvest."

Kate watched the process, fascinated once again with how Ben had turned his small holding into a full-time business. Where she was from, hobby farms weren't uncommon, but they rarely made a sustainable living without an extra hustle or two. Bee Hill was doing surprisingly well and, while the estate wasn't generating substantial amounts of income, she also knew it had the potential to become something more in the future. Making a mental note to broach the subject she turned her attention back to making honey and grabbed the glass jars Liam had requested.

Twenty minutes later, a lanky teenager sauntered inside without an excuse, dressed in gym clothes, a brand-new pair of white Nike Jordans, and large cubic zirconia's winking from each tawny ear. His arms were littered with random tattoos, though Kate seriously doubted there had been much thought behind them, unlike the artwork she'd spied on his brother.

"Sup?" greeted the boy, taking the only seat in the room.

"You must be Jack."

"See, Liam. Even Ben's bird knows who I am," he said confidently.

Liam closed his eyes as though he were praying for strength and patience, after which he crossed the room in two strides and wrenched his brother out of his seat by the earlobe.

"Ow, let go!" Jack yelped. "I just got it pierced."

"I know," said Liam, baring his teeth. "Outside. Now."

Kate felt sorry for the boy...kind of. Then she remembered what he'd said. "Hey Ben, why did Jack call me your bird?" It wasn't a term she was familiar with and assumed it was part of the local vernacular.

"Because he's seventeen," he replied brusquely.

He looked flushed. Kate decided the heat in the room was either getting to him or he needed to eat. She could go for another scone herself, or an order of fish and chips—aka fries—from the pub, hold the mushy peas.

"Okay, but what does it mean?"

Ivan and Krish gave each other knowing looks. "It's slang for girlfriend."

"Oh." But she wasn't Ben's girlfriend.

You want to be, sang her heart, totally on board with the whole bird-slang-thing.

"Most people don't use it anymore. My girlfriend would hand me my a—"

Krish gave Ivaan an elbow to the ribs and a look which clearly said shut it. "What he means to say is, it's old fashioned and some people find it demeaning."

"Ah." She looked in Ben's direction for his reaction, but he was busy pouring the honey into jars. He hadn't bothered to correct anyone about their relationship status. Her heart gave another leap before she remembered this was all a misunderstanding, and villages were like small towns everywhere—rumor mills.

They left shortly after, returning their protective clothing to the other cabin on the trek back to the cottage. Unusually silent as he walked beside her, Kate didn't feel inclined to pull Ben from his revery. Had the bird comment made him uncomfortable?

Surely, Ben knew the comment hadn't offended her. Jack was only a kid, and courtesy of Liam, he'd come back inside one earring short with a sullen apology on his lips. After that, he'd finally set to work bottling honey.

Agnes was cooking dinner when they arrived back at the cottage, and though Ben invited her to join their trio, Kate suddenly felt like an intruder. Or rather, an imposter.

"Thanks, but I should be getting back." *Because we're friends but I want to be your bird.*

Ben raked a hand through his hair, disheveling it more than the veil already had. Her stomach flipped at the sight, which was why she needed to leave before she did something dumb like taking him by the shirt and yanking him into her lips. *Oops, sorry, I tripped,* only sounded good in her head.

"Next weekend is the lavender harvest. Can I count on you to help?"

"Sure," she said surprised. "Shorthanded this season?"

"Not particularly."

"Oh."

Ben hesitated and ran his hand over his hair again, mussing it until a wave fell haplessly over his forehead. The man was unequivocally sexy without any trying.

"Kate, my darling girl."

She sucked in a breath. There was that endearment once again, casually slipping off his tongue and turning her world upside down.

"Don't you know yet, your presence is always needed."

Be cool. Be cool. Be cool.

"Well, since you asked so sweetly, I wouldn't want to disappoint Henri."

Ben nodded in the negative. "Of course not," he said solemnly. "And for the same reason, I expect you'll join us for the regatta at the end of September."

"Henri would no doubt be distraught if I didn't."

"Utter despair beyond all reason."

"I guess there's nothing for it then; you're stuck with me."

"Quite."

Ben opened the driver's side door, waiting for her to slide behind the wheel. Leaning in close enough for her to smell a hint of the harvested honey behind his usual scent and causing her heartrate to ratchet up, Kate gripped the gear stick tightly. So much for playing it cool.

"To be clear, Henri isn't the only one who would be distraught if you stopped coming around. Goodnight, Kate," he said with a kiss to her forehead.

Whoosh went the breath she'd been holding as she released it and started the ignition. If she grinned the entire way back into the city, no one but her knew.

The next day, she took a blanket and her latest read to St.

James's Park, entering by way of Birdcage Walk near The Blue Bridge. The entrance next to the Queen Victoria Memorial in front of Buckingham Palace was always crowded with tourists taking photos and trying to catch a glimpse of the Queen's Guard. Kate had learned to avoid the area at all cost, especially on such a nice day. Perhaps she was starting to think more like the locals, avoiding less trafficked areas wherever possible.

Reveling in the green space, towering trees, and ducklings bravely wading into the lake, Kate stretched out beneath the sun the way Merlin often did in front of the cottage door. She soaked in the pleasant warmth of the day, glancing up from time to time at the calls of children playing a game of tag in the distance. In her failed attempt to hide from herself, she'd also kept herself from enjoying life fully. And hiding is exactly what she'd been doing, hiding from her feelings and what she wanted out of life.

One day she wanted to be brave enough to risk it all again, to fall irrevocably for someone who could love the real her, not a version of who he wanted her to be. Hopefully, it would be Ben, but if not, the possibility of someone someday was progress and the best excuse to spend a lovely English summer day outside getting lost in *The Pirate and His Thief* by her new favorite author, Jinn Royce.

Chapter 15

Kate

A year to the day after Kate exited the train at Oxford station for The Isis Sculls the previous September, she and Ben did so together with Henri and Hamish leading the way. The little boy had been insistent about bringing Percival, as if he needed an extra sense of familiarity to deal with the crowds that would undoubtedly swell due to the pleasant autumn weather. It wasn't the first regatta he'd attended, but his dad said they took everything out of him and created a low tolerance for coping days afterward.

The school psychologist Kate knew had explained how certain situations might create sensory overload for Henri, but there were ways to negate the effects. Today, they were trying out noise-cancelling headphones and Percival. So far so good. The pup had even managed to stay clean and keep his bowtie on, as if he understood his boy's success was partly dependent upon him.

"I still think the hamper would've been the better choice," said Hamish, taking Kate's side of the argument.

"Why thank you, Hamish," she said giving Ben her cheekiest smile.

"Right, then," he said, and slipped his arms into the backpack he'd filled with bicuits and thermoses of tea.

It wasn't pretty or nostalgic, but Kate could admit the walk to the Isis would be far easier. She'd also switched her customary heels out for a classic oxford in burgundy. It was a concession of sorts, but not a total surrender. She made every effort to stay true to herself whatever the situation, which was one of the things she'd promised herself after leaving Preston.

"Kit-Kat," called Eliza, waving them over to a grassy spot near the river ten minutes later. "And don't you look dapper today, Percy."

He barked in agreement.

"Kate bought him a new bowtie to mark the occasion," said Ben, with a smile.

Her breath hitched at the sight, and she reminded herself to keep any attraction on the down low for the day. It was one thing to live rent free in her head, but she had no delusions about her future status as Bee Hill's mistress.

"I would have bought you one too, but I prefer you in a tie," she replied, turning away quickly, her cheeks warming with the words. So much for keeping her feelings about Ben private.

Ben

Well, well, well, Ben thought smugly, but only long enough to reconsider. Kate enjoyed fashion as a hobby and putting together a smart look, he reasoned. Certainly, it wasn't anything personal. "I'll be sure to dress accordingly next time." Ben deposited the backpack and started pulling everything out while Kate laid out a second rug to accommodate the size of their group.

"Felix should be here any minute," said Hamish mildly, sitting on a low stone wall behind the group.

"He doesn't usually compete in the regatta. In fact, he's never even been to watch."

"I know, but when I mentioned we'd all be coming, he wanted to give it a go."

"Right." Ben closed his eyes and prayed for patience. He knew his father hadn't done it on purpose.

"The two of you used to be so close. What happened?" Hamish asked.

His father wasn't being deliberately obtuse. He'd simply been more absent than present between his wife's death and the births of his grandchildren. And he wasn't wrong. Ben and Felix were close… before Monique.

Ben had hoped their shared love for Henri would eventually build a bridge between them, but the wedge had only grown over the years. He turned his gaze to Kate, who watched him knowingly, but without judgement. She knew the truth and understood, which was enough for him to let the old jealousy fade away. A bit of healthy competition between brothers was normal, and while Monique hadn't turned out to be the love of his life, by some miracle, he'd gained Henri out of the ordeal.

"You are the better man," Kate declared under her breath, handing him a cup of tea and a plate of raspberry chocolate torte—his favorite. "Henceforth, you shall be my champion for the day. Go forth and win, Sir Galloway," she said solemnly, knighting him for the quest with a nearby stick.

Medieval role playing coming right up, he thought with an internal grin. No doubt her book pile currently featured one or two historical romances. He ducked his head, placed his hand over his heart and promised, "Milady, it shall be done." Being playful wasn't his modus operandi, but as usual, Kate had drawn something out of him that didn't exist, or he was becoming a different person for having her in his life. There was no denying she had a way of bringing out the best in him. "Where did you get the torte?"

"The same place as the cupcakes—Sweet Bitter Bakes. Come to think of it, everything they make has fruit and cocoa in it," she said, passing out pieces to Hamish and Henri, who gave her matching grins of anticipation. "Althea mentioned how your mother used to make it, and I figured it would be a fun way to celebrate today's win.

Talking with his mouth full, Sam said, "Because today we hit the swing."

Ben dug into his own piece with a half-smile. Win or lose, the day had already been a success. Henri had yet to meltdown, Kate had brought his favorite dessert, and his father hadn't accidentally mooned anyone on the way here. Granted, the day was young, and Percival was conspicuously absent, but he was also the likely culprit for the vehemently shaking hedge directly behind them.

"Da, can we go find a spot to sail our boats?" Henri asked, holding up the tall ship models built and painted by his great grandfather when Felix and Ben were lads. Percival chose the moment to exit the bush he'd shaken down to its bare branches, stopping at Hamish's heel to snatch up a dropped crumb and berry.

His father stood, taking one of the boats from Henri. "I know a good spot, lad. Come with me. 'I must go down to the seas again, to the lonely sea and the sky, and all I ask is a tall ship and a star to steer her by,'" Hamish quoted from John Masefield's "Sea Fever."

It was the poem Ben's mother had recited whenever they took the boats out for a picnic by the stream near the estate's easternmost boundary. If intimacy was the act of being vulnerable, his parents had done so through a lifetime of opinions, concessions, and innocuous gestures. It was a rare thing indeed for two people to accept each other wholly, yet his parents had somehow achieved it.

Kate let out a throaty laugh, drawing his attention and causing him to smile until he caught sight of Felix over her shoulder. Honestly, he'd hoped his brother would flake out in typical fashion. Ben went to tug at his collar, his temperature rising with his emotions, and rolled his sleeves for good measure.

"Old chap."

"Little brother," said Ben, knowing how much the term would rankle. "No models in need of your particular expertise today?"

Felix ignored the dig. "Care to make a friendly wager?"

"I'm in!" Eliza exclaimed from where she leaned against Sam on the second blanket.

"All right," Felix replied without giving her a second glance. Her engagement to Sam meant nothing; gingers had simply never been his type. Unfortunately for Ben, blondes and brunettes were fair game in equal measure.

"What are the terms?" Ben asked tersely.

"If you win, I buy the pints."

"And if you win?"

Felix smirked. It was smarmy, and Ben wanted nothing more than to wipe it off his face.

"Kate goes on a date with me."

Ben schooled his features and turned to Kate, who was glaring at Felix. "I'm afraid I have to decline on the lady's behalf."

"Fine," said Kate simultaneously, with a determined gleam in her eye and a hand to Ben's chest as if she could read his murderous intentions. "If Ben and Sam win, you buy the pints. If you do, we can go to lunch."

"Kate," Ben said firmly, placing his hand on her lower back in a possessive show. It was a moment of weakness on his part, but she didn't move away, and he let out the breath he'd been holding.

Felix smirked again. "I was thinking a candlelit dinner for two and a bottle of wine at this cozy restaurant in Southbank."

"Too bad. Lunch at the pub today or no deal."

"You drive a hard bargain, but I like a girl who knows what she wants."

Kate rolled her eyes as Felix turned on his heel and headed for the starting dock. "Your brother is starting to get on my nerves."

"Kate, you don't have to go through with this."

"Sure, I do. But you won't lose because you already promised me you'd win. Now, go kick some ass, sea bass."

"I love it when you speak American."

Kate grinned all the way to her dimples. It was the only incentive Ben needed to wipe the Isis with Felix's loss.

Divesting himself from a linen shirt and the trousers he'd worn over his athletic wear, he dropped them into a pile, quickly making his way with Sam to the boathouse to pick up the double scull assigned to them. Scheduled for the next alumni heat, they hurried for the starting dock. Setting the boat onto the water, he and Sam settled into position.

"Nervous?"

"No."

"Good. Felix is a knob."

The announcement coming from a bull horn nearby drowned out Ben's response.

Sam shifted his weight, rocking the boat again. Ben took a

couple of deep breaths to steady his churning gut. He looked to the left, taking in their immediate competition, and his brother on the far side. The torte had been a bad idea.

Felix met his stare with a hard one of his own. Life was one big game as far as his brother was concerned, and since Felix usually came out the winner, who could blame him for playing it the way he did? Sometimes Ben wondered if he ever considered or cared about the damage he caused in the process. Being obtuse would be easier to forgive than selfishness.

"I see Felix finally decided to find out which of you is the better man," commented a familiar tobacco-roughened voice. "In the water, anyway," said the former coach with a knowing look.

"He does seem rather eager all of sudden," conceded Ben.

"Eager for a beating, you mean," mumbled Sam.

The older man guffawed, coughed, and finally wheezed until he was a vibrant shade of puce.

Neither Ben nor Sam acknowledged the fit for the sake of his pride.

"Pretty girl you have here with you, Ben. Same one as last year?"

"Kate Howard is my business partner and friend."

"So is my Hilde," he remarked, before walking off in the direction of a silver-capped woman surrounded by a gaggle of grown children and their young families.

"How long do you think they've been married now?

"No idea. Do you think he's right?" asked Ben.

"You're asking the wrong person. I can't imagine Eli not being my best friend or partner. It's why I asked her to marry me."

Ben nodded with understanding. "Let's win this one for Kate and Coach. We don't want to disappoint him by letting my brother win."

"The old codger has no appreciation for those born under a lucky star."

"Loyalty, hard work, and mettle are the only things in this life worth anything." It was the mantra their coach had drilled into each man who raced for him. Anyone who hadn't believed in those qualities hadn't earned a spot in the boat, including Felix. His brother had rowed for Keble College, but not for the prestigious Oxford University Boat Club or against their archrival Cambridge. It had been a sore subject between them, made worse by their mother's passing and father's absence.

Ben closed his eyes briefly to center himself. Rowing was as much a mental game as a physical one. Getting into the right head space was crucial. Felix may be flawed and a royal pain, but he was still his brother. The goal was to win, not destroy him.

The gun went off and they set the pace for their muscles. Half stroke, half stroke, three-quarter stroke, lengthen, full stroke; pushing first with their feet, keeping their cores engaged, and the layback short until they settled in. As they lengthened their strokes, they moved into a working pace, gaining speed and distance in front of the team to their left and Felix on the far side.

As always, the cheering from the sidelines receded to nothing but a distant hum. Demanding more of his body until everything burned with fire and fatigue, Ben pushed himself beyond the crippling discomfort until they crossed the finish line a full stroke before the other crews.

"We hit the swing," Sam breathed heavily into his ear as he dropped his head in exhaustion.

"I know," Ben replied between labored breaths. He was getting too old for this.

"Congrats, you saved Kate from your brother."

"I didn't do it to save her, she can handle herself. I did it to save Felix from me."

"At least you're finally being honest. C'mon, mate," he said, offering Ben a hand up. They pulled the scull from the river and hiked it back to the boathouse, each taking an end and carrying their oars in the other hand, accepting congratulations from the other crews along the way.

Felix stepped onto the path, effectively blocking the way, and held his hand out.

"Not too shabby, old chap."

Ben shook his brother's hand, and noticed Felix didn't bother to congratulate Sam.

"You made me work for it. Nice rowing," Ben complimented, though it was the last thing he wanted to do.

"Next year, then."

"Right." So much for looking forward to the regatta.

Felix held out fifty quid. "For drinks."

Ben took the money. After all, a gentleman should always pay his debts. "You're welcome to join us."

But only because I won.

"Yes, well, tell Kate it was lovely to see her as always. As it turns out, I have other plans."

Ben watched as Felix walked away with a buxom brunette he'd left dithering in the warm sun. The poor woman's milky complexion was rapidly turning pink. His brother was officially a cad in designer clothing.

"Your brother is a real piece of work."

Ben gave Sam a barely there, closed-lip smile. He couldn't blame his friend for noticing the obvious. Loyalty ranked high on Ben's list of priorities, but he could admit his best friend wasn't wrong in his assessment.

Chapter 16

Kate

"Tickets please," said the train's porter, stopping to look at each one as he passed a filled seat.

Henri sat next to Hamish, their heads close together, one white and thinning, the other dark and thick with the vitality of youth. They were quietly discussing Boudica of the Iceni and her battles against the Roman forces in 60 AD. She had successfully defeated the Romans 9th Legion, destroying the capital of Roman Britain in Colchester and eventually London.

Kate smiled as she listened. History rarely recorded the feats of women, but for those who made it into its hallowed halls, they continued to be the rally call for every woman who came after, including herself. She turned in her seat slightly, catching sight of Eliza snuggling into Sam, both wearing earbuds and listening to their preferred play lists, rock and classical. By their own account, they shouldn't make any sense, but from what Kate had seen, they made more sense together than they ever could apart.

Beside her, Ben had fallen asleep immediately after leaving the station. Taking out the sketchbook she'd purchased on her last bookstore run, she opened it to a blank page a quarter of the way through. Inspired by her recent self-revelations, she'd decided it was time to take back yet another thing Preston had stolen. She'd planned to sketch some of the images stuck in her head from the regatta. Folly Bridge gathering the Thames to herself the way a mother gathers a child to her bosom had stood out, as had the rowers crossing the finish line, exhaustion and varied emotions marking the lines on their faces. But sketching Ben's profile was a more tempting prospect at the moment.

The muscle memory in her hand had grown steadily with daily practice, making it easier to start without overthinking. Touching pencil to paper, she began with the curves and swirls of an ear, constructing the rest of his face by drawing lines toward his nose and eyes. His chin was trickier, and she switched to a three-quarter view to capture the dent she'd once found dismissive. Admittedly, it was a lie born of self-preservation at the time. But now she could see how it added character and helped define the rest of his features into a total dreamboat.

Inner office memo: remove high school sweethearts and small-town tropes until words like "dreamboat" cease to be a primary description.

"Next up, Kings Cross Station," said a voice over the intercom.

Kate opened her eyes slowly and wiped the corner of her mouth. She must have fallen asleep. Worse, she'd fallen asleep on Ben's shoulder and drooled a puddle on his sleeve. Oh well. This was real life, not some romance book where the main characters woke up disheveled but sexy, instead of dry mouthed and cranky about their bed partner snoring all night long.

"I didn't know you liked to draw," he said close to her ear, sounding surprised.

Kate looked down to see the sketchbook still open to the one of him.

Put me out of my misery, she pleaded to no one. As if falling asleep on his shoulder uninvited and drooling weren't bad enough.

"It's been a while."

"May I," he asked, reaching for the book.

"Sure."

In other words: Why not? What could be worse than you seeing my sketch of your profile?

Ben smiled softly, not lingering on her sketch of him, and flipped through the ones before it. "These are good. Did you take classes?"

"In high school and college. It's actually how Eli and I met during freshman year. Long story short, I didn't know what I wanted to major in yet, and she was interested in one of the nude models."

His brows rose, but his lips quirked into a smirk.

"What?" Kate asked with a shrug. "She wanted a look at the goods to see if it was worth her time."

"And was it?"

Kate grinned, but said, "I told her she was circumspect, and the rest is history."

"How come you stopped sketching?"

She stalled, taping the pencil in her hand against her leg. "I got married."

"Too busy to be creative, huh?

"Not exactly."

Please don't ask, please don't ask.

"Kate, did your ex—" Ben started, a frown forming between his brows.

"Kings Cross Station," said the voice over the intercom again.

Not saved by the bell, but close enough. Kate stood up and quicky grabbed her bag. It wasn't a leap to assume her marriage had been less than ideal after what she'd shared with him last Christmas, but she wished Ben were less astute sometimes.

He handed her the sketchbook, leaning down slightly to meet her eyes. "Whatever the reason you stopped, I'm glad you've picked it up again."

"Thanks."

"And I'm happy to model for you anytime," he said, winking.

Cheeky fella. "Are you offering to take your clothes off for me, Mr. Galloway?"

"Art is sacrifice, after all."

Were they finally going to do this, cross the line they'd been toeing since honey harvest?

"Da, I got to take a wee," whined Henri, dancing in place.

"Me too," said Hamish. "Stop lollygagging and move it along to the loo, everyone."

"Right, then," Ben said, stepping into the aisle and waiting for Kate to exit in front of him.

So much for crossing lines. She had, more than likely, been imagining any flirting on Ben's part anyway. He was only teasing her about the sketch she'd made of him, and she needed to stop torturing herself. They were friends and partners.

Kate's hormones didn't bother to argue to the contrary this time, despite the protest of her heart. There was a strong cuppa and a Belgian chocolate bar waiting for her at home.

Hamish waved her past the crowd of those disembarking from the other cars.

Tea and chocolate, she recited internally—after everyone used the restroom.

. . . .

Kate kicked the last of the leaves lining the street in front of Henri's school, the satisfying crunch beneath the heels of her boots lost in the bustle of families filing inside. She tucked her cold hands into the pockets of her wool coat and burrowed into the scarf wrapped around her neck. The temperatures had plummeted overnight, and what had been a warm autumn now stood at the precipice of winter.

Inside the large multipurpose room, she looked left and then right, spotting Ben near one of the booths, with a protracted line of parents and children waiting to win a prize. Henri held his hand, shifting from one foot to the other, looking agitated.

"Excuse me, good sirs, it would seem I've lost my way. Have either of you seen where they put the apples for bobbing?" Kate asked, enjoying the sight of Ben wearing a woolen cap, his scarf hanging loose over a henley shirt, coat in his other hand.

"We don't bob for apples anymore. The school said it was a liability," Henri replied, sounding crabby, and Kate noted his lack of greeting and enthusiasm.

They stepped forward as the line moved up. "Sorry, he's a bit out of sorts tonight," apologized Ben stoically.

"No problem. I'm kind of disappointed about the apples too," she joked.

Ben gave her a small smile, looking worn out. "Hayley left school with a fever today."

"Got it," she said, understanding Henri's disappointment over the absence of his friend. "No headphones tonight?" she asked quietly to keep from drawing anyone's attention.

"Henri didn't want to wear them in front of everyone. Honestly, I'm not sure why we're here."

"Do you want to leave?"

"I don't know what's best."

Ben seemed as frazzled as Henri, but Kate would rather be with them in the middle of their chaos than anywhere else. Book boyfriends had ceased to be enough company as soon as she'd accepted her desire for the real thing.

"Benny!" exclaimed a woman behind the booth as they finally made it to the front.

Benny? Since when does he go by Benny?

It was like the movie about losing a guy in ten days. Nowhere in the plot did it suggest giving a man like Bennett A.K. Galloway a ridiculous nickname unless you wanted to repulse him. Yet, this woman with bouncy chestnut curls to match a set of bouncing double Ds had committed the cardinal sin without an ounce of compunction.

"Janet, nice to see you," he said, sounding more welcoming than he'd been with Kate.

"Here you go, love," said the woman wielding atrocious nicknames, handing Henri a set of plastic balls to toss at the wooden pins set up on a table.

Kate watched as the leech latched onto *Benny's* arm, gripping the closest bicep and tittering like a chickadee instead of a grown woman. To make matters worse, a group of well-dressed women clustered across the gym were eating him up with their eyes like a tasty pack of hot cross buns. Not that Kate blamed them. His buns were exactly the right height and firmness for devouring.

Jealousy squeezed her heart within its ugly grip. She hated feeling insecure, but this was the first time Ben and Henri had invited her into their world away from Bee Hill. Taking a deep breath, Kate let it go and focused on the child who'd asked her to attend his school's harvest carnival.

She could see Henri's frustration mounting with every throw he missed. How did they expect young children to knock wooden pins down with lightweight plastic balls, Kate wondered. It was terribly unfair, especially for a child who was already feeling overwhelmed with his surroundings. She glanced over her shoulder to see if Ben had noticed, but he was still engaged in conversation with Janet. Kate rolled her eyes and turned back around.

The sixth and final throw sailed over the tops of the pins, causing one to wobble momentarily before gaining purchase again. Henri stomped his feet and clenched his fists at his side.

"It's not fair; the game is rigged," he yelled at the top of his lungs, tears streaking across his cheeks and his excellent vocabulary on display.

Kate stepped forward a beat too late as Henri sent the pins crashing to the floor with a swipe of his arm. The entire room stopped moving, an unnatural hush descending in the large space. Ben rushed forward and swept his son over his shoulder and out the doors into the refreshing night air. She walked swiftly, catching up as he reached the rover parked across the street.

"I'll follow you back to the cottage," offered Kate. "I can read Henri a story while you take some time for yourself."

"Not tonight, Kate," he said firmly.

"I thought you might—"

"Not tonight," he said again, his voice slightly raised before he caught himself. "Thank you, but I'd be poor company."

Translation: I neither need nor want your help.

"Okay," she whispered and pivoted on her heel, walking quickly to her car and ignoring the ache in her heart until she arrived home.

Trying unsuccessfully to get into her latest read, she finally discarded her book along with a flute of prosecco and sank beneath a layer of bubbles in the clawfoot tub. Being underwater helped block out everything else while she sorted through her feelings. She held her breath for as long as she could before heaving herself above the water line, displacing water over the sides of the tub.

He didn't mean to hurt your feelings. His priority should be Henri, she reassured herself. Why then did it feel like a big, fat rejection? Kate sank beneath the water again.

Ben

He made his way down the stairs, skipping over the ones he knew would groan loudest in protest. Ben had tucked Henri in with the weighted blanket Kate had brought the weekend before, hoping it would relieve the sensory overload from the evening. It had been a while since the last tantrum, and he'd foolishly hoped they were past them.

Tonight had been a series of bad decisions on his part. Primarily, giving in to Henri's request to attend the carnival. They'd skipped the event in past years due to his challenges, but his recent progress had given Ben hope. Secondly, he should never have asked Kate to join them.

He usually looked forward to seeing her, but he'd never had to focus solely on Henri in her presence before. Bee Hill and family were safe places to be himself, but amongst the staff, parents, and other children, Ben always felt like he needed to protect Henri from ridicule, whispers, and ignorance. Going to school stressed him out as much as it did his son.

Not only had he ignored her all night after inviting her to attend, but Ben had also shut Kate out as soon as Henri melted down. Logically, his child's needs came first, but the hurt etched all over her face as she walked away made him wince even now. He should call and apologize; it was the right thing to do. But he didn't pick up the phone.

Instead, he shoved his feet into a pair of wellies and grabbed his beanie from a hook by the door. Henri had always been a heavy sleeper and Ben needed to clear his head. He walked toward the stables, zipping up his coat and admiring the galaxy shimmering above, the stars winking with the secrets of the universe. He took a deep breath and let it out. Bee Hill had always helped him get his priorities straight, and tonight was no different.

Whinnies and snorts greeted Ben as he pushed open the door to the stables, spotting Dobbs in the corner. "Evening," said Ben.

Eugenia's book club met at their house the third Thursday every month, which explained the older man's presence at such a late hour. Dobbs doffed his cap in greeting, donning it again as he left, closing the door behind him without ever saying anything.

"Hullo, beautiful creatures of destruction."

Pale snorted and shook her head to the contrary, making Ben's lips rise gently at the corners. He ran a hand over the marking between her dark, unfathomable eyes. She was the unspoken leader of her cadre, the one the others followed and watched to read the room. It only made sense when Kate chose to ride her. In fact, it wouldn't surprise him at all, if it was the other way around. Horses were highly intuitive creatures after all, and Kate was...well, more than he deserved.

He'd messed up and had no one to blame but himself. Ben had been busy admiring her from behind while Janet prattled on in his ear about nothing. Distracted, he'd missed the warning signs and Henri had paid the price for his misplaced attention. That was the real reason he'd pushed Kate away.

He sat down on the stool Dobbs had vacated and scrubbed his face with his hands. What was it C.S. Lewis once said? Ah yes, *"I sat with my anger long enough until she told me her real name was grief.*" He understood the sentiment well. How many times could a man grieve the same thing, he asked himself. The answer seemed to be infinite.

Except now his grief had doubled. Monique had never been his to begin with, and technically, neither should her son. But it didn't change his current reality. Ben had accepted full responsibility for Henri when Felix casually handed over the best part of himself. He wouldn't refuse to do what was right now, even though it meant not having the life he hoped for.

Henri might always have obstacles to overcome and while it was Ben's job to love and guide him through those, Kate hadn't signed up for moments like tonight. It would be unfair to expect her to get any more involved than she already had. She was a friend and business partner, but she would never be anything more, and he needed to let his hope of it go.

Pale nudged his arm to gain his attention, pawing at the ground in irritation. She clicked her teeth, snapping close to an ear and forcing him to retreat a step.

"Right, then, message received. But it doesn't change anything."

Chapter 17

Kate

"Last Christmas I gave you my heart, but the very next day you gave it away," Eliza sang as she and Kate walked through the Chelsea Christmas Market, one of several dotting London's various neighborhoods during the holiday season. Avoiding the crowds, running the shop, and feeling homesick, she'd excused herself from going the previous December. Unfortunately, this year didn't seem to be falling out any differently aside from a decision to buck up and make the most of London anyway.

Kate sighed loudly, rubbing her mittens together to warm her hands before admitting defeat and stuffing them into the pockets of her Harris Tweed wool coat in coffee and cranberry. London was a treasure trove of charity shops selling high-end secondhand, and she was always happy to buy for a good cause, though admittedly, her wardrobe had begun to bulge after a recent shopping trip.

Unfortunately for Kate, Eliza had insisted on a girls' night out instead of the classic movie and pizza she'd pictured when her friend called the night before. On the flip side, the shop's manager, Byron, was a godsend—or an elf in disguise. Either way, he shooed her out the door at five o'clock sharp every night, shared the homemade gingersnaps in his lunch, and welcomed every customer who came through the doors of Lavender Honey & Co. as if it were his own home. Of course, the man himself was a dark chocolate truffle with a champagne liquor center—in other words, a gorgeous, smooth, and decadent encounter. Every. Single. Time.

If he wasn't married and gay, she might have thrown herself at him to soothe her sore heart. Fine, it wasn't entirely true since she was his boss. But Benny, Benny, Boo had somehow managed to bruise the heart Preston had once annihilated with words and actions no one should ever put up with. While Ben may have hurt her feelings, he also hadn't been cruel, simply a good father. It's not like they were dating. She had no right to expect more from him.

Inconsiderate romance books, dishing out happily ever after and hope like they grew on trees.

"Will you please stop singing," Kate begged.

"Blame it on Wham!; it's annoyingly catchy."

"It's annoyingly accurate is what it is," she complained. "No one should ever give their heart away during the holidays."

"Well, emotions do tend to run high or low at this time of the year."

"Doesn't make it right."

Eliza smiled and bumped Kate's shoulder. "Come on, Scrooge, let's go get something to eat and a cup of mulled wine."

"Fine, but there'd better be chocolate involved," whined Kate.

"I got you, girlfriend. Something sweet coming right up."

They meandered down King's Road, the twinkling lights and festive decorations declaring the joy of the season despite the cold temperatures. At least it was dry instead of drizzling, conceded Kate, trying to find a modicum of Christmas spirit in the silver lining.

She had stopped leaving messages and sending Ben texts after the first week, when it became glaringly apparent he would only return an email regarding business. The hardest part was feeling as though he'd cut her out without explaining why or giving her a chance at rebuttal. Though they weren't in a romantic relationship, Kate genuinely believed their friendship was a two-way street. Or, it had been. Were they still friends, or simply business partners? She was so confused.

"Ooh, look over there," Eliza said, pointing to one of the elaborate windows displays London's stores were famous for. "Let's take a closer look."

Lost in her maudlin thoughts, Kate followed blindly, missing the other couple in front of the window until it was too late.

"Well, well, well. Look who else is out and about this fine

evening," said a familiar brogue.

"What a fun coincidence," replied Eliza, kissing Sam's cheek.

Kate's head swung left at the same time Ben's swung right, their eyes locking briefly before staring at their companions.

"Right. As if the two of you had no idea where each other was going tonight."

"I might have mentioned checking out the market," Eliza said, giving Ben a wicked grin. "Sam are I are drawn to each other; we can't help it."

"Like magnets, huh?" Kate said, raising a brow in accusation.

"We were on our way to the pub, but Ben insisted we walk through the market first."

"I'm fairly sure it was your suggestion," said the accused, sounding none too happy over the run in.

"Does it matter who came up with the idea? Now we're all here, we should enjoy the company," declared Sam, hugging Eliza close to his side as they walked away, leaving their duped friends to fend for themselves.

Kate and Ben walked a short distance behind them, trying to navigate the crowd without getting too close to one another. It reminded her of a junior high dance, where no one talks to each other, let alone dances. She grinned over the picture in her head, a snort-chortle combo escaping in the process.

Ben

Ben smiled widely in response. It was quite likely the first genuine one in weeks, but he couldn't help himself. Those dimples were going to be the death of him, and her laugh the nails in the coffin. It would be a good way to go though. Better than the morose existence he currently lived. He and Henri were back to their routine; dull and drab as ever without the sunshine Kate brought into their small world. "Do I want to know?"

"Know what?"

"Why you're laughing."

"I highly doubt it since we've hardly spoken in weeks."

Well, she wasn't mincing any words. It was one of his favorite things about her. Which was part of the problem. He liked everything about her, and it scared him witless. The worst part though was knowing the distance he'd forced between them wasn't making it any better.

If anything, he'd spent more time thinking about her—what she was doing, whom she was with if not him in her spare time. But it was worse for Henri, who didn't understand the complexity of grown-up relationships and blamed himself for her sudden absence, as if Kate would ever abandon either of them over something as trivial as having a bad day.

"I'm a foolish man," he admitted.

"Oh?"

"Let's not pretend you don't know what I'm talking about,"

he said with a resigned look before continuing, "I was embarrassed about what happened at the carnival, both for myself and Henri. I ignored the cues, and his struggles are my responsibility, not yours."

"Hold on," she said looking left and then right. "With this being merry ole England, there's got to be a sword around here somewhere."

"What are you—"

"You know, so you can fall on it, like a proper martyr."

"Ha, ha. Point taken."

"Ben, I'm in your life because I want to be. We're more than partners, or at least I thought we were. Friends help each other out. Especially when things are hard."

"I didn't want us to be a burden," he confessed quietly, causing her to move into his personal space.

She stopped him with a hand to his arm, waiting for him to face her. "You're not. And if you had talked to me about this to begin with, we could have saved ourselves all of this nonsense," she said, waving her arms around at the crowds and scenery.

He huffed a laugh. "As always, you're right."

"Not always, but as close as damn is to swearing."

"There's the American vernacular I adore." Ben offered her his arm, glad she didn't reject it. The weight in his chest from the weeks apart eased with every step they took together.

"One more thing," Kate said.

"Anything."

"Don't ever decide what's best for me again without consulting me. It isn't fair to either of us. I'm perfectly capable of setting my own boundaries."

"I promise," he said, a hand over the left lapel of his charcoal peacoat. He still wanted her as much as he ever had, but keeping their friendship intact was worth the residual ache in his heart.

According to the GPS, he was five miles from the house Sam and Eliza had rented near Cairngorms National Park in the eastern Highlands. Kate had taken the train north to Scotland on Christmas Eve, which is what Ben had wished he could do, but family holiday obligations were what they were. The trussed-up tree at Althea's had, at least, had the decency to droop in solidarity with him.

Ben had chosen to drive, thinking solitude would be good for his peace of mind, except he'd done nothing but think about seeing Kate. In fact, he was giddy with it. They'd spoken on the phone every day since their walk through the market to make up for the time lost. Most of it was purely trivial, but with the busy sales season and preparing to go out of town, she wasn't able to come to Bee Hill for a proper visit. He also had a nice long chat with Henri to explain the situation, but in the end none of it mattered anyway.

"So, what you're saying is she can't come 'round because the shop is busy."

His son had taken a ten-minute diatribe, on Ben's part, and reduced it to a single sentence. If only everyone communicated with such brevity, surely the world would be a more efficient place. It would seem he had as much to learn from his child as Henri did from him.

Ben turned onto the gravel drive and followed it out to the house overlooking the River Tummel. He parked, hopped out of the car, and grabbed his bag from the boot. Most of the landscape was obscured by the loss of daylight, but he could hear the water burbling nearby and smell the Douglas firs and pine surrounding him. *Click* went the latch on the front door as he pushed while someone else pulled from the opposite side.

"Yay!" Kate cheered, clapping her hands and bouncing on the balls of her feet with a full smile. Dressed in yoga pants and an oversized sweater, she reminded him of lazy mornings under the covers, rainy afternoons spent reading over tea, and winter evenings with a smoky dram and jazz in the backdrop. In other words, the best life had to offer.

He dropped his overnight bag and reached for her. It was instinct, one she graciously allowed him since she didn't try to pull away. Kate gave as good as she got in return, as if there were no other place she'd rather be, and he buried his face in her soft tresses. She ran her hands up and down the column of his spine in a soothing motion, causing Ben to nearly purr with content. His cat might be on to something.

After a dinner of grilled steaks, roasted garlic potatoes, and sautéed Brussels sprouts, Sam and Eliza headed for the hot tub on the back deck. Ben followed Kate to the couch in the living room, where they settled in toe-to-toe, the falling snow captured picture-perfectly through the windows by the light on the porch.

"Still glad you didn't go home for Christmas?" Ben asked, swirling the whisky in his glass, admiring the legs left behind on the side. Leave it to Sam to bring not just one, but three bottles. It was hard not to, with distilleries producing a scotch to match nearly anyone's palate.

"Yeah. I'd rather be there in the spring for my niece's arrival. I still can't believe Laura's going to be a mom. My baby sister's all grown up now," she said, her lower lip jutting out in a pout.

"You called it when you said it wouldn't be long."

"And now she doesn't need me anymore," she said morosely.

"She may not need you like a chick needs a hen, but she still needs her sister."

"Was Henri excited to stay with his cousins?" Kate inquired, switching gears.

"Aye, and as it turned out, my father also decided to go."

"I bet Althea will be glad to have all of her soldiers under one roof for a couple of days."

"She keeps us together when all else fails. You might say she's our glue," said Ben, gently directing Kate back to the previous topic.

She nodded in understanding; the loss of one role could be the beginning of a new one if she was willing to embrace the change.

"And the shop is closed until after the New Year?"

"Actually, my manager was looking for a way to avoid his in-laws, who are visiting from Canada, and volunteered to cover the shop."

"In my limited experience, in-laws are either the golden goose or a Chimera."

"My sister hit the jackpot. The Kellys are like winning the lottery."

"And your ex's family, what were they like?"

"Preston didn't have any. His parents died when he was young, and he grew up in the foster care system. He didn't like to talk about it."

"A bad situation?"

Kate shrugged. "Your guess is as good as mine."

"What about your parents?"

"They don't leave the farm very often. My dad doesn't know the definition of retirement and my mom only leaves his side for weddings and funerals. But they are excited to be grandparents, and they adore Nick, so…" she trailed off, leaving him to draw his own conclusions.

"Did they like Preston?" he asked out of curiosity.

"Not exactly," she said with a tight smile. "Want to watch a movie?"

Subject change noted. Still, he wondered why her parents had disliked Kate's ex, and why she was so reticent to speak of it. "What are my options?"

She looked at the stack of Blu-ray discs on the coffee table. "Hmm, how about *Charade, Quantum of Solace,* or *Notting Hill.*"

"Anything but the last one."

"Not a fan of rom-com or this one in particular?"

"The main male character is an idiot," stated Ben.

"Now this, I've got to hear. Please proceed."

"First off, he says meeting her is 'surreal but nice.' Secondly, he can't climb a fence," he said, tersely ticking the reasons off with his fingers. "Third, he lets her open the door when he knows what awaits her on other side. And don't even get me started on his rejection of her heartfelt speech at the end."

"Wow. You are extremely passionate about this. Okay, I'll give you the 'surreal but nice' comment—a low point for sure," she said, wiggling her toes in her socks and bumping his with the motion.

Ben pulled her feet, stretching out as he tucked her legs between his and the couch in order to see her better. If he also reveled in having more physical contact with her, no one but him was the wiser.

Kate continued with her case. "But he's not supposed to be suave. His character is the average joe, which is what earns her affection. And the paparazzi situation, while unfortunate, was a necessary plot twist," she said confidently.

"I would never put someone I care about in that situation," he said, refusing to budge. "And his rejection? I mean, she brings him Chagall's *La Mariée.*"

"Oh, come on, the character is an actress! Besides, once he opens her gift, he realizes her sincerity."

"She's 'just a girl standing in front of a boy, asking him to love her,'" he quoted.

"Yeah," said Kate, wistfully.

"You'd never guess, but Althea gobbles up celebrity romance novels like a Christmas turkey."

"Too much 'do they like me for me' drama—but I can see why it's such a popular trope."

"I'm sure social media doesn't help," said Ben. "Having one's personal life bandied about like fodder for the public is unpleasant at best."

Kate's nose scrunched up as she said, "I avoid it as much as I can. Wait a second, what do—"

"So, what's your favorite trope then?" Ben interrupted, hoping to distract her. Kate didn't need to know about the high-profile relationships he'd found himself in during his misspent youth. He much preferred the quiet life at Bee Hill to gallivanting around London with a certain crowd, trying to avoid the paparazzi and subsequent tabloid articles. Not everyone was so lucky to have the option.

"Honestly, anything with a reasonably realistic happily ever after. I don't mind a book hangover every once in a while, but trauma is what therapy is for, not romance," she said, swinging her legs over his and standing. "Ready for dessert?"

"Ladies first," he said, holding out his hand for her to lead the way to the kitchen.

She tore open the cellophane wrapped around two bags of popcorn and poured the white and milk chocolate chips Eliza had already decimated earlier into different bowls. "Popcorn with chocolate drizzle and coconut, coming right up."

"Should I be worried?"

"I'm going to pretend you didn't insult my microwave skills."

He grinned. "Oh, I see how it is. There's no actual cooking involved."

"Precisely." She licked the chocolate from the spatula after drizzling it over the popcorn, handing Ben the coconut to sprinkle on top.

He dropped the bag and spilled some of its contents onto the floor. Kate had more skills in the kitchen than she realized. "You know, I could teach you how," he said, the pitch of his voice dipping with dark promise.

"How to what?"

"Cook." *In the kitchen, the bedroom, pretty much wherever you want to, darling.*

She put her hand out and waited for him to shake it. "Deal."

In the end, they didn't watch anything, choosing to talk about books and music until the clock struck midnight, declaring it 2013 with every ting of the bell struck by a wooden figurine with a miniature hammer. Sam and Eliza had gone from the hot tub to their room, leaving Ben and Kate to find their own beds.

She stretched and yawned, rubbing her tired eyes and he took the cue. "I'm on the couch tonight," said Ben.

"Sorry, I'm not usually such a night owl. I bet you've been waiting to go to bed for hours," said Kate, putting her hands out for him to pull her up.

He could hardly breathe for want of her as she stepped into his space. Ben kissed her forehead instead of the lips he wanted to ravish. "Happy new year, my darling girl," he said, watching as she stumbled away, looking back over her shoulder with a sleepy smile.

Coward, beat his offended heart. *Or sensible*, he countered. The problem was, Kate wasn't a random girl he'd met in the pub or someone he could avoid if things didn't work out. And then there was Henri's relationship with her to consider. The heart might want what it wanted, but sometimes staying the course was better for everyone involved.

Ben stripped down to his flannel pajama bottoms. Tossing back and forth on the narrow couch, he punched his feather pillow into a lumpy hill. Wide awake with thoughts of Kate an hour later, he finally gave up and turned on a James Bond film.

Chapter 18

Kate

Kate juggled the books she'd borrowed from the library with Thai take away, and a canvas tote filled with self-care items from Boots pharmacy, trying to insert her key into one of the narrow mailboxes lining the outside of her apartment building. Miraculously, she held onto everything, slipping the pile of bills and a small box into the bag before climbing the stairs, the pile between her chin and chest balanced precariously as she climbed the stairs to the fourth floor.

"I need to get in more cardio," she huffed out as she reached the top of the landing, a sheen of perspiration lining her forehead.

Valentine's Day had fallen on a Thursday, making the day feel more like every other day of the week. Opting to close the shop by herself, she'd sent Byron home an hour early to enjoy the evening with his spouse, who'd made special plans for them. Both Ben and

Henri had been sick with a stomach bug the previous weekend, sadly preventing a repeat of last year's valentine-making party, but Kate had made hers and sent them through the post on Monday.

Ben had mentioned a visit with Althea the following weekend and suggested they check out London's West End for a performance and dinner while Henri stayed with his cousins. Until then, she was counting down the days. Fine. She was counting down the hours, but since he would never know how much she looked forward to their time together, it didn't matter.

She dumped her pile on top of a waist-high bookshelf doing double duty as an entry table and dug into her tote for the mail. Written in chicken scratch across the front of the box was her name and address, with a printed label for Bee Hill in the upper left corner. Using a kitchen knife, she carefully tore through the top at the seam, assuming whatever lay within must be related to business. Kate grinned so wide her cheeks hurt.

Bennett A.K. Galloway had sent her a homemade valentine card and three baby succulents. A handwritten note lay tossed amongst the layers of quality stationery hearts, glued together at various angles and trimmed with bows.

Dearest Kate,

Happy Valentine's Day from Bee Hill. Henri has used the ribbons for his own words. May you find the adjectives endearing if also practical. Put your chicks and hens in the windowsill and water them sparingly. They love the sun like someone else I know.

Forgive me, but elegant words have never been my forte, and thus I leave you with those of a poet who understood the full depths of love.

Yours,

Ben & Henri

Kate stopped to put the plants in the sill before reading the individual words on each length of ribbon, laughing when she came to "orderly" and "punctual," then tearing up over the word **FRIEND**, written as it was in all capital letters. Swiping away the telltale moisture, she devoured the stanzas by Elizabeth Barrett Browning, a woman who, by societal standards, had been a rebel both in her career and for waiting to marry later in life. It was by no means her most romantic poem, but Ben's thoughtfulness sent Kate's heart soaring as she pulled the Valentine to her breast. Whether he intended to or not, the proprietor of Bee Hill saw her all the way to her soul.

Postscript: Return cozy reads to the TBR pile.

Ben

He watched as Kate mixed in the four-cheese blend he'd spent twenty minutes grating to make her first lesson easier. When he'd called to ask what she wanted to learn to make first, she had answered with an adamant, "Mac 'n cheese."

"Comfort food," he'd said in response, completely understanding the choice.

She measured the milk the way she did everything, with precision and order, making him smile. The woman never did anything halfway, whether it was coordinating an outfit or learning how to convert ounces to grams and cups to milliliters. Ben knew she loved others with the same determination. Now all he had to do was convince her being together was worth the risk of their partnership.

Sam and Eliza were scheduled to arrive at any minute. Before he could psych himself out, he poured four glasses of pinot noir into the stemless glasses Kate had brought to say thank you—as if he needed any incentive. Ben had every intention of making tonight a more regular occurrence.

Agnes came down the stairs holding tightly to the rail, having tucked Henri in after a dinner at the pub in order to give Ben and Kate space in the kitchen uninterrupted.

"Don't forget to cover it with aluminium foil."

Kate gave him an amused smile. "I'm sorry, what did you say?

"Cover it, so it doesn't burn, then remove the aluminium for the last ten minutes to achieve the perfect crunch on top."

"You mean aluminum foil?"

"Everyone knows the proper pronunciation is aluminium."

"Like schedule or privacy," she mocked in her best impression of his accent, making the shh sound at the beginning of the former and turning the long "i" sound in the latter into a short one.

"Exactly," he said, not giving an inch, but enjoying the mirth in her eyes.

Kate bent over to place the nine by thirteen glass dish into the oven, and he followed the movement with his eyes, appreciating the rear view. She set the timer and pursed her lips, double checking the recipe card and temperature setting one more time, making him smile again.

He walked Agnes to the door and helped her on with her coat, taking a brolly from the bin by the door. It was a short walk to her car, but the ghastly weather outside had been pelting the windows of the cottage all afternoon. Ben stared out the panes and contemplated a trip to Spain's Costa Del Sol with Kate and Henri: sun drenched skies, olives and wine, languorous strolls on the beach, stolen kisses at the water's edge.

"Remember, what I said," Agnes said conspiratorially, pulling Ben from his sunny vision and down to her diminutive height as though he were hard of hearing. Unfortunately for him, her hearing aids were absent, causing her whisper to come out at full volume.

How could he forget? Kate had arrived early for tea and Agnes had been more than a bit insistent about reading the tea leaves in the bottom of her cup. Ben had been slightly mortified, but Kate had merely grinned with excitement.

"This is just like *Outlander* by Diana Gabaldon" she said, ever the good sport, and moved to sit beside Agnes.

"Kidding," she added when he didn't say anything. "I walk

through standing stones to visit the past on a weekly basis," she teased, trying to draw him out.

Ben made a mental note of the book title for future reference.

"Mm-hm. It's as I thought," said Agnes, ignoring their tête-à-tête. "You have unfinished business."

"The good or bad kind?" Kate asked.

"If you don't take care of it, bad. Very bad, indeed."

"And if I do?"

"Better. Ben, pay attention," Agnes snapped.

"I'm right here and all ears," he replied calmly.

"Yes, but you're not hearing me."

Ben started to reassure the older woman, who had his best interest at heart even if he didn't always agree with her, when Henri came rushing in with Hamish and Percival quick on his heels.

"Kate, the sultan has a new female!"

"Oh my, how's the rest of the harem feel about her?"

"She's at the bottom of the pecking order."

"They're jealous of the newer model," said Hamish.

"Someday, the tables will turn. Men aren't the only ones who enjoy a newer model," Agnes said with a knowing wink in Hamish's direction

His father blushed, and Ben averted his gaze. The less he knew about anything going on between his father and Agnes, the better.

Sometimes, Ben wondered how his life had become so full in such a short time. It was truly remarkable, and not at all what he'd expected when Eliza sent him to pick up Kate. She'd gone from being a reckless inconvenience to becoming the center of his world, aside from Henri.

He stomped his boots at the door and put them into the tray.

"Agnes get off okay?" Kate asked, sipping her wine from where she sat on the counter next to the stove.

The timer on the oven buzzed obnoxiously. Waltzing over, Ben reached for the trivets on a shelf above Kate's head, the faint sound of a caught breath in his ear. She uncrossed her ankles beneath the long maxi dress she wore, inviting him closer and placing her hands on his waist. His gaze flickered to hers in question and at the silent plea he found, he gently pushed her cardigan from one shoulder to bare for his inspection. He kissed one freckle and then another, her gasps of pleasure urging him on before moving to capture her wine-sweetened lips.

Ben shook his head to clear it from the indulgent daydream. "Aye," he said more brusquely than he'd intended. "Be a love and hand me the trivets will you?"

. . . .

"Do your siblings have four names each like you do?" Kate asked as she and Ben walked from the warehouse to the office a week later. They were going to go over the sales reports from last quarter in order to project for the next one.

"Aye. Felix William Shelley and Althea Joan Rosetti."

"Okay, there's got to be a rhyme and reason to it. No way someone haphazardly gives their children so many names."

Ben chuckled. "There is, as you say, a rhyme and reason. My mother decided in order for it to be fair, she got to pick two and so did my father. Since Galloway was a certainty, she chose family names from her side for our given names."

"So, Bennett…"

"Was her maiden name."

"And the first middle name?"

"A warrior, though not necessarily a hero, depending on your viewpoint."

"Thus, Alexander the Great," she said, beaming. "Your sister lucked out. She could have had Boudica for a middle name."

"It would have suited her better than the pious Joan," he said, dryly.

"Since your third name is Keats, and your mother was fond of poetry…"

"Specifically, the Romantics."

"Hmm. Though technically, you're *Lord* Bennett Alexander Keats Galloway, 9th Baron Bennett, aren't you?"

"I see you put two and two together from the family portraits in the gallery."

"Yeah, about five minutes into our visit to Clatter Hall. But since I know the story behind your mouthful of a name now, I decided it would be okay to bring it up."

"Aside from having an old house and estate to keep up, the title is essentially one of inheritance and tradition," he said, feeling both burdened by and proud of his familial obligations.

"Do you serve in the House of Lords?"

"No, fortunately my family isn't one of the ninety-two hereditary peers required to."

Kate gawped at Ben in realization. "Oh my gosh, have you met the Queen?"

"Aye. She has a keen mind, and her dogs are astonishingly well-behaved."

"Well, one would hope so, considering their royal pedigree," she said, regaining her composure.

"Any other questions about my useless title?"

"Will Henri inherit it one day?"

"If I don't have any other children, the title will either pass from me to Felix or directly to Henri, depending on the circumstance."

"Because Henri isn't your biological child?"

He nodded in the affirmative.

"Do you want more children someday?"

"Honestly, I don't know," Ben replied evenly. "It might depend on Henri's needs, and that of a significant other. What about you?"

"Do I want kids?" Kate asked, blatantly stalling.

He waited patiently for her reply. It wasn't his intent to ambush her, but he wanted to know—no, needed to know either way. As a single father, he didn't have the option to be with someone who couldn't picture themselves raising a child.

"Yeah, I think so," she finally replied. "Though I swear every magazine out there has a fertility warning for women over thirty. It's mind boggling."

Ben chuckled, used to her oversharing.

"Probably more information than you were hoping for," she said before continuing, "My point is, I'm okay with motherhood if it finds me, however it finds me."

"And if not?"

"Honestly, when I was married it wasn't an option and when I left the plan was to be single indefinitely."

"Are you still determined to be single?" Ben asked, waiting anxiously this time. If Kate planned to keep her single status, then she had absolutely no interest in a romantic relationship with him.

"Not if the right person were to come along," she squeaked, and cleared her throat. "What about you? I mean you've been single since Monique and Henri came along."

"I've dated here and there."

"Oh," she said and stumbled. Ben steadied her before she could do a face plant. "Of course you have. I'm sure you're the catch of the village.

Ben grinned but said nothing more as he opened the office door for her.

Chapter 19

Kate

"You're the catch of the village?" Eliza asked.

"He caught me off guard." Kate had left Bee Hill the previous Sunday feeling like she was playing a game for which she didn't know the rules. It was like throwing a rock past the tenth square on hopscotch. Did it mean she missed a turn? Or was she supposed to hop through all of the squares to the end?

For consideration: google the rules of hopscotch.

Eliza laughed hysterically, bringing her back to the conversation. "Understatement of the year."

"I was flustered," said Kate, unpacking the boxes stamped with Bill Hill's signature branding of bees flitting through a lavender bush. What did she care if Ben was dating every single woman within a half-mile radius looking for a baby mama? It was none of her beeswax.

Subject line: No more books with sexy single dads who think bookworms are hot. Wait, those are separate ideas, right? He had her so discombobulated, she was mixing up her book pile's meta data.

"Because he was asking if he could fertilize your field?"

"He was not!" Kate said, denying the full-body flush the word picture produced, and fanning herself at the same time. She needed to put in an extra order of Althea's "special" tea. Hormones were hormones, after all, and Ben A.K. Galloway made them sing like an opera on steroids with what was surely an innocent glance. No one smoldered as much as Kate imagined he did.

"Not directly, but trust me, the implication was there. Congratulations Kit-Kat, someone wants in your pants."

Another heat wave swept over Kate as she re-lived their encounter in the kitchen, or rather the one she'd imagined was going to happen until the oven timer went off. She probably needed to have her eyes checked, but she could have sworn he'd smoldered in her direction before asking for the trivets. "Don't be crass," chastised Kate without any bite, switching the phone to speaker. The store didn't open for another hour, and she preferred early mornings to late evenings.

"Since you can't see me, I'm doing the eyeroll of eyerolls."

"Ben and I are friends and partners."

"Except, you want more."

"It doesn't mean he does."

"No man asks if you want children, unless he's considering you as a candidate for his, born or unborn."

"Fine."

"There's no way you're letting me off the hook this easy," Eliza said, followed by a pop. She'd been chewing loudly since she picked up the phone.

"What's wrong? You only chew gum when the creative juices are in a slump."

"Sam and I can't agree on the lyrics for a new song. Now, stop changing the subject. What did you tell Grumpy?"

"In his defense, he only gets grumpy when he's hungry...or Felix comes around."

"Big shocker there. His brother is a total tool. The only reason Sam puts up with him is because he respects Ben.

"The man acts as if he's responsible for the choices his family makes and their less-than-honorable behavior."

"Good men do what's right even when it's hard."

"And he's one of the good ones."

The best, said her heart staunchly, leaving no room for argument.

Ailis Sebina Kelly wailed louder than her daddy's fire engine as Father Hugo poured the chilly water of baptism over her head. Leo stood opposite Kate, promising to guide the newest Kelly in the ways of God, and she took note of the short, dark hairs growing in on his previously bald pate. The bruises beneath Leo's mischievous eyes had also done a disappearing act since his last chemo treatment shortly before the wedding. She was relieved to see him doing so well.

Shipped off to New Orleans the week before in the name of Howard business, Lon had missed another celebration, but she and Laura both recognized the decision for what it was—a hail Mary. After his no show at the wedding, their father had come to the end of his patience. It was something Kate hadn't known was possible, until now.

Someday, her brother would realize everything he'd missed, and when he did, she hoped he would grovel for their forgiveness. Not actually, but the possibility made his actions sting less. Hopefully, Louisiana would be the fresh start Lon needed.

Kate recited the words the priest prompted, officially becoming a godmother in addition to an aunt. To her way of thinking, it meant she had double the responsibility but also twice the excuse to shower her niece with gifts. Ever practical, Laura had done an exaggerated eyeroll over the personalized onesies and embroidered spit-up rags she'd bought at a posh children's store—until she reached the end of the stack.

"Property of Squad 2 and Future Nerd," her sister read aloud, and promptly cried a bucket's worth of hormones.

"No one ever tells you how brutal postpartum is," said Laura as they walked down the front steps of the church. "You leak from every orifice of your body, sleep deprivation wreaks havoc on… well, everything. And then there are the hormones. One second, I'm all sorts of badassery, and the next I'm a blubbering nitwit."

"I think it's okay to be both, moon pie. Some might argue strength is born from tears."

"Aria and Gina are amazing as far as sisters in-law go, but I'm glad you're here," Laura admitted, her relief evident in her expression.

"Me too," said Kate, wrapping an arm around her. Ben was right; her sister didn't need a mother hen anymore, but she could still be there for Laura in other ways. "No postpartum depression, right?"

"Nope, but Gina had it after Sofi was born. She tagged the notepad on the fridge with symptoms to watch out for. Nick checks it every time I cry."

"You have to admit, under normal circumstances, you're not exactly the most emotive person."

"You think?" Uncle Joe asked sarcastically, kissing a cheek each as they reached the top of the stairs. "I'm off to do a delivery run for Ruth," he said with a gentle squeeze of Ailis' chubby cheek.

"I'll come by to catch up before I leave," said Kate.

"Sounds good, doll," he returned with a wink, trotting in the direction of Ruth's Deli.

Laura leaned in and lowered her voice. "Mama's driving me crazy, and while Nick does his best to back my play, she's like a gale-force wind. I've never seen a guy with so much muscle move as fast as The Flash when she gives him *the look*." The look was Beth Howard's first weapon in her arsenal. Half disappointment, half challenge, she was scarier than any witch in a fable.

Kate snorted. "Sounds like her. Now, hand over the baby," she demanded, taking Ailis from Laura when they reached the sidewalk. "I could kiss these cheeks forever—so soft and squishy."

"You won't be saying the same thing when she's got spit up stuck in the crevices of her neck. Sour milk is sour no matter where it comes from."

Kate wrinkled her nose. "Gross."

"Exactly. Wait until she has a blowout and ruins what you're wearing. This is my second outfit today."

"Geeze, you make having kids sound like a day at the park." But Kate kept thinking back to her conversation with Ben. If she were honest with herself, she did want kids—with him. Whether they only ever had Henri or more, if it was with him, then she wanted everything.

Laura grinned. "It's not all bad. Look at those cheeks."

"Yeah, they're pretty spectacular. How's the pub coming along?"

"So far, so good. The re-opening is set for the beginning of

June. Thanks again for letting go of the apartment."

"Of course. It only makes good business sense to increase the usable space."

"So, does this mean you're staying in London indefinitely?"

Kate came to an abrupt halt before saying, "Yeah, I think it does."

"You sound surprised."

"Honestly, I hadn't taken everything into consideration until just now."

"Are you staying for the shop or a certain grumpy Brit?"

"Both," said Kate without hesitation. "I don't know if Ben feels the same way I do, but I want to stick around and find out."

"Do you hear that, Ailis?" Laura cooed at her daughter. "Your Auntie Kate found her grit again."

"I did, didn't I," said Kate, smiling to her dimples.

"Damn straight, you did."

"Keep it up and your daughter's going to have a potty mouth," said Beth Howard, stepping up directly behind them.

"Shitake mushrooms, Mama!" exclaimed Laura with a jump. "Stop sneaking up on me; it makes my boobs leak," she said, looking down at the blouse she'd worn to be sure nothing had gone through the pads of her nursing bra.

"Give me my grandbaby," said Beth, taking Ailis from Kate. "She's not wrong. Grit looks good on you, sweetheart," she sang, striding for the car and gabbing with Nick's mother, Luna, like they were best friends.

"Something tells me those two are a dangerous combination."

"Amen," said Laura, making the sign of the cross.

Ben

"How was the trip home?" Ben asked, standing and admiring the woman who had stepped into his office. He'd been trying to tally the books for the week and failing miserably, mostly because he kept daydreaming about Kate. And like his dream, she'd appeared out of thin air, without a phone call or text, looking as if she'd come directly from the airport. *Had she?* he wondered belatedly.

"Okay, I guess," she replied on a sigh. "Walker's Pub opens again in June. It's coming together well, and with the extra space from my old apartment, not to mention the roof for special events; it's going to be a real money maker."

"How was it playing Aunt for the first time?"

"Ailis is a doll. She has the most kissable cheeks, and my sister is deliriously happy."

She'd been away for a week, but he'd missed her desperately. Used to their weekly chats and visits, it was as though Kate had become an extra limb—one he relied on as much as the other four he had.

"It's slightly nauseating, huh?" Ben asked, understanding the tone beneath the sentiment.

"Exactly. Don't get me wrong, I'm happy for them, but..." Kate said, trailing off.

"It makes you feel the teensiest bit envious?"

"Uh-huh," she said, bobbing her head up and down. "Not because she and Nick don't deserve to be happy," Kate rushed to explain.

"But you wonder if it'll ever be your turn?"

"Yeah," she said, wearing her heart on her sleeve.

Stepping into her space, he pulled her into his arms, enjoying the way she melted into him.

Friends hug. They comfort one another in times of distress. And if everything went the way he hoped, they would be more than friends by the end of the lavender harvest. All he had to do was patiently warm her up to the possibility of being something more. As for himself, he knew the only thing keeping him from making a declaration at this point was their friendship. He could live with the potential business loss, but losing Kate altogether was unthinkable.

Courage, dear heart, he told himself, channeling the wisdom of C.S. Lewis's Aslan. Per usual, Narnia contained the wisdom of the ages, because a true classic never went out of style.

"Kate, what happened with your ex?" he asked, worried her marriage had cast a shadow over any potential relationships. After all, he'd experienced firsthand the spell Kate wove. Fortunately for him, she had never returned the sentiment where several strangers were concerned, let alone Felix. Still, he would have to be a complete dolt to ignore what she claimed to want and her actions to the contrary.

"I might need a drink first," she mumbled into his neck, her breath feathering the sensitive spot there and causing a shiver to course through him.

He held on tighter for another moment before stepping back and changing course. "Well, as it happens, I have a bottle in the drawer I keep for difficult stories."

Thirty minutes and two empty teacups later, Kate came to the end of her tale, and Ben promised himself if he ever came face to face with Preston Toliver, he'd dump the man's body into the Thames where no one would ever find it. The worst part was knowing how she'd skimmed over the details. He had no doubt she'd endured more than she let on and draped an arm over the back of the couch, not touching her but close enough to reassure them both.

There were those who never made it out of an abusive relationship. Ben wasn't so naïve as to think it was as simple as leaving. Isolation, shame, and fear often kept someone from ever seeking help, let alone the financial, emotional, and mental hurdles a person would need to overcome.

"Anyway, two months later the court dismissed my battery case," she said, taking a shaky breath. "I've always suspected Preston had half the state of Georgia in his back pocket, including the District Attorney. At least the court granted me a divorce on the grounds of spousal abuse," she said dryly.

The irony did not escape Ben's notice. "A right arsehole, huh?"

"Something like it." Kate shrugged, her emotions laid bare for him, and he wanted nothing more than to wrap her up in his arms and keep her safe. But he couldn't fight this battle for her. Only she could come to terms with her past. All he could do was walk beside her as she did.

Ben took her chin in hand and gently brought her eyes to his. "You are not to blame for anything he did."

"I know."

"Perhaps, but I'll keep saying it until you believe it."

"Therapy was expensive, but at least it showed me no one deserves to be a punching bag in any form."

Ben's jaw clenched tightly, and he forced himself to relax before asking, "What is it then?"

"Preston was larger than life. He was charming, well-connected, and wealthy. What if I only attract toads who look good from afar but are far from good?"

"Well, I for one think you're right—you are rather shallow," he teased leading her away from the edge of self-doubt.

She swatted at him with the back of her hand, and he chuckled low in response, capturing it with his own and giving it a light squeeze before releasing it reluctantly.

"I can't believe you called me shallow."

Slinking inside through the cracked door, Merlin weaved in and out of Kate's jean-clad legs, purring when she picked him up to lay in her lap.

I know exactly how you feel, you bold moggy; there is no other place I'd rather be than beside her.

"Monique and I spent weeks in each other's company, working closely on the estate, sharing meals, and getting to know each other. Not once did I ever suspect she was seeing Felix," he shared to equalize the vulnerability between them.

"Your brother never said anything or suspected your interest in Monique?"

"No, I refuse to believe Felix could be so underhanded, though the men in this family can, admittedly, be obtuse when it suits our purpose. I suspect he planned to have a little fun and move on. At least, until Monique announced her pregnancy."

"So, he tried to do the right thing by them?"

"Aye, I think he meant to make an honest go of it."

"Still, he walked away when it counted most," Kate said, her nose scrunching up with apparent dislike.

"Or he did what was in everyone's best interest in the end."

"I shouldn't speak ill of the dead, but doesn't it seem odd you were spending so much time with Monique, and she was sleeping with Felix?"

"My brother can be quite dashing when he wants to be."

"Which I've been a firsthand recipient of—and not at all

interested in," she finished, lifting her left hand up to stop his interjection. "My point is, you spent enough time with her to think there was a connection between the two of you, yet she was sleeping with your brother, and no one was the wiser until she was pregnant."

"Are you implying Monique…"

"Was stacking the deck in her favor in order to land one of the Galloway brothers?"

"Well, that's one way to put it," he said, feeling a bit horrified over the idea.

"I'm sorry, Ben. I shouldn't have said anything."

"Actually, I've wondered the same thing a few times myself, but guilt always gets the better of me."

Kate regarded him with solemn eyes. "Why is it so hard to forgive ourselves when we weren't in the wrong?"

"I suspect it has something to do with fear. We're afraid if we forgive ourselves, we'll forget the lessons we've learned. And neither of us wants to make the same mistake again."

"Some people might venture to say we aren't the ones in need of forgiveness."

"And those same people might also say neither of us are the same people we were once upon a time anyway," he said, extending his hand to help her stand. "Want to see the abbey?"

The feel of her hand in his was like coming home every single time, and Ben let himself fall all over again, sliding her fingers through his and locking them together.

"Well, what's left of it, anyway," he said meeting her gaze. "It's crumbling into a pile of dirt and rock with every passing decade, but there's enough of an outline to appreciate what the monks left behind."

Chapter 20

Kate

Kate looked down again at the hand still holding hers and sighed in recognition. Of what exactly, she'd examine later. But her hand in his was a good place to start something new, she decided.

"There's an abbey nearby?" she asked, tumbling into the varying skies of his gaze for the millionth time since meeting him.

"Aye, and maybe we'll catch a peek at the bees on our way. They're starting to wake from their winter slumber."

They are not the only ones. A tingly warmth filled her abdomen as her ovaries tap danced.

Holding hands does not equal knocking boots, so knock it off, Kate internally shouted at her reproductive organs. They merely worked double time to prove otherwise. Fortunately, Ben didn't appear to notice as he rambled on about hive life, saving her the disgrace of throwing herself at him in the middle of a muddy lane.

Kate sighed with content as they rounded the corner of a stone wall lined with shrubs. Sharing her story had given her a new sense of freedom and a clearer perspective. Her relationship with Preston wasn't a burden she had to continue carrying around. Regardless of why she fell for him, only her ex was to blame for how he'd treated her. And while there was no changing the past, the future held better because she was no longer the same person she'd been then. These days, she was a new creation, bold and unafraid to shine her light for all to see.

The abbey, as it turned out, was mostly a hill of rubble with an outline. Still, Kate reveled in its history, which had nothing to do with her own sad past, meandering in and out of its ruins. Whoever implied moving forward meant forgetting what came before had obviously never experienced anything traumatic, she mused.

Spooling her wool gathering for another time, she said, "This would make a perfect wedding venue." Kate took note of the daffodils and bluebells sheltered against the stones, the lingering snowdrops welcoming their more delicate neighbors to the Easter season.

"I can't imagine anyone paying top dollar for a crumbling abbey in which to say their vows."

"Unusual venues are all the rage right now and a crumbling abbey is the epitome of romantic." Ignoring his look of doubt, she continued, "The stars above, candlelight, and nature, all entwined with history. It makes for the perfect ambiance. Not to mention, a couple could use a registrar to officiate the ceremony and satisfy any family religious expectations at the same time—previously holy ground, but not sanctimonious. Admittedly, it would only work for two or three seasons out of four."

"And when it rains?"

"White event tents and butane heaters to keep the chill away."

"And a reception?"

"The ballroom at Clatter Hall or tents in the garden."

"Brilliant, darling. Positively brilliant. I would need to procure a license from the local council, but I think Agnes can help with the application," he said with an appreciative gleam in his eyes.

Kate ate up his compliment, while Ben played an undeclared game of hide and seek with her, weaving in and out of the various columns and stacks of stone.

"The sheep keep the grass mowed, so be careful where you step," he warned, while she continued to grin until her cheeks hurt.

"Duly noted," Kate acknowledged and checked the bottom of her new rainboots. A few weeks ago, she'd shown up at Bee Hill to find a pair of wellies in beetroot waiting in the shoe tray beside those of the other occupants of the cottage. They were the exact pair she would have picked from the garden catalogue in his office and matched the trench coat she'd bought for the spring weather from one of the charity shops on Portobello.

"This way you don't have to bring yours back and forth from

London. There's also a pair in the office, for the days we leave from there," he'd added bashfully, as though she might object to his thoughtfulness. He couldn't have been more wrong. If anything, her adoration of him had reached a whole new height of skyscraper proportions.

After tromping around for a while longer, they headed toward the estate to discuss her ideas for renovating the orangery into a café or venue for afternoon tea. Kate melted into a puddle for the umpteenth time. Somehow, *this* man knew the way to her heart lay in asking for and valuing her opinion.

She wasn't a complicated woman. Fine, she was kind of obsessed with sustainable fashion and completely unrealistic in terms of book boyfriends, but those were reasonable quirks when one considered the whole package. And since when did she categorize herself into pros and cons? It's not like she needed to create a list of selling points for Ben—they were friends.

Kate looked over her shoulder to find Ben watching her, causing her heart to race, his gaze intense with purpose as he took long strides in her direction, eating up the distance between them. *Oh my gosh,* she wondered nervously. Had he finally come to the same conclusion she had and decided to confront the situation head on? Her lips were dying for attention and so were other parts south of the equator, but was she ready to cross a line they couldn't come back from?

He walked past her, a mere hair's breadth away, to the far wall.

Kate shook her head and came crashing back to reality.

What a feather-brained ninny muggins, she chided and followed it up with a hard eyeroll for good measure.

From now on, only biographies, memoirs, and non-fiction were acceptable reading material. She could probably find a self-help book on the subject. *Removing Romance for a More Productive Life* sounded like an excellent title or something like *Getting a Life for Dummies.* Kate sighed. She was hopeless.

"I don't think we'd do any structural damage to the rest of the space if we bumped out the walls for a kitchen right here. What do you think?" Ben asked, knocking on the wall for good measure after analyzing the structure intently.

Pathetic. Utterly pathetic, Kate berated herself. And yet she knew it wouldn't change anything. She was a total goner for the man who only had architecture and business plans on the brain. Putting aside her disappointment for the time being, she smiled beatifically. "Actually, I was thinking the exact same thing."

Ben

Lavender Honey & Co. finally had a responsible manager, freeing Kate up regularly on the weekends. Henri didn't seem at all upset by the change in their routine, used to her presence more than her absence. The trio spent their free time together reading, riding, and walking the estate to visit the newly blooming beds and waking hives.

Percival and Merlin inevitably sought her out, demanding their due along with the black sheep Betty couldn't seem to keep with the rest of the flock. Kate may as well have been a fairy-tale princess come to life, casting a spell over man, child, and beast alike with her dimples and optimism. And when she left, they returned to their less-colorful lives, waiting for the weekend to come around and her with it.

Ben looked down at Percival. "Everyone wants to be Cary Grant. Even I want to be Cary Grant," he quoted, thinking of Kate's infatuation with the man's films, and ignoring how the actor had actually been referring to himself when he'd said it.

Something had grown from the barren, fallow ground of his soul—a longing for more—and to settle for less would be a self-betrayal. Ben could feel it in the crackle of tension whenever Kate was near, similar to the way his knees predicted a change in the weather. Whoever said forty was the new thirty had never been a collegiate athlete. Wear and tear on the body was a very real phenomenon.

Regardless, the feeling was as ominous as a storm on the horizon and knowing what was to come provided no relief other than confirming how much he wanted Kate in every part of his life, whether at home, work, or in his bed each night. Ben ran his hands through his hair as he remembered their afternoon at the abbey and the orangery afterward.

He had come so close to kissing her then, changing course at the last moment, lest he ruin everything in his haste. Kate was worth waiting for and wooing properly. Now, all he needed was a plan.

"Agnes says the rain is coming in this afternoon." Ben reached for his knee out of habit, stopping the telltale motion and spreading a rug on the grassy knoll.

Kate looked up and around. "There are only a handful of clouds in the sky, and the view is amazing from here."

"Aye, but it's May."

"I know, which means flowers instead of showers."

"This is spring in England, which means all four seasons are possible in a day."

"Then why didn't you grab a raincoat or umbrella, Oscar the Grouch?"

"I'm sorry, who?" he said, playing dumb.

"How do Brits learn to be kind humans without *Sesame Street?*" Kate asked, her feathers ruffled. "Please try being anyone other than Darcy for the next hour."

"Right," he grumped.

"You seem hungry."

"I could go for some quiche and tea," he admitted, feeling unaccountably out of sorts. *Best batten down the hatches, old chap,* his left knee seemed to say as he waited for the impending storm to break. Henri had chosen to spend the afternoon with Hamish and a book, as if he too could sense what was coming though it contradicted logic.

"On it," she said with a knowing grin.

He took the plate from her, waiting for her to serve herself before digging in. He'd fed Henri lunch and, in a hurry to pick his father up in the village, had completely forgotten to feed himself. It was one of the hazards of parenting, he supposed. They were eating cherry cordials, when the wind picked up its pace, hastily forcing the cloud bank on the horizon to move in and block out the sun. Ben sighed. So much for pleasant weather.

"Those clouds look kind of ominous" said Kate.

His look clearly communicated, *I told you so.*

Kate shrugged as if to say, *Oops.*

Quickly packing away the used cups and plates, Kate put the food back into its paper containers as the sky opened up with rain and hail. Lightening cracked in the distance, the roll of thunder a deep rumble throughout the earth around them. "Come on," he said, grabbing her hand and making a run for it. "There's a folly between here and the house. We can shelter there."

By the time they reached the carved marble columns designed after a Grecian temple, the nearby pond had overflowed its banks. Ben closed the sturdy wooden door behind Kate and immediately searched for any sign of available warmth. While the folly provided a roof from the elements, the construction left little in the way of preventing hypothermia. At least the narrow horizontal slits cut into the stone, directly below the roofline, provided enough light for the time being, dull as it was.

"Is it me, or did the temperatures plummet when the rain started?" Kate asked, beginning to shiver.

"It did, but being drenched isn't helping."

"And neither is the marble."

"Aye. My great-grandfather designed the folly to be a retreat for summer picnics and the like."

Kate took in their surroundings. "Laura sent me a postcard from Greece once, but the temples on the front were only replicas."

"As a rule, most ancient things are also decrepit," he replied, finally locating what he was looking for. "Ah-ha!" Ben exclaimed, opening the rectangular wooden crate in the corner.

"What did you find?"

"Althea's hidden stash. She used to escape out here when she wanted to be alone."

"What's in there?"

"Candles, matches, a blanket, and…"

"And?"

"Nothing," he mumbled, trying to scrape the image of condom wrappers and a box of cigarettes from his mind. No man wanted to think about his sister and those items in tandem.

So much for Althea coming here to be alone.

He took the matches out of the sealed box, and, hoping it had staved off the moisture, he struck one and then another. He placed each lit candle into a niche, illuminating the room and the resident goddesses.

"Wow," said Kate in admiration, walking around the room to read each plaque. "Aphrodite, Athena, Artemis, Demeter, Hera, Hestia, Persephone, and Astraea. They're exquisite."

"Aye," he said, watching her from the shadows. "Here, let's warm you up."

She snuggled into the tartan throw he put around her shoulders as he rubbed up and down over her arms, trying to infuse some warmth into her, their lips a mere breath apart. He leaned in, giving her the chance to pull back. Surely, this would be the best way to warm them both up.

Ben dipped his head, sliding one hand to the nape of her neck.

Kate lifted her face in turn. And then her teeth began to chatter in earnest.

It was like pouring ice cold champagne over his head and his ardor.

Abandon ship, I repeat, abandon ship, signaled his addled brain.

Adjusting the blanket around her slender neck and stepping back from the lips he wanted to taste, Ben tossed his soaked jumper to the side. He wrung out the cotton shirt beneath, forming a tiny puddle between them.

Who was he kidding, Ben asked himself, sitting down lengthwise on the crate with his back to the wall. No doubt he'd misread the situation anyway. "Come sit," he invited, patting the spot in front of him. "It's sturdy enough."

She hopped up and settled into the space left by the V shape of his legs, leaning back into his chest the way he'd imagined a million times before, and lining up their lower extremities. Ben tucked her close, caging her in with his arms.

"And for your information, Oscar wasn't a bad sort," he confessed. "He just needed Big Bird to lead him into the light from time to time."

"You did watch *Sesame Street!*" Kate accused, sitting up straight and chastising him with a look over her shoulder.

"Aye," he laughed low, pulling her back in. "In fact, I was rather sad to realize it had been cancelled." Everyone could use a few role models to help navigate the world, and Elmo would have made an excellent one for Henri.

Kate settled in, her breathing deep and steady as she relaxed further into the cocoon he'd created.

"I read somewhere that the best way to keep hypothermia at bay is to get naked and share body heat," she casually blurted out.

Ben coughed, his chest spasming beneath her. It was almost certainly one of the random facts she collected ad nauseum with all of her reading. If he had to guess, Kate had it filed away under *Worst Case Scenarios* in the labyrinth of her intelligent mind. Nonetheless, that didn't make him any less eager to try out her theory, except he knew she hadn't meant it as an invitation.

"Are you okay?" she asked, fully alert again.

"Fine, fine. Carry on," he answered, hoarsely.

Falling asleep at some point, Ben woke up warm and insulated with his arms wrapped around Kate. Darkness had fallen, but from what he could tell the rain had finally stopped. They *should* head for the house, where they could start a fire and call Hamish with their whereabouts, but he hated to rouse the woman in his arms, especially when there was nowhere else he'd rather be. He closed his eyes and allowed himself for a few more moments to pretend she was well and truly his. "I would not wish any companion in the world but you," he whispered, knowing she wouldn't be able to hear his whimsical confession from the Bard.

Chapter 21

Ben

The best way to keep hypothermia at bay is to get naked and share body heat.

Kate was trying to kill him, but only a wanker would have taken advantage of the opportunity she'd thrown out like scraps for a hungry animal. Nearly kissing her had been bad enough. She deserved the moon and the stars, not a guy who took advantage of his circumstances. He didn't want her to consent today only to lose it tomorrow; he wanted it for the foreseeable future.

His father's advice at luncheon the day before had been, "Throw the lass over yer shoulder and make yer way to Gretna Green for a quick elopement. How do you think I won yer mam?"

"I always assumed she was attracted to your intelligence."

He shrugged, "Or my virility. Yer mother liked a hard—"

Ben had stopped his father with a raise of his brows and a long stare. "Sorry, I forgot who my audience was," Hamish said, looking sheepish.

Well, this certainly explained a few things he'd always wondered about. Namely how his mother wound up married to the irreverent Scotsman. Given the circumstances, Ben should ignore his father's ill-conceived advice. Still, he did have a point.

For the sake of his sanity, it was time for Ben to stop wallowing and take charge of his destiny. It would also be slightly less pathetic than pining, he decided. If she wasn't interested, then he would fade into the shadows of their business partnership without making things overly awkward between them. However, if she was interested in something more than friendship it was time to put the kettle on to boil.

He couldn't hide his feelings from Kate forever. Besides, courage always won the day even when defeat seemed imminent. Deciding self-respect was as good a motivation as any, he said, "*Carpe diem, old chap.*" The walls of the office stared back without reply, and Ben took their cue for encouragement.

Rolling a pencil back and forth, he waited impatiently for her to answer, jazz coming from the 1956 radio he kept on the drafting desk. Awakened by the birds nesting nearby and plans for an addition to the cottage rattling around in his head, he'd been eager to get them on paper before he could forget. He was about to hang up when a velvety, deep voice finally came over the line. "Good afternoon, Lavender Honey & Co., Byron speaking."

"Is Kate in?" Ben asked, forgoing his usual manners and wondering if he'd dialed the wrong number. Who was Byron? He could've sworn Kate had said her manager's name was Bronwen.

"Sure, mate. Hold on a minute."

Ben listened to the muffled voices in the background as Byron passed the phone off but couldn't distinguish who was saying what.

"Hello, Kate speaking," she said, breathless.

Why was she breathless? And who was this Byron guy with his dark chocolate and caramel voice? He shook his head over the description. Kate was rubbing off on him with her dessert comparisons.

"Have dinner with me and Henri on Saturday. It's time you had another cooking lesson." It wasn't what he'd planned to say, but it still met the criteria for a date—sort of.

"Um, Ben?" she asked as though it weren't perfectly obvious.

"Do other men call to invite you to dinner?" he asked tersely and tugged at his collar. Except he wasn't wearing one. *Blasted pullover.*

"Well, not lately, though if this is what you consider a dinner invitation in Britain I'm not sure why anyone would ever accept," she delivered dryly.

Point taken. "Kate, please do me the honor of joining Henri and me for dinner."

"I'd love to, on one condition."

Of course, she had a condition. He went to tug at his collar again and blew out a breath of frustration instead.

"Let me bring dessert," she qualified, the sound of her voice a sultry caress sliding over his whole body.

As far as he was concerned, Kate was the dessert—sweet, luxurious, and exquisite.

Ben shifted in his seat and went to roll his sleeves, having to push them up over his forearms instead. Bloody knitwear. Why was it so hot? His father must have played with the thermostat earlier. Or his imagination was in overdrive. The sooner he found out if they were on the same page the better. "Done," he said, and hung up without saying goodbye. When he looked up, it was to see his father standing in the doorway.

"Certainly, one way to throw her over yer shoulder."

Ben glared at his father, who merely gave a Gallic shrug and walked away, his kilt swinging in triumph with his gait.

No going back now, old chap. Time to lay his cards on the table, as the saying went. What could go wrong? Right. Losing his best friend and partner.

Four days later, Ben met Kate in the soon-to-be paved-and-painted car park. Opening the car door, he admired her long legs as she shimmied out in dark denim jeans, an amethyst blouse, and those heels he'd come to appreciate but hadn't seen in a while. Was she marking the occasion, or was he reading into things?

"Here," she said depositing a familiar bakery box into his hands.

"Chocolate marmalade cupcakes or chocolate raspberry torte?"

She shook her head in the negative. "Devil's food cake, layered with apple pie filling, and salted caramel frosting," answered Kate with a knowing smirk.

God, he loved this woman.

One foot in front of the other, old chap—no sense in getting ahead of yourself.

Too late, declared his heart. Too late, indeed.

Kate

After a dinner of mushroom and game pie with baked sweet potatoes on the side, Ben suggested they remove to the living room for a night cap.

"Good night, Henri. Sweet dreams," she said as the little boy sleepily shuffled up the stairs, Ben following behind him.

"I'll only be a moment."

"No need to rush on my part. Your library could keep me busy for weeks."

He chuckled. "Why don't you pick out something to listen to instead? I don't want to lose you in Wonderland tonight."

Kate gave him an impish smile and walked over to survey his vinyl collection filled with Jazz, Big Band, and the Blues. It was the kind of music her grandparents had listened to. They were always spinning around the kitchen during her childhood visits, twirling and dipping until she'd grown dizzy from watching them.

She sat down on the floor and ran her index finger across the rows of covers, reading the tiny print as she went, until she found her favorite. Plucking it from amongst the rest, she put it on top of the restored gramophone, gingerly setting the needle into place for fear of scratching the record.

For tonight's dinner, Ben had taught her to make a cheater version of the crust used for the pies to cut down on cooking time and though she mostly watched and took mental notes, she enjoyed being in the kitchen with him. He wore an apron when he was in chef mode, and he patiently explained every step as if she were planning to pursue a culinary arts degree at some point in the future. It was sexier than it ought to be.

She looked down at her outfit. Dressed for a date, despite their friend status, she'd worn heels and spent extra time on her makeup. Laura would call her out for going above and beyond friend protocol, and she would be right. At least Ben had dressed to match in slacks and a tie, instead of the more relaxed style he preferred at home. No doubt he'd gone to town or had a meeting at the office earlier in the day.

Had Althea mentioned something about it when she called to confirm her pick up for the following week? Kate couldn't remember, but then again, she'd been busy making plans for her non-date with Ben. She was becoming more delusional by the day.

Getting caught in the rain and taking shelter in the folly certainly hadn't helped dim her overactive imagination. She could have sworn he was going to kiss her. If only her teeth had behaved instead of ruining everything with their obnoxious chatter. Then she wouldn't have any room to wonder if he would or would not have kissed her senselessly.

Kate blew out a breath, trying to dislodge the whisp of hair dangling in front of her eyes. She should consider getting bangs. A fringe might add a little sass to her strut. Every woman could use some Audrey Hepburn inspiration now and again.

Looking up as Ben rounded the newel post, the aged stairs alerting her to his presence with their numerous creaks and groans, Kate lithely rose from the floor.

"He fell asleep after two questions, instead of the usual five. I think he stayed up late reading last night."

"I used to hide beneath the covers with a flashlight, and hope Laura wouldn't tattle. Some stories are too good to set aside before they're finished."

"Agreed," said Ben pushing open a couple of windows to let in the night air, the fragrance of late spring blooms wafting in from below. "Shall we?" he inquired, having eaten up the distance between them and opened his arms in invitation.

"Dance? Here? Now?" she asked, becoming increasingly pitchy with each question.

"There's no time like the present."

Why did he sound so calm? Didn't he know he'd shocked her all the way into next week? *Calm down, girlfriend,* she told herself, but her ovaries were sounding the alarm.

This is not a drill. We repeat, this is not a drill, dancing is involved—snuggle up, buttercup.

Ben waited patiently for her to step closer, his hand ready to take hers, not looking the least flustered. She, on the other hand, was about to start flapping her arms to match the flapping she was doing inside her brain.

Be brave, be brave, be brave.

Kate placed her hand in his, the same way she'd done on multiple occasions, except this time, Ben pulled her in until his arm encircled her, holding her securely in place. It was somehow more intimate than any hug he'd ever given her, and as she met his eyes, she instinctively stepped backward at the same time he pushed forward. She kept her gaze locked with his, and though they moved in the small space left between the fireplace and furniture, she pictured an opulent ballroom at Clatter Hall, women dripping in jewels and men in black tails as they circled the dance floor.

The music petered out with a jarring scritch as the needle sought purchase and Ben released her, breaking the spell. Kate took a deep breath, as though she'd been underwater instead of on solid ground. She stayed where she was, immobile, uncertain of her next move.

Taking a bottle of amber liquid from a hiding spot beside the gramophone and pouring a finger's worth into a wide, squat glass, Ben asked, "Fancy a drink?"

A small amount of liquid courage couldn't hurt, so long as she kept her wits about her. "Sure, anything but bourbon."

"Scotch all right?"

"With a splash of water, please," she requested. "Bourbon was Preston's favorite." The words slipped past her lips without permission, the phantom smell of sweet, distilled corn filling her nose. Kate closed her eyes in irritation.

"My father would tell you the only true whisky comes from Scotland," said Ben in understanding.

"I knew I liked Hamish, though I bet the Irish would beg to differ."

Ben flashed her with one of his rare full smiles, causing her to feel a smidge bedazzled. "Since they spell it the same way the Americans do, it doesn't count."

"Don't tell my brother in-law. If it doesn't end in EY and have an Irish label, Nick thinks it's dirty."

"Triple distillation doesn't make it better, only smoother," Ben countered amiably.

She took the glass he offered and followed him to the couch, tucking a leg beneath her as she sat, and trying not to fidget.

"To being partners, friends…and us," he toasted, staring intently into her eyes.

Kate tapped her glass to his and lifted it to her lips, sipping once, and again, waiting for the contents to take the edge off her sudden case of nerves.

Friends and partners, she told herself repeatedly.

Ben cared for her, but his priorities were Henri and Bee Hill. There was no way he felt the same way about her as she did him. It would mean all of those happily ever after's she read about in novels were possible and not the delusions of a lonely woman.

She eased further into the cushions and sighed with resignation, finally meeting the eyes pinned on her profile. Here was a man capable of real love. Kate had seen firsthand the way he cared for his son, gently and patiently. And Ben always tried to treat those around him with the utmost respect, despite being hungry. What wouldn't she give to be the woman who sweetened him up whenever his blood sugar dropped?

"Kate, my darling girl," he said, tucking a loose piece of hair behind her ear. "If all you want is to be friends and partners, I promise to find a way to make this less awkward someday—possibly from the other side of eternity. But the truth is, I am hopelessly, impossibly smitten with you."

At his low words and the tenderness shining in his eyes, the dam holding her own ardent feelings in check broke like a flood.

Kate pressed her lips to his without thinking. Ben only hesitated for a second before catching up and reaching for her. She let him pull her into his lap as his hands took hold of her hips and gently tugged, while hers were already reaching for the buttons on his shirt.

He caught her wrists in a hold she could break at any moment and deepened the kisses between them, lavishing her lips with attention until she began to moan with need.

"Kate, what do you want?" Ben asked, breaking the kiss and breathing harshly.

"You. Preferably without your shirt on," she said without any shame. She couldn't wait to get her hands on the well-honed shoulders and chest she'd caught fleeting glimpses of.

He laughed softly and brought her wrists to his lips, inhaling deeply and kissing each one in turn before placing her hands gently in her lap. "Good, because having your hands on me sounds like a dream."

His words didn't match his actions though. Wait. Was he turning her down? She flushed with humiliation.

He made no move to stand up. "Heaven help me," he whispered.

She squirmed under his gaze and his hands shot to her hips, stilling her movements. "Keep it up and I won't be able to concentrate."

"On what, exactly?"

He chuckled in response to her disgruntled question. "On doing this right."

She arched a delicate brow in his direction.

"One step at a time, darling," he said softly into the shell of her ear, causing a full body shiver to run through her as his fingers began kneading the hips he continued to hold in place. His lips kissed down the column of one side of her neck and up the other, his hands moving to take her jaw in hand and control the kiss he swept over her lips.

Once, twice, three times, until he nipped, making her whimper with suppressed frustration. He merely chuckled, devilishly. Kate melted into a puddle of desire as she pulled him closer by tugging on his tie in retaliation. When he growled in response, she smiled briefly against his lips, until he stole her attention again with his torturous ministrations.

The next morning, Kate woke to a warm body at her back, and slobbery puppy kisses on her face.

"Good morning, Percy," she said, her voice hoarse from not enough sleep.

Kate stretched as much a she could with Ben's arm anchored around her waist, feeling more feline than woman at the moment. Not exactly satisfied, but certainly more relaxed than she'd been in years. She'd forgotten how sinfully good the endorphins from oxytocin could be.

They'd made out on the couch until Ben had drawn a firm line. "I refuse to make love to you for the first time with Henri in the room next door, let alone on a couch."

"I understand," she'd said, pragmatically. And she did. Ben was a single parent. The last thing she wanted was to create a confusing situation for the little boy who'd stolen her heart as much as his father had.

"No, I don't think you do." Ben kissed her passionately again before resting his forehead on hers, their breaths mingling in the desire between them. "You are worth every attention to detail and ounce of pleasure I'm going to wring from you. Neither of which I expect you're going to be very quiet about," he said, a seductive promise shining in his eyes.

"Oh," she said, swoony with anticipation.

"Aye."

Starting immediately: All sub-genres, tropes, and spice levels may return to the TBR pile. Love is the order of the day, every day.

Chapter 22

Ben

"Morning," said Henri from his typical place at the kitchen counter. Kate squeaked and Ben pressed his hand to her stomach to keep her from falling off the couch. He'd hoped to have more time to revel in the feeling of her in his arms. And a minute of pillow-talk before reality set in would've been nice.

She had offered to leave last night but Ben didn't like the idea of her driving home at such a late hour and, selfishly, he'd wanted this. Sex with Kate would doubtless be amazing when they found the right time, but he'd always considered conversing at breakfast the next morning more challenging than the physical act.

Biology could be the culprit behind the first instance, but connection usually drove the second. Unless, of course, a person was simply trying to be polite. Manners were manners after all. But his only design had been to keep Kate for as long as she would let him. Forever should be long enough.

"I can hear you thinking," she whispered over her shoulder. "How do you want to handle this?"

And Ben could hear the panic in her question. "Henri is fairly logical about most things," he whispered back. "Follow my lead."

Her hair caught the stubble on his chin as she bobbed her head up and down in response.

"Morning, my brave boy. Ready for eggs?" he asked, releasing Kate.

"Aye. Would you like some too, Kate?" said Henri with nary a glance in her direction.

"Please. Thank you, for asking." Kate stood up, smoothed her hands over her impossibly wrinkled silk blouse and trousers, and tucked her loose hair behind the ears he'd nuzzled the night before. She met his eyes and flushed as if she knew exactly where his brain had gone off to.

Ben smirked and made his way to the kitchen.

"Da says manners are important; they keep the world civilized."

Kate sat on the stool Ben pulled out for her at the counter, next to Henri's. "I think he's right. What book are you reading?" she asked.

"*The Hobbit.*"

Kate didn't bat an eyelash, as if seven-year-olds read Tolkien all the time. "What do you think so far?"

"It's not very realistic."

"Neither are the Tales of King Arthur or Merlin."

"No, but those have historical context."

A laugh left the lips Ben wanted to spend the day kissing, and he sent a silent thank you to the universe for a woman who took Henri's behavior in stride. *Who am I kidding? She does the same thing where I'm concerned.*

Kate poked her finger into Henri's side, causing a giggle to escape and a cheeky grin to appear. "It's called fantasy for a reason; it's supposed to offer an escape, but it still reflects real life because we can relate to how the characters feel and behave."

Ben had tried to teach Henri the very same thing using picture books and children's stories the school counselor recommended, but his son had tired of their simplicity quickly. Kate had suggested using fantasy or fables instead thinking they might challenge him intellectually enough to keep him engaged, teaching him empathy at the same time.

He watched the two of them, heads bent together as they moved on to discuss the plot, Kate sharing her favorite scenes and listening intently to Henri's responses. Teaching his son to read between the lines of people's words and actions was tedious at the best of times. Life, more often than not, was an experience in the nuanced not the literal. Most of his peers gave up with time, and the teacher had an entire classroom of kids to be concerned with, not only Henri.

"Remember," continued Kate, "people often make choices or react based on their feelings."

"Logic makes more sense."

Kate shrugged nonchalantly, refusing to argue and letting him come to his own conclusion based on her non-verbal cue.

"But it's okay for people to approach things differently. Someone else's feelings are as valuable as my logic."

Kate gave Henri an approving smile.

"Eggs are up," said Ben, sliding the cheesy scrambles onto the three plates lined up on the counter, beside toast and fruit. He liked the way their prime number filled the space. Percival waited expectantly at his feet, and he obliged by adding a scrap to the wee dog's bowl. The absence of the bowtie, along with Henri's lack of notice, made him grin widely as he sat down beside Kate at the oval table.

Ben had a mouth full of breakfast, as did Kate, when his son decided to ask, "What was your nightmare about?"

Kate looked at Ben, eyes wide with confusion. He chuckled because he knew exactly where this line of questioning was going. She gulped down the toast in her mouth with a large swig of tea.

"Um," she stalled.

"Henri usually crawls into bed with me after a bad dream," he explained, calmly.

"Oh."

"Da is the best nightmare slayer around," said Henri, shoveling another fork full into his mouth before his father reminded him of his manners.

"Actually," Ben said, "I'm the one who had the nightmare, and Kate was kind enough to let me sleep next to her."

Henri nodded in understanding. "I guess Kate's a slayer too."

Kate smiled with pleasure and a measure of embarrassment if the stain on her cheeks was anything to go by.

Grinning widely, Ben said, "I think you're right. Kate is now an official member of the 'Bee Hill Order of Nightmare Slayers.'"

Laura

Meanwhile, in a galaxy far, far, away. Oh, right. Sorry, dear reader, sometimes this fairy godmother mixes up her genres. It's a literary habit…I mean hazard. Let's try this again, shall we?

In a land, far across the sea, another leading lady wiped the bar at Walker's Pub clean and pulled out dessert menus for a table of four, instantly spotting the newcomer as he came in. He looked exactly the way she remembered, even with his hair cut short. The tie around his neck was an exact match for the icy color of his eyes and his tailored suit, which couldn't disguise the cruel twist of his mouth no matter what it cost, a perfect fit.

"Laura, it's good to see you," he greeted, all smarmy charm.

"I wish I could say the same, Preston

"If that's the way you want to play it."

"Kate's not here, so why don't you go back to whatever slimy hole you crawled out of and leave her alone."

"Your sister and I belong together," he said, plainly annoyed with her attitude as he adjusted the expensive cufflinks at his wrists.

"Whatever. You sound like a creep. Get out before I call the cops," she said with no room for argument.

He laughed harshly, revealing the monster lurking beneath his polished surface. Laura turned on her heel to walk away. Engaging was what he wanted, and she had more important things to do, like warning Kate off. If Preston poked around enough in Brooklyn, it wouldn't take him long to track her to London, especially if he found her boutique.

His hand shot out and grabbed her upper arm in a bruising grip. "I see not much has changed where you're concerned. You always were a brat."

Laura met his glare reluctantly, refusing to yelp despite the pain; she wouldn't give him the satisfaction.

Leaning in close to her ear so no one else would overhear, he said, "I like what you've done with the place. So much nicer than before."

A sense of foreboding slid over Laura, setting her teeth on edge as she clenched her jaw.

Preston pulled a folded piece of paper from the inside pocket of his suit coat and laid it on top of the bar. "Thanks for the help, little sister."

Laura cringed at the familial title and waited for the door to close before reaching for the newspaper he'd left. Front and center were the picture of her and Nick kissing at the 9/11 Memorial next to the original column with a follow-up interview they'd done to promote the reopening of the pub. Laura gasped and froze in place, chills snaking down her spine. There, in a tiny block print at the end of the story, were the words she feared.

"It would seem business is blooming in Brooklyn this spring, especially for these two sisters." The wedding announcement photo her mother had insisted on flashed like a Las Vegas neon sign beneath, and though it was slightly grainy, there was no mistaking Kate for anyone else.

"Swing by Walker's Pub for their grand re-opening on Friday, and while you're in the neighborhood, check out my favorite skin care line at Lavender Honey & Co."

Apparently, Hatta Mann was a better reporter than her fictional predecessor, except the villain in Kate's story was real. Laura had no doubt Preston Toliver would use every resource at his fingertips to make her sister pay for leaving him.

Kate

She and Ben spent the rest of the day together canoodling on the couch and chasing after Henri and Percival before heading back to

London. She had a shop to run after all, even if she would prefer to spend all of her time at Bee Hill. Lavender Honey & Co. was her baby, and it had been a huge part of her healing and recovery from Preston. Still, Kate could admit the shop was no longer the lifeline it had previously been.

Other things, or rather people, had begun to fill in any cracks left behind from her marriage. When she started the shop, it was to give herself purpose and hope for the future. While she had no intention of selling in either Brooklyn or London anytime soon, she was excited to see what else the future held for the first time since she'd walked out into a wealthy suburban neighborhood, covered in bruises.

Kate jiggled the doorknob and pushed her shoulder against the door at the same time, a curse slipping out in the process. The phone stopped ringing as she entered the apartment. She needed to let the property manager know the door stuck with the change in seasons. It wasn't uncommon for older buildings to encounter issues when the temperature dipped or rose. Doorjambs and windows swelled and shrank with the heat and cold regularly, but having to cajole, wheedle, shove, and sometime swear it into opening was getting old.

A red number five blinked furiously on the answering machine. She hit the play button and dug down to the bottom of her purse looking for her cell phone, or "mobile," as Ben liked to call it, pronouncing the long vowel in each syllable. He was less than impressed when she informed him "mobile" was pronounced like Mobile, Alabama, and "mobile" as in "mobile home" or "look how mobile the toddler is." Kate chuckled again, getting a kick out of British English. Of course, she didn't tell him how often his accent appeared in the characters she read about, or that they were always her favorite. She sighed with content and re-played the messages she'd missed while daydreaming.

"Kate, call me back," said her sister's voice over the machine.

"You better not have your phone off because you're making out with Grumpy."

Sister intuition is creepy.

"Pick up the effing phone, Kate!"

No need to get your Wonder Woman undies in a bunch, sweetie. Kate grinned and plugged in her cell phone. While she and Ben were… busy with other things, the battery had died sometime in the middle of the night. She tuned back in as the next message on the machine began.

"Kate, please call me back," Laura whined.

Maybe she and Nick were fighting, Kate worried, until the last message began to play. Her heart jumped into her throat and her stomach filled with bile.

"Preston is in Brooklyn, and he's been snooping around. I think he's trying to find you," Laura finished, sounding scared.

The green battery symbol on her cell lit up and Kate brought up her voicemail. All of them but one were from Laura, and each said the same thing as the others. Using a technique her therapist had taught her; Kate squeezed her fists to ground herself and forced herself to breathe deeply and evenly to keep the panic at bay. She refused to let her ex consume any more space in her life. Once she was certain her voice would come out sounding fairly normal, she rang Laura.

"Kelly residence," answered a deep voice on the other end.

"Hey Nick, it's Kate. Is Laura around?"

"Hey, sis," he said, the relief evident in his tone. "Laura's kind of been freaking out since last night."

Kate forced herself to laugh as though it were nothing new. "I'll bet."

"Here she is," Nick said, the sound muffled as he passed the phone to Laura.

"It's about time," said Laura, clearly miffed.

"Glad to hear from you too, moon pie," replied Kate, refusing to give in to panic or her sister's tizzy. She did, however, allow herself to make a dramatic eye roll. "Start from the beginning. I'm sure Preston's presence in Brooklyn is a coincidence. He didn't contest the divorce, and I highly doubt he hired a private investigator to find me."

"He didn't have to. I led him straight to you."

"Somehow, I doubt it."

Kate took off her heels and hopped onto the counter, twirling the chord around her fingers and swinging her legs back and forth.

Laura went on to tell her about the article announcing the reopening of the pub, along with several photos, one of which starred Kate. "And to top it all off, a mention of Lavender Honey

& Co."

"I'm glad Hatta Mann likes the shop so much, but who are they?" Kate asked.

"It's a *nom de plume*, and she's the same reporter who took the photo of Nick and me kissing in front of the Memorial to use in her Valentine's Day column," Laura complained, apparently still disgruntled over the incident.

"It's an amazing photo."

"I know. She gave me a copy of it when we met to talk about the pub. It's in a frame on the mantle. But we digress. Preston is coming for you, so how do we keep you safe?"

"Don't you think you're blowing this somewhat out of proportion? Why would Preston come looking for me now? It's not like I'm flashing my life all over social media. The only page I have is for the shop and Stephanie is the gatekeeper of it."

"Yeah, here's the thing," Laura said hesitantly before diving in. "Preston has been snooping around the store. Steph got the stalker vibe and called the cops, but it doesn't bode well. It won't take him long to find you in London at this rate."

It was a good thing Kate was sitting, otherwise the floor would have fallen out from beneath her. Gripping the phone in a strangle hold, she told herself to breathe. In and out, in and out, in and out, but her breathing was too quick and shallow for the repetitions to work. When her hands began to shake and her body followed suit, she slid off the counter gingerly and laid herself out on the floor.

"Are you still there?" asked Laura, concerned over her prolonged silence.

Nope, thought Kate. "Yeah," she said instead, and tried to swallow past the dryness coating her mouth. "I'll book a flight and speak with Byron. I'll call you from the airport once I have my flight details."

"I didn't mean you should come running into his arms, Kate! I wanted you to be aware so you could make a plan or get help from the local police. Sheesh. Do you have a death wish?"

"Preston won't kill me." At least not right away, she reasoned. It wasn't his style. He got off on causing her pain—emotional, mental, and physical. For whatever reason, having control over someone else made him feel better about himself. Besides, if he were looking for her, it could be for a couple of reasons. He either wanted revenge for her leaving or he had a misguided—looney toons—notion he could somehow win her back. It didn't make sense, but it wasn't uncommon in abusive relationships for the abused to return to the abuser. Stockholm Syndrome was trippy, and she'd been fortunate to avoid it.

"I'll explain everything when I see you, but there is no way in Hades I'm staying here for him to find me." *Or Ben and Henri*, she finished mutely.

She hung up with Laura and immediately dialed Eliza's number to give her a brief rundown of the situation and swearing her to secrecy in hopes she'd be back before Ben realized she was

Stateside. In the meantime, she'd inform Byron of her last-minute "business trip" to Paris and try to keep the man she loved in the dark with a handful of texts. Her heart neither picked up its pace in fear nor skipped in denial at the admission.

She had loved Ben for months. In fact, she couldn't remember when friendship had turned to infatuation and then solidified into a feeling so deep it defied definition, the two becoming intertwined over time. Someday, she would give him the words she hadn't said yet, perhaps over a cup of tea or while reading toe-to-toe on the couch. It didn't need to be a dramatic declaration or planned out, only sincere. And with any luck, she'd be back in London within seventy-two hours.

Chapter 23

Kate

Less than twenty-four hours later and mentally exhausted, Kate used the brass knocker on the glossy black painted door to announce her presence. She smiled at the willow wreath with lavender and thistle tucked inside the branches at regular intervals. She'd brought it as a housewarming gift all the way from London, the last time she visited. Somehow, it had miraculously survived the flight.

She breathed in the scent, taking comfort from the now familiar smell, a constant reminder of Ben.

Keep counting sunrises. You'll be back at Bee Hill in no time. She knocked lightly a second time, hoping Ailis would sleep through it if she were napping.

Micky barked in response from the other side of the door, and she could hear her brother-in-law's heavy tread moving steadily through the living room. When the door opened a moment later, she was immediately swept into a bear hug by Nick before she could step inside.

"Hey sis, we missed you." Coming from anyone else, Kate might have construed it as a required pleasantry, but Nick was entirely sincere. Family truly was everything to him. She couldn't have asked for a better man for her sister.

"I was here a few months ago," she said as he released her.

"Doesn't matter."

Kate smiled and bent down to give Micky ear scratches and fluff the ruff at his neck. "Good boy. Taking care of everyone as always, I see."

"Told you she was a dog person," said Laura, pulling Kate in for a hug as if she weighed nothing. It would seem carrying a baby around was paying off in the bicep department.

Kate, on the other hand, wanted a piece of cake, preferably chocolate, but her sister's preference for peanut butter would also do the trick under current circumstances.

"I know, I know," capitulated Nick, with his palms in the air. "You only tell me every time she visits."

Laura smirked to rub it in some more.

"Micky was always Laura's. I knew it the moment I saw him, didn't I, boy?" Kate asked the canine. "Besides, leaving him behind was kismet."

Nick grinned. "Fair enough. Mistaking "Mick" for my name

while wearing earbuds did make for a pretty great meet cute."

Laura took Kate by the hand and pulled her along while Nick brought in her suitcase from the stoop. "It's about time you got here. I've been worrying away my fingernails ever since Preston showed up at the pub."

"Don't be so dramatic," said Kate. "I told you I needed to take care of a few things before I left."

"You wouldn't be here if I was wrong," poked Laura.

"I hate it when you're right." And yet it was the reason behind her leaving without telling anyone other than Eliza about Preston's sudden presence in Brooklyn. Her manager at the shop in London believed she was on a business trip to Europe, and Kate had been deliberately vague about her return in hopes her ex wouldn't stick around if he came snooping. She didn't want Preston hurting anyone else with whatever game he was playing.

"Like I told you on the phone, Steph said Preston stopped by the shop on several pretenses. Eventually, he asked to speak with you when it became apparent you weren't just hanging around." Laura stopped momentarily to listen to the baby monitor before continuing, "Thankfully, her creep radar went off and she only gave him vague answers. I think it's why he tried me at the pub."

"This is where it gets interesting though," said Nick jumping in as they all moved toward the kitchen, Micky trotting faithfully after them. "When he came into the shop again the following day, Steph called the cops."

"Preston left before they got there," Laura continued for him. "But as it turns out, once she gave them the name he'd given her, he showed up in the system."

"He doesn't have a record though."

"Not under Preston Toliver, but as it turns out, your ex has been very busy since you left him," said Nick.

"Let's face it, he was waist deep in manure back then," interjected Laura.

"Busy doing what? And how do you know?" Kate asked.

"I still have contacts at the police department, thanks to Miles," said Nick, referring to his deceased brother in-law.

"When Laura told me what happened, I wanted to rip Preston to shreds with my bare hands, but then I remembered to work smarter not harder."

"So, he called his connection at the precinct. After explaining what had happened at the pub and giving them a physical description and name—"

"All of the dominoes fell into place," finished Nick.

"Apparently, Preston is on the FBI's most-wanted list for racketeering in several states, including New York. The white-collar-crime division has been investigating him for the last two years."

Kate's mouth dropped open.

"Yeah, that's pretty much how I reacted when Nick told me."

"Which means—" Kate started.

"He could go to prison for a very long time."

"And you'd finally be free of him for good," said Nick.

All of the air left her lungs, and Kate dropped into the dining chair Nick pulled out to catch her.

Kate checked the screen of her cell phone, but nothing had changed since the last time she looked. She'd sent Ben a text right before boarding her flight and had yet to hear back from him. Had he changed his mind about her?

Data roaming rates were ridiculously expensive, but she was willing to pay any price if it kept Ben blissfully unaware until she'd handled the situation with Preston. Kate sent off another text, but the longer she went without hearing from him, the more she second guessed herself.

She wasn't worried about the shop. Byron had things well in hand, and his only request before she left had been to promise she'd visit the fashion exhibition at the Louvre. "It's to die for, Love."

Kate justified the lies by telling herself she'd confess the truth to both men as soon as all of this was over. She tucked her phone away and made a mental note to check in with her cell phone company to confirm everything was working on their end. If they were, she would deal with what it meant then. In the meantime, she needed to figure out what she was going to do about Preston.

"I'm here! Where's the body?" Aria asked, as she entered the house a couple of hours later. She came to an abrupt stop when she caught sight of Kate and Laura chatting it up at the dining table on the opposite side of the living room.

"What body?" Kate inquired, totally confused.

"You know, the one you wanted me to dispose of," said Aria in a tone suggesting the word "duh" would've been more *apropos*.

Nick laughed, his whole body shaking with the sound as he came out of the kitchen with a glass of water and a granola bar for Laura. "I didn't actually mean there was a body," he said watching his sister like she'd lost her mind. "I wanted to surprise you with Kate's visit."

He walked over to introduce himself to the stranger standing behind his sister. "Hi, I'm Aria's brother," said Nick, extending his hand in the direction of the other man.

Aria waved behind her when her companion didn't return the gesture.

"This is Sully. He doesn't speak much and prefers not to make contact," she said blandly on his behalf. "We work together."

Kate eyeballed the tall, muscular guy dressed in black cargo pants and a T-shirt stretched tautly over arms the size of battering rams. "At the bank?" she asked skeptically. Sully looked like he could bury a body with ease, and his dead eyed gaze confirmed it.

Aria brushed Kate off. "He's the interim branch manager at the bank. So, there's no body?"

"Sorry to disappoint you," said Laura, coming into the room with a bottle for Ailis in hand. "Duty is calling." She handed Nick the bottle, who eyed the new guy once more while Laura hugged Aria.

Kate couldn't blame Nick for being wary. Her brother in-law was a beast of a guy, but Sully made him look like a kid's action figure in comparison.

"Brunch on Saturday, and I expect to hear all the juicy deets about your new friend."

Laura was anything but subtle. Kate smiled and kissed the top of her niece's head, receiving a gurgled babble for her efforts.

Aria started to protest but fell silent when Laura raised an eyebrow in disbelief. All three women knew it wasn't worth the argument. She would get the information one way or another.

Kate watched her sister and brother-in-law walk up the stairs, Laura giggling and Nick pinching her bottom on his way up behind her. She was happy for them, but sometimes she wished she didn't have a front row seat for the show. She'd finally fallen for someone worthy of her affection, and though the other night had made it seem like Ben had similar feelings for her, the words her risk-averse heart longed to hear were noticeably absent.

Her love life might as well be a Shakespearian play for all the tragedy it held. Admittedly, some of it was her own fault, but did it mean she had to suffer the rest of her life over one measly mistake? People married the wrong person all the time, yet she seemed destined to have Preston with her for the rest of her life.

Kate's heart ached thinking about Ben and Henri. If she'd had any other choice, she would never have left without saying goodbye but keeping them safe was more important than what she wanted. She shoved the depressing thought away and grabbed Aria's arm, dragging her over to the couch.

Aria cocked her head in Sully's direction. "There's probably something in the fridge if you want it."

Sully left without a word to go and fend for himself in Laura's kitchen.

"He's like a human garbage disposal. The man has absolutely no discernment when it comes to food, other than requiring enormous quantities of it," said Aria.

Kate smiled. "He doesn't fit the usual banker mold you prefer to hook up with when loneliness threatens to abolish whatever's left of your humanity—your words, not mine," she said, teasingly.

She and Aria had made an instant connection at the wedding festivities and again for the baptism. Maybe it was because they were both older sisters and shared similar concerns about their ability to have healthy romantic relationships in the future. Regardless of the reasons, Kate was grateful for the bond they'd forged.

"What gives it away?" Aria asked.

Kate ticked the reasons off on her fingers. "The haircut, the clothes, a striking physical similarity to the hulk—I swear there must be something in the water here. Or were you referring to the two of you sleeping together?"

"We're not, which is part of the problem," grumbled her friend. "But enough about me and Sully. Why are you in town? And where is the grumpy Brit you were languishing over the last time you were here?"

Kate didn't know how to answer the question other than to say, "It's a long story, but I still might need you to bury a body at the end of it."

Aria grinned wickedly. "Sweet! Sully," she called in the direction of the kitchen, "we still have a job."

He gave her a thumbs up with the hand not shoveling leftover Chinese food into his mouth. Whatever her friend claimed, Aria and Sully traveled the same wavelength.

"He's surprisingly dexterous with those chopsticks."

"That's what she said," Aria deadpanned, causing both of them to burst out laughing.

Ben

Ben punched the code into the gate's control pad ensconced within the newly constructed brick wall and drove the short distance to Eliza and Sam's house, parking next to his best friend's prized 1959 Austin-Healy Sprite. Not bothering to knock as he entered through the kitchen door on the side of the house, he reasoned if the couple didn't want company they should lock the door—which, considering the high-end gated community, one would think they'd make an effort. Living outside of London offered a certain amount of privacy, but fans had still been known to go to extremes to get close to Eliza in the past.

His panic over Kate's sudden disappearance had absolutely nothing to do with his recently acquired bad manners. Or so he told himself and tried to ignore the worry gripping his heart in a tight snare. "If *anyone* ever answered their phones, I wouldn't be on this wild goose chase to begin with," he snapped at the empty kitchen.

Yelling a greeting into the cavernous, modern space comprised of cement, steel, and glass, Ben didn't wait for a reply, instead taking the stairs down to the ground floor and the recording studio the couple spent the majority of their free time in when not on tour. He stepped into the booth where Sam was making minor adjustments to the sound board, while Eliza did voice warmups and ran her bow smoothly over the strings of her violin in the adjacent soundproof room.

"Where is Kate?"

"Mate. It's good to see you too."

"Kate hasn't answered her phone or returned my call for at least forty-eight hours."

Sam went back to fiddling with the knobs on the sound board. "Maybe she's busy."

"I'm neither an idiot nor an overbearing buffoon."

"Could've fooled me, but you do have the look of a man who is frantic and lovelorn."

"As if this is any great surprise. Who won the bet, you, or Eli?"

"Eli. I don't want to talk about it."

"Serves you right."

"Bawbag. Would it have killed you to give in to your feelings for her sooner?"

Ben ignored both the insult and the question. He had more important things to worry about than Sam's wallet or Eliza's betting habit. "Do you, or do you not, know where Kate is?" he asked, his frustration mounting to match his worry and making his left eye twitch in irritation. He knew in his gut something was wrong.

When he hadn't heard back from her about the upcoming delivery, he had decided to drop off the scheduled inventory himself, leaving Henri with his father for the day. "She would never ignore a phone call about the shop, regardless of our personal relationship," he said, tugging at his collar.

"Did you ask the shop's manager?" Sam still wouldn't meet his gaze. "What was his name again?"

"Byron, who as it turns out, is quite nice and married to another man. But then again, you already knew as much when I brought it up the first time," said Ben, knowing how much Sam enjoyed needling him. "He was also less than helpful in case you're interested. Some nonsense about a last-minute business trip to Paris. Kate is a planner. She doesn't do anything without careful preparation, and either way she would have checked in about the delivery."

All of that was negligible because Ben knew she would never ghost him without a good reason. She was too classy for such a move, not to mention professional. Something must be very wrong; he could feel it niggling at the back of his mind as much as his lovesick heart. "My calls go directly to voicemail, and she hasn't answered a text since yesterday morning."

"Have you asked Agnes?" As a true Scotsman, Sam was a firm believer in the older woman's ability to "see" the future.

"She rang yesterday. I couldn't have stopped her if I'd tried."

"And?"

"She said, and I quote, 'There's trouble. Kate needs you.' Nothing else. No hint as to why or where to find her," Ben said pulling his hands through his hair and causing it to stand on end. He frantically paced the room, out of his mind with worry for the woman he loved.

"Well, well, look who's a believer now." Sam punched the intercom button for the booth. "Eli, Ben is here," he sang with glee.

Eliza set down the violin and opened the door. "It's about time," she said, clearly exasperated, though Ben couldn't fathom why since she'd won the bet about when he and Kate would become more than friends.

"Under the circumstances, I was positive you'd show up last night, Loverboy," she continued, wiggling a five quid from the front pocket of her jeans and laying it in Sam's outstretched hand.

His best friend grinned and raised his winnings in a fist. "Victory is mine," he shouted, the r's of his burr rolling in triumph.

"There will be no living with him now." Eliza looped her arm through Ben's. "Come on, something tells me you're going to need a cuppa and a dram for what I have to tell you."

"Bad, huh?"

"How much has Kate told you about her ex?"

"Enough."

"Kit-Kat always did have a way of skirting the details," she said, giving him a sad smile.

Chapter 24

Aria

The next afternoon, Aria stopped midstride when she spotted an unfamiliar, non-descript black sedan parked across the street from her brother and Laura's house. She knew Nick kept in contact with a handful of the detectives Miles used to work with, and had asked for some assistance on Kate's behalf, but the guy sitting in the front seat with a pair of binoculars looked a lot like her current bank manager.

She refused to refer to him as her boss. The zombie apocalypse would happen before she ever let him dictate anything she did—at work or otherwise. After running into each other at Walker's Pub the night before and imbibing one or three cocktails—on her part—he'd insisted on walking her home, which was when Nick had called. She still didn't know what could've induced her to invite

Sully inside.

Aria waved to Kate, who was standing in the doorway, expecting her arrival, and made a beeline for the car instead. She tapped her knuckle against the window even though Sully could clearly see her and waited impatiently as the passenger side window lowered at an exasperatingly slow pace. The look on her bank colleague's face resembled a declawed cat—irritated, but without any available recourse at his fingertips.

"What are you doing skulking out here?" she asked, confused.

He pinched the bridge of his nose in frustration, looked at the driver beside him, and then back at her. "My job."

"What do you mean? You're the branch manager of a bank."

"About that," hedged Sully.

Aria shook her head rapidly in the negative. "No, no, no. This is not happening," she denied, piecing together in rapid succession the recent events at work and his random appearances elsewhere in her life.

Sully opened his door slowly, giving her time to back away.

"You are not—"

He wasn't listening to her diatribe though, his attention having shifted over her shoulder to whatever was happening behind her.

"Are you even listening?" she shouted.

"Aria, get in the car. Do it now," he commanded as he pulled a firearm from the holster at his waist and steadily made for her brother's front stoop.

Sully

"Preston is a businessman. Granted, a dirty one, but I still don't understand why he hasn't tried going after the shops," said Kate.

"I think we all know the shops are low-hanging fruit," replied Nick, bouncing with Ailis, who cooed in delight while Laura played with their youngest nephew on the floor.

Aria's younger sisters were setting the dining table at the other end of the room and her brother in-law had taken the two older nieces and nephew to pick up ice cream for dessert, giving the grownups some space to discuss the situation.

"Ultimately, your ex wants to get his hands on you," said Nick, looking directly at Kate.

Sully took the cue and added, "Going after someone's business takes time; legitimately or otherwise. If your ex is playing the long game like I think he is, then he isn't going to do anything rash unless we force him into it." He looked first at Kate, and then the crowded room filled with Kellys for Sunday dinner, before coming back around to land on Ben.

Or the grumpy Brit, as Aria had referred to him, once she'd stopped shouting from the back seat of the car he'd locked her inside of. He could admit he'd had a brief moment of panic when he spotted the man in front of Nick's house. In retrospect, Ben Galloway looked nothing like Preston, but for a moment the only thing he'd known was rabid fear for the woman who'd recently turned his world upside down. It was irrational, but it didn't change anything.

Sully sighed. Aria might as well have the word TROUBLE tattooed across her forehead. He had no idea how she'd gotten mixed up in the middle of both of his investigations, but he also couldn't say he was surprised. Pinching the bridge of his nose, he counted to five, trying to find any semblance of Zen.

When he'd started his undercover assignment at the bank two months ago, he never dreamed she'd have an association with the other case he was working on, the case he'd steadily sold his soul for the last two years. Hell, he'd moved to the New York office when Preston Toliver—aka, Alfie Ransom—showed up a year ago in the last place he'd expected to find him. If anyone wanted the man behind bars, it was Sully.

The only person who wanted it more was the ex-wife he'd abused and manipulated. She didn't know how fortunate she'd been to get out when she did. He knew too many women who hadn't been. With any luck the POS would get what was coming to him on all counts. Now all he had to do was flush the man out of hiding.

He had all the evidence he needed to convict the dirtbag of racketeering in three states, assault-and-battery-related charges in two, and sex-trafficking in the state of California. The file was thick enough to fill an entire drawer of the metal filing cabinet in his office at the bureau. He crossed his arms over his broad chest as everyone started to speak all at once.

Nick gave a high-pitched whistle to get everyone's attention. "The floor is yours, Agent..."

"Tobias Sullivan, but you can call me Sully."

"At least you didn't lie about everything," mumbled Aria from where she sat on the arm of the couch. She crossed her arms and legs in a synchronized movement, turning her profile away from him.

Aria was the most beautiful woman he'd ever met, especially when she was spitting mad. *Oh well, it comes with the job,* Sully told himself and returned to the matter at hand.

"Whether Preston wants Lavender Honey & Co., or believes Kate is still his, he's not going to jeopardize the opportunity by putting her at risk."

"And if he only wants revenge for her leaving?" Nick asked.

"Either way, we can flush him out if he thinks he's going to miss his chance."

"How?" Kate inquired.

Ben was two steps ahead of everyone. "No. Not an option," he said, starting forward until Kate put a hand on his arm to hold him in place.

"What isn't an option?" said Laura.

"Using Kate as rat bait." Aria stood up, glorious in all of her fury and indignation. Sully's favorite part was the way she waved her index finger in his face. "Nah-uh. Not going to happen."

He met her stare for stare when what he wanted to do was kiss her until she finally gave into this madness between them. But women like Aria were never a one and done. She was the dream of a lifetime, and he was her worst nightmare. Everything about him screamed risk, including his previous stint in Special Forces.

His life would be less complicated if he weren't so good at what he did—putting the bad guys away—in a coffin or prison, it didn't matter which, so long as they paid for their crimes. At least working in the white-collar crimes division allowed him to sleep better at night.

Kate

Ben pulled her into his chest and wrapped his arms around her. She needed zero encouragement to snuggle in and melt against him. Finding him on the other side of the front door had been the most amazing surprise of her life, which spoke volumes, since Kate didn't do surprises.

"Hullo, my darling girl. I'm fairly certain you forgot to tell me something," he'd said, his eyes swimming with affection and concern.

She'd thrown herself into his arms and started blabbering.

"I didn't want to leave, but I was afraid—" Kate's excuse flew out of her head as Ben crushed his lips to hers and pulled her body flush with his. Her entire body became one giant flame as she granted him the entry he sought, letting his tongue dance with hers. A breathy moan escaped as his hands found the strip where her shirt had ridden up, his fingers like fire against her exposed skin. She was fairly sure it was from her. Yeah, it was her, but she didn't care how desperate she sounded. "Please," she whispered when he drew away.

"I would normally say, whatever you need. But I think we should continue this later…in private," he'd promised, as breathless as she was.

"Good idea." But no sooner had the words left her mouth than the sun behind Ben disappeared, a looming shadow taking its place.

"All right, folks, what do you say we move the show inside in case Kate's ex is watching."

Kate blinked back to the present, and the danger at hand. "Okay," she said quietly. "I'll do it."

Ben tightened his hold. Now that he was here, the last thing she wanted to do was leave his side. Kate should have been angry with Eliza for disclosing the information about her whereabouts, but instead she was immensely grateful. At least she had this time with him if everything went into the outhouse, as her father was fond of saying.

Her parents planned to arrive tomorrow night and would be staying with Uncle Joe, who'd ignored her wishes and rang them up as soon as Laura gave him the details. It was hard to stay mad when she would have done the same thing if she'd been in their shoes.

The expression "you could hear a pin drop" accurately described her audience's reaction, but the look on Ben's face spoke volumes.

"No. Not happening," denied Ben and Laura at the same time. At least the man she adored and her sister were in step with one another.

"It's the only way," Kate said, laying her hand on his cheek, his five o'clock shadow bristly against her palm. "You need to go back home to Henri, and I can't hide forever. What kind of life is that—waiting and worrying? Preston deserves everything he's got coming, and I'll do whatever it takes if it means putting him behind bars."

"My darling girl," Ben whispered, placing his forehead to hers. "Don't you know you've already sacrificed enough. When will you forgive yourself for being human?"

A tear spilled over onto her cheek. "I should have known."

"You were not to blame for his actions. *Ever.*"

"No, but I should have walked away sooner."

He pulled a monogrammed handkerchief from his coat pocket, wiping away the collective storm gathering in her eyes. "Ending a relationship of any kind is never as simple as walking away."

She knew he spoke from experience, but still, this was different than his stepping into his brother's life. In the end, she believed Ben had done what was right for everyone involved. How could she ask anything less of herself? She shuddered, whether with pent-up emotion or fear for what was to come, she couldn't distinguish.

"Your courage is admirable, but we'll find another way," assured the man she loved with every fiber of her being. "Please, Kate."

She swallowed hard and met Laura's gaze across the room. Her sister blew her a kiss and tugged Nick's hand, pulling him behind her toward the kitchen. Ailis babbled in her daddy's arms, blowing raspberries with her cupid lips and unaware of the silence weighing down the rest of the room.

"We'll let you talk without an audience," said Luna, patting Kate's arm on her way to the kitchen, the rest of the Kelly clan following in her wake as if they wouldn't be eavesdropping. She would have laughed, but there was a fine line between funny and hysteria, and she was standing on the edge of it.

"I'll be parked outside for another hour," Agent Sullivan tossed out on his way to the front door. "The guys in blue will take the night shift on the off-chance Preston decides to show up. Call me when you're ready."

Ben

Her decision was a foregone conclusion. Everyone in the room knew it and had abandoned Ben to his fate. He wanted to throw her over his shoulder and haul her home to Bee Hill, fully prepared to take out anyone who stood in his path. Surely, his years of fencing and boxing at school had all been for this moment. But doing so would only reinforce Kate's doubts about her ability to use good judgment and he'd be damned if he ever belittled her decisions or made her feel less than the incredibly brave creature she was.

Agnes Winthrop's premonitions and tea leaf readings aside, every touch, word, and interaction he had shared with Kate over the past twenty months only confirmed what he'd known deep within his soul from their first meeting at Heathrow. He was hers from now until eternity and whatever lay beyond—or for however long she would have him, in any case.

She grazed his cheekbone with her thumb, garnering his attention, and he forced his eyes back to hers. "Go home to Henri. I'll join the two of you as soon as this nightmare is over."

"Not a chance, darling," Ben said firmly. "Or have I not made myself clear? Where you go, I go. Your people are my people," he said with a wry smile and a glance toward the kitchen. "Though there does seem to be a whole horde of them suddenly, and all of the other pish posh people promise under duress," he finished, caressing her cheek tenderly.

"Eli told you everything, didn't she?" Kate asked, leaning in to kiss him, her lips soft against his, causing Ben's breath to catch.

"She may have. I love you," Ben whispered. He'd planned to tell her in a more romantic way, but there was nothing like fear to make a man spill his secrets, so the present would have to do.

"To the sun and back?" Kate asked in the cheeky manner he adored.

"And then some," he said, kissing her forehead.

"Well, as it turns out, I'm rather fond of you too," said Kate in a reserved manner worthy of any Brit.

He loved her all the more for it. "Hmm. Only fond, huh?"

"All right, maybe more than fond," Kate confessed, her dimpled smile giving away her feelings.

"Good, because I know this crumbling old abbey someone once said would make a good wedding venue," said Ben, stopping himself short of dropping to his knee on the spot. He was going to do this right, with all the pomp and circumstance Kate deserved, even if it killed him to wait.

Her breath caught, eclipsing the space between them.

He kissed her lips again, before saying "Let's get all of this behind us, so we can go home. Henri will never forgive me if he and Percy don't get to be a part of the planning."

"Don't forget Merlin and the girls," she said, still wearing an impervious grin to match his own.

"Of course not. What would a proposal be without the wizard and muses of Bee Hill?" he said dryly, coaxing a laugh for his efforts.

What he wouldn't give to keep this memory in a jar the way Henri collected treasures on their walks. Instead, they would eat a solemn supper and tomorrow she would walk away from him. He'd left London with a purpose and determination to bring Kate home, but none of it mattered in light of her decision.

Chapter 25

Ben

The front door swung open, and two more people entered the fray, unaware of what had passed in the last half an hour.

"Sorry we're late!" exclaimed a man who looked similarly enough to Nick to be related, like every other person present but himself.

"We got stuck on the bridge," said the woman next to him, blushing as she tossed a messy braid over her shoulder and adjusted her clothes into some semblance of order.

The guy's smirk and the way he pulled her close for a kiss to the temple suggested their tardiness had less to do with traffic than a quick tussle in the car.

Laura came forward, greeting them both with hugs. "Leo, Vinny. This is Kate's grumpy Brit. Ben Galloway, this is Nick's brother and his wife."

Ben shook Leo's hand while Kate hooked arms with Vinny, the two of them whispering conspiratorially as they all made their way to the dining table.

"Glad to see you finally made it across the pond, man."

Ben gave him a side glance in response.

"Laura's been rooting for the two of you since Kate mentioned you at the wedding."

If the circumstances had been different, Ben would have relished the tidbit. But they weren't. "I wish it were under better circumstances," he said with a restrained smile.

"Don't worry, we've got this. Laura's part of the family, which makes Kate part of it by extension. Kellys take care of our own." Leo clapped a hand on Ben's shoulder in reassurance.

"Aria, say grace," commanded Luna as everyone took their seats. "You can walk a plate out to Sully after dinner."

"But Ma—" she started to protest.

"No buts, Aria. There's room at the table and I like him for you," said Luna with a shake of her thick, silver-streaked bob.

"He's in law enforcement and even worse, he lied about it," baulked Aria.

"You need a strong partner and he's not intimidated by you. Take care of your business," said the Kelly matriarch, an Italian accent creeping in.

Has she always had one? Ben wondered.

Aria's corresponding huff was loud enough to earn a chuckle from everyone around the table.

"Looks like someone's finally met her match," lobbed Nick.

"Careful, baby brother. I'm fairly certain Agent Sullivan knows how to bury a body where no one will ever find it—for real," retorted Aria, sending her brother a death stare.

If looks could kill, Nick would have bled out all over the garlic linguini at his elbow. Instead, he grinned as wide as the gap between London's trains and platforms.

"Bring it."

All of the children at the table gave a resounding "Ooh."

Ben's head swiveled back and forth between the siblings as they bantered, which is how the meal continued, everyone talking over each other, ribbing one another, and exuding so much love it was possible to push his previous worries into a box for later. Ben committed every laugh and smile from Kate to memory, his fears about tomorrow stifled, if only for the time being, against the backdrop of family.

Kate

Kate slipped from Ben's arms, causing him to stir before letting out a soft snore and rolling onto his back. She took in the clean, if run-down, extra bedroom they were staying in as she lifted her hands above her head and stretched up onto her tiptoes to work out the night's kinks. Nick had sheepishly apologized for its state the night before.

"I'll get to it eventually."

"Maybe in ten years, Clark Kent," said Laura, pragmatically. "Not even your alter ego could remodel this house in less time."

Nick had sighed in defeat at first but then smirked. "Superman, huh? Want to put on our Halloween costumes, Tink," he said, suggestively.

Her sister had blushed profusely before saying in her most serious tone, "Race you."

"La, la, la. We don't need to know your plans," said Kate, pointedly.

"Don't worry, we're on the opposite side of the hall, so at least you won't get a play by play," Laura promised with a devious gleam in her eyes.

Kate looked at Ben. "You see what I'm dealing with."

"I do." He kissed her temple. "Let's go to bed."

Being the gentleman he was, Ben offered to sleep on the couch or the floor, but Kate had wanted him close to her. God only knew what tomorrow held and his nearness would help keep her fears tethered to reality, though not completely at bay. They kissed and whispered into the early hours of the morning, until she had finally fallen asleep listening to the percussion of his heart.

No wonder her dream had been so incredibly vivid last night.

With all the trappings of a historical romance or past life, she'd ridden across the moor bareback in nothing but a billowy nightgown, her long tresses flowing out behind her. She was simultaneously at one with the powerful beast beneath her and watching from the sidelines like a spectator—the woman, yet not. Mist lay heavy on the ground, but the longing for freedom had been too great, a yearning she couldn't deny.

She raised her face toward the orange light cresting the horizon, the orb pushing away the last of a grey curtain. But it had come too late to save her from her own foolishness. Before her lay the hedge, and beyond nothing but a short path to the cliff. Panic swept through her, causing her thighs to tighten their grip. The black reared in response, and then there was nothing.

She awoke in the dream, her head aching and the sound of her name coming from a distance. Had she jumped, or had the horse thrown her?

There it was again, her name carried from the woods in front of her. She walked toward the sound of the panicked voice. And then he was there, assessing her from head to toe.

"Are you hurt?" Ben asked in the authoritative tone she both admired and refused to acknowledge on a regular basis.

She nodded in the negative.

"What have I told you about riding in this weather?" he scolded, as he wrapped her in his long coat and drew her close, his tone at odds with his actions.

"I admit it was rather foolish. At least the horse had better sense."

"You could've been seriously injured, or worse," he chided again, the words losing their sting as he gently rubbed circles up and down her back.

The linen shirt beneath her cheek was soft and reassuring as she clung to the vestiges of the dream, wishing she could keep reality away a while longer.

"What then, my darling girl? How would I ever live without you?"

Her subconscious had obviously conjured up her heart's desire—to stay safely in Ben's arms. Kate squared her jaw. Whatever happened today, everything would work out in the end. It had to. She refused to let Preston ruin her happily ever after twice.

She watched Ben from where she sat cris cross applesauce on top of a bookcase in need of a sanding, stain, and varnish. Her hands itched for a pencil to capture him without the responsibilities that normally furrowed his brow. Spying her bag next to the door, Kate hopped down to pull out a pen and small notebook, leaning against the wall to get a better view of her subject.

She started with the lock of hair lying across his forehead, moving steadily down toward the eyes and cheekbones, and finally the cleft chin. It was where Ben kept his stubbornness hidden and the tenderness he reserved for her and Henri in quiet moments. Kate had gotten lost in his eyes on more than one occasion, but the dent in his chin had become her weakness in direct correlation to the love she had for him.

Flipping to a new page and trailing her eyes down the length of him, she sketched the broad shoulders and torso encased in a threadbare undershirt. She was just filling in the defined muscles of his chest, where she'd laid her head the night before, when a loud knock sounded on the door, rousing the subject of her scrutiny. "That'll be Agent Sullivan. I had Aria call him last night."

"I imagine she was less than thrilled," he said, frowning.

"As thrilled as you look. Come on, let's get some breakfast. You know how you get when you're hungry," she tossed out lightly to avoid an argument.

His lips instantly formed a straight line to dispute her statement, and it was the tug on his uncollared shirt that gave away the real truth; Ben was worried about the plan they'd come up with over dessert. He hadn't been the only one. Every Kelly sitting around the table had put in their two cents, all of which amounted to a hill of coffee beans as far as Kate was concerned. This was her life, and she didn't intend to spend it running from her ex.

After throwing on some clothes, they sedately made their way into the kitchen, where Agent Sullivan and Aria sat in a staring contest over mugs of hot coffee. Laura handed a cup of tea to her and Ben, whispering, "They've been doing this for the last five minutes."

Kate would have laughed but her nervous system was pumping enough adrenaline through her body to short circuit her brain into thinking something was funny when in reality it wasn't.

Agent Sullivan looked away from Aria first, which was telling, concluded Kate. Obviously, there was more to their story, but her curiosity would have to wait until later.

"You ready for this?"

Taking a deep breath, she said, "As ready as I'll ever be."

Last night, as part of the plan they'd formulated, Kate called Stephanie and asked her to contact Preston at the number he'd left with his current alias printed in bold block letters as if he wasn't a felon.

"When you get to the shop, stay calm. Let him approach you. I'll be nearby; you'll never be out of my sight," said Sully.

Kate bobbed her head up and down in response.

"You never did explain why Kate has to be the bait. Is it because you can't find him without her?" Aria taunted.

Agent Sullivan ignored her, choosing to look at Kate when he answered the question. "As it turns out, Preston's no dummy. In the time since I started looking into him, he's either made some friends in high places, or they were the ones pulling the strings to begin with," he said without compunction. "Unfortunately, for him and his cronies, the mob doesn't take kindly to outsiders dipping their hands into the family cookie jar. I know someone on the inside who'd be more than happy to make your ex go away without any help on your part. Just say the word."

Kate took a deep breath. If Sully was implying what she

thought he was, she could walk away now and be on a flight back to Bee Hill with Ben tonight. It would be no less than what Preston deserved if he were guilty of everything Nick and Agent Sullivan had hinted at. But would it be true justice? She wasn't the only one who had suffered at his hands. Didn't everyone who had been on the receiving end of his duplicity and abuse deserve to have their day in court?

"Death would be an easy out for both of us. Preston deserves to have the full weight of the law come down on him. He should serve time for every person he hurt, not just me," she finished, watching Ben's face.

"Of course you'd think that." Ben pulled her to himself and kissed her forehead. "Sometimes I wish you weren't quite so brave, but then again, how could I ever ask you to be anyone other than yourself?" He switched his focus to Agent Sullivan. "I'm going with you."

"You're a civilian. You aren't going anywhere."

"I'll stay out of the way."

"So will I," said Aria, crossing her arms in a defensive motion. "I'm coming too."

"Aria," Sully warned.

"You owe me, and you know it. I'm the only reason you have an inside man," she stated smugly, a feline smile gracing her mouth.

"Way to be subtle," Sully fired back, closing his eyes briefly. "I was trying to keep you out of this."

Nick's jaw clenched as he turned away from his daughter's highchair, the tiny spoon with mushy glop stopping halfway to Ailis' gaping mouth. "Are you saying what I think you're saying? Because if you are, Ma is going to flip her lid six ways to Sunday!"

Everyone went still at his rare outburst—everyone except Aria.

"Who do you think sent me to see Uncle Guido?" she said, waving away her brother's concerns and turning back to her main opponent. "When do we leave?"

Chapter 26

Kate

Kate got ready, enjoying the rare sight of Ben without his shirt as he shaved the stubble from his face—cheekbone to jaw, rinse and repeat. He'd opened the bathroom door at her knock in nothing except a pair of well-worn jeans slung low on his hips, his already dark hair a jet black from the recent shower. She wanted to tackle him and make out but reached for the tube of toothpaste he passed her instead. Unfortunately, they were once again in a bustling house filled with Kellys, not that they had time to indulge in any of her fantasies anyway.

Ben finished and kissed her cheek, leaving without a word. She sat down on the closed toilet seat, twisting the toothbrush back and forth, mulling over what the next couple of hours might hold. Agent Sullivan seemed certain she wouldn't be in any real danger, but even thinking of Preston made her break out into a cold sweat.

Kate stood and spit into the sink, slurping water from her brush and rinsing once more before reaching for the travel-sized roll-on in her toiletry bag. She gave herself an extra swipe to be sure and checked her reflection in the mirror, the mask Preston preferred perfectly in place as if she hadn't changed in the four years since she'd walked away. Hair straight, sleek, and pulled into a tight ponytail, it accented her cheekbones and exposed the column of her neck—check. Every button of her shirt, including the top one, fastened, and makeup lightly applied in a neutral shade—check.

Anything more, and he'd think her tacky.

"Sluts wear heavy makeup and reveal too much cleavage." Kate cringed as if she were still sitting beside him at an upscale restaurant in downtown Atlanta. The dress was new, and she'd taken extra care with her appearance for the special occasion.

"Any woman who dresses like a whore is begging for it," he'd said, staring pointedly at the stilettos she'd paired with a long sheath dress, the side slitted to her knee.

As if a woman couldn't dress or primp to please herself. Preston wore what he liked, or so she assumed, yet he'd had a double standard for her, not to mention the creep factor. How had she ever married a man who believed a woman was "begging for it" with the way she dressed?

In his deranged thinking, had her ex justified trafficking those women because of how they presented themselves? Or had they simply had the misfortune to be lonely and without anyone to watch out for them?

Kate placed her hand on her stomach and forced the bile back down her throat. Though Agent Sullivan had been less than forthcoming with the details, she knew enough to know Preston's criminal activities preceded his marriage to her. She also knew her father had refused to invest in any of his so-called lucrative schemes after the wedding.

She would always wonder if her parents' money had been the reason Preston pursued her to begin with. Breathing in through her nose and out through her mouth, she steeled her nerves with every piece of jewelry she put on.

They were classic: pearl earrings from her momma, a dainty gold watch—a match of the one Eliza wore to commemorate their undergrad—and the amethyst ring her grandma Howard had left her. Nothing Preston would think out of place or over the top, but if she was going into battle, then she was also taking with her the women who had loved and cared for her in countless ways.

Tugging the cuffs of her starched, white blouse into place and tucking the bottom fully into her pencil slacks, Kate adjusted the thin, black belt at her waist until the shiny buckle was front and center. Last, but most importantly, she slid her feet into the ballet flats she'd borrowed from one of Laura's sister in-laws. They were tight but met the requirement. Giving herself a once over in the full-length mirror hanging on the back of the bathroom door, she accepted the ensemble for the armor it was.

Tomorrow, I'll be me again.

Like every day before this one, tomorrow sat on the horizon with a promise of hope for something better. It was a promise Kate would cling to for the next few hours. Convinced of her future, she turned away from the specter in the mirror and made her way down the stairs. "This isn't a funeral," she said, trying to lighten the mood of the group who waited below in the foyer.

Ben's smile didn't quite reach his eyes.

Ben

Kate always looked put together, regardless of what she wore or the way she did her hair, but this was a different version of the woman he knew and loved. Her usual bold colors and the heels she adored were nowhere in sight, as if she'd tried to mute herself, or blend in with someone else's expectations. This was careful cultivation instead of the vibrant confidence Ben was used to. He found it infuriating.

"Give us a minute," he requested quietly and watched as Aria left with Agent Sullivan through the front door. Hugs and a half second later, Laura disappeared with Nick into the kitchen, where Luna Kelly waited with food no one had the stomach to eat.

"No heels today?" Ben asked as calmly as he could, his temper simmering near the surface, and threatening to boil over in as much as it ever did.

"Preston prefers me in flats."

"And everything else?" he asked evenly, controlled.

"A mask. Or armor, depending on how you want to see it," she replied, cupping his clean-shaven jaw in her hand, the cold stare she'd adopted finally softening beneath his panicked gaze.

Ben refused to let Preston take anything more from her—*from them.*

Taking the hand at his jaw, he placed it over his heart, the beat steadying beneath her touch. "Soul to soul, mask, or no mask, I see you. *All* of you," he said placing his forehead to hers. "I'm yours Kate, in every way a man can be."

She bobbed her head in agreement and kissed his firm lips, lingering long enough to reassure him and ease some of the earlier tension between them.

They rode with Agent Sullivan and Aria to the shop, the silence fraught with emotions and fears no one wanted to give into. If the circumstances had been any different, Ben might have enjoyed the short tour and arrival at Lavender Honey & Co., Brooklyn. As it was, he tried to keep the weak tea and bagel he'd had at breakfast from making an abrupt appearance in the back of the car. He wiped his sweaty palms on his pants and took one of Kate's hands in his, giving it a gentle squeeze.

They parked a couple of blocks away, but with a clear view of the shop. Trees waved hello, greeting every passerby with their early summer garments of dark green, the breeze easing the humidity and temperatures momentarily. Thunder cracked in the distance, the dark clouds above threatening to make the weather report right.

"Stephanie called Preston yesterday to let him know you'd be at the store after closing to go over inventory. My guess is he's already keeping a lookout and will try to intercept you at the door," said Agent Sullivan into the otherwise silent car.

"Do I try to get him inside?" Kate asked.

"No. We don't want a hostage situation."

Kate visibly blanched, and Ben fisted the hand not holding hers.

"Preston will try to keep things casual, make it seem like it's a coincidence running into you. Try not to spook him, but you don't have to be overly friendly either."

Kate took a deep breath. "Okay."

"I'll have eyes on you the entire time, and I have people stationed throughout the area. If he's playing a long game, he'll only want to make initial contact. We can try again if we don't get what we need this time."

"Again?" Aria demanded. "You didn't say anything about Kate needing to meet with him repeatedly."

Ben would've jumped in, but Agent Sullivan wasn't paying attention to anyone but the woman sitting next to him.

"He's gone to ground before. We don't want to alert him and risk doing so again," he reasoned. "The more information I have, the better my case. It might take time."

He turned to Kate. "Get him talking, but don't act like you know anything about his…extracurricular activities. Miller hook you up with a wire?"

She nodded.

"Grim," Agent Sullivan said into the air. "Are we coming in loud and clear?"

"Crystal, bossman," crackled a voice over the radio at his shoulder.

"Aria's right. Let's get this over with," said Kate, resigned.

Taking another deep breath, she stepped out of the car and onto the sidewalk without a backward glance. Ben watched the sway of her hips as she walked away, his heart beating furiously in revolt and damning him for letting her go so easily. The three of them watched her cross the street, the keys to the shop already in a protective grip. She stepped up onto the curb as a man in a suit approached, his pace unhurried but his stride purposeful. Despite the distance, Ben could see the cost of the suit by the perfection in its tailoring. Aside from that detail, he only noted the fair hair, hard jaw, and self-assured smile the man flashed.

Ben wanted nothing more than to beat Preston to a bloody pulp, especially when he touched Kate. At first, the gesture appeared light and flirty, the kind of touch used to imply interest or a degree of comfort with the other person. It made Ben see red, and he checked his emotions to the cargo hold of his brain.

Now was not the time for jealousy or anger. He needed to keep calm and focus on her—except now Preston had his hand wrapped around her elbow and appeared to be steering her away from the shop. "Where's he going; where's he taking Kate?" Ben asked loudly in the small space. It didn't matter. One second she was there and the next she was gone.

Occupied with giving his colleagues directions over the radio, Ben used the momentary distraction for the opportunity it was and exited the car before Agent Sullivan could stop him. Running in the direction he'd last seen Kate and looking around frantically, he caught sight of the wire she'd been wearing smashed on the corner where the shop met up with a cross street.

Preston had obviously found the device, or he'd known law enforcement was watching him the entire time. Ben's earlier suspicions about the FBI and Agent Sullivan's previous comments coalesced into one horrifying concept: Kate was the bait, but not to trap a lowly pawn like her ex-husband.

No, what they were after were Preston's connections to the city's upper echelons. The FBI wanted to take down the puppets pulling Preston's strings; the ones who would expect him to tie up any potential loose ends unless he wanted to find himself without their protection, or worse, dead in a ditch. This was so much worse than Ben had ever imagined.

My darling girl, where are you?

His head snapped back up as though someone had called his

name. *There*, said his inner voice—a glimpse of long blonde hair at the next block.

"Kate!" Ben ran, the frantic beat of his heart trying to keep pace with his feet and failing. Agent Sullivan and his team would have to put things together on their own. He couldn't wait or else he chanced losing her all together. Rounding the corner where he'd last seen her, he came to an abrupt halt. Between the rows of buildings was a neighborhood park with a modern art installation in the center of it. The towering pieces of marbled sculpture offered a degree of privacy from prying eyes but couldn't quite disguise the pair within its cluster of stones.

Sully

"Great, now you've lost Kate *and* Ben."

He knew better than to bring civilians into a case, but his judgment where Aria was concerned tended to skew in her favor. Even now, she was telling him what to do in her bossy, take-charge demeanor as if he were a rookie who'd landed the job by chance. In all fairness, she didn't know the full extent of his background, but as a former operator this entire situation was child's play.

Sully stared hard at the woman who barely came to his shoulder, willing her to zip it with a glare. Finding Ben would have to wait. The guy wasn't his priority anyway; Kate's safety came first.

Besides, the Brit didn't seem like the type to go running into danger. Chances were, he'd give up and come back to the car.

Curtly giving directions to his team over the radio clipped at his shoulder, he side-eyed the woman to his left. With enough agents and tech to cover every block for a square mile, time was still of the essence. He'd underestimated Preston, and while he would have preferred to take down those behind the man, he could live with picking them off one at a time.

Kate's ex would likely turn state's evidence for a deal anyway. The bigger the rat, the better the deal, it seemed. Sully's jaw clenched painfully. He needed to find a new line of work, and soon.

The radio crackled. "Yo, bossman, I've got something from the camera at the light on the corner of 4th Street and 5th Avenue. A couple veered into the park there."

"You got that, Miller?"

"Yes sir, on it," she replied.

"Stay here," he ordered Aria.

Aria analyzed her nails as though doing otherwise had never crossed her mind.

"Whatever."

The woman was the biggest pain in the craw he'd ever met. Sully took off at a run in the direction of the park going the opposite direction Ben had and threw a quick glance over his shoulder. Aria stood by the car studying her nails and looking bored, but she didn't fool him. He could see the rigidity in her stance, and the fear lining her face as she refused to look his way.

"Talk to me, Grim," he commanded. Isaac Grimaldi was a former Army Ranger and one of the best tech specialists he'd ever worked with. The man was a genius with computers and operation systems. Fortunately for the United States government, the techie was one of the good guys, because he could hack into anything. He was also one of the best sharpshooters Sully had ever seen, though he preferred the van to field work these days.

"I can't get a clear view, but they're inside some sort of art display at the center of the park."

"I'm entering through the southeast gate now. Miller?"

"Ready when you are, sir."

"Move in slow, and don't do anything until we have a clear view of the perp and Kate."

"Got it."

"Everyone else, remove the other occupants as discreetly as possible. We don't want to create panic or draw attention."

He and Miller steadily crept across the park and into position, taking note as other undercover agents quietly removed children and families from the playground until the area was cleared of bystanders. Fortunately, it was dinner time on a weeknight, and sparsely populated.

Later, he'd admit it was the last thing to go right.

Sully got into position behind one of the sculptures. Distracted, Preston kept his back toward them as he shook Kate violently and threatened to do her bodily harm if she didn't cooperate. Sully had prepared to move in when, at the last second, he noticed the gun concealed by a hand and loose clothing; things had gone from complicated to disastrous in a blink. Shaking his head from side to side, he conveyed the necessary information to Miller with his eyes. She nodded in the affirmative from her vantage point.

To make matters worse, Ben now stood out in the open five feet away, looking like he was about to do something foolish and heroic.

Eff me.

The only way this scenario could get any worse was if Aria ignored his instructions and joined in on the unfolding idiocy. May God have mercy on his soul if she did because he wouldn't hesitate to kill Preston as soon as he had a clear shot. Not only was she his best chance at closing his other case, but his feelings for her had surpassed any a handler should have for an asset months ago. It was a boundary Sully knew better than to cross, but there was no turning back now.

Giving Kate another hard shake, Preston finally noticed the bystander in his field of vision. "This isn't any of your business. Move on," he said pointing the gun at the other man.

"Right. I'm afraid I can't do that," Ben said, inching forward.

Daylight was beginning to sink behind the nearby buildings, the light playing tricks on the eyes as it turned to dusk. Did the Brit still have his vest on or was the shirt he'd worn navy, Sully asked himself.

Shit. He was losing his edge.

"No, Preston, don't!"

Sully watched as Kate grappled for the gun, trying to wrest it from her ex's hands. He stepped forward to intercede, but it was too late.

Bang! Bang! Bang!

Ben stumbled back under the assault of bullets and crumpled to the ground. Kate used the moment to escape Preston's hold, sprinting forward as he turned the gun on her. Without a second thought, Sully pulled the trigger of his standard issue Glock and dropped Preston with a direct hit to the chest.

"No, no, no," Kate pleaded, dragging Ben into her lap and searching for the source of blood pooling onto the dark pavement beneath the first stars in the night sky. "God, please, no," she rocked. "I love you; please don't leave me," she begged helplessly.

"Civilian down. Agent requesting an ambulance," Miller spoke into her radio.

Sully placed his fingers on Preston's neck, searching for a pulse, but already knowing he wouldn't find one. Curse or gift, the outcome never changed. Kate's ex was simply another death at his hands. "Perp is dead. I repeat, the threat is gone," he said into his radio.

Chapter 27

Kate

Three months later, Kate watched a warmly lit Clatter Hall come into view as the car made its way down the long drive. She smoothed the skirts of her ivory, duchesse silk ballgown with gold embroidered lavender bushes and bumble bees and nervously adjusted the locket at her neck as she tugged the bodice of her dress up. In her limited experience with them, strapless dresses were a gravity disaster waiting to happen, but Beth Howard had insisted this was the perfect gown for Bee Hill's first annual gala to raise awareness about domestic violence.

In fact, her parents, Laura, and every single Kelly family member were all going to be in attendance to show their support for her. Even Uncle Joe had come, despite his fear of flying. Kate teared up. She'd come so far from that first phone call for help, and farther since her arrival in London two years ago.

Never in her wildest dreams did she think she'd be the face of abuse, but she was one of the lucky ones, thanks to her family and friends. Now, it was her turn to advocate for those who weren't so fortunate, and it was the least she could do under the circumstances. Kate double checked to be sure she'd put her speech notes and a Cadbury Twirl into the evening clutch her mother had loaned her. One could never be sure when a need for chocolate would strike, and nerves always made her hungry.

Patting the back of her hair to make sure her intricate chignon was still in place, she took the hand of the gentleman who opened her door, stepping onto the newly poured gravel in gold, strappy heels, her toes painted a creamy pink to match her nails. When she'd agreed to confront Preston, her sole consolation had been that she'd return to London with Ben, so they could start their life together. Kate looked at her naked ring finger and sighed in resignation, stowing her hopes away into the pocket of her dress next to the handkerchief her mother insisted she take for the occasion. She ran her thumb over the initials sown into the fabric.

True to his word, Ben had brought her home to Bee Hill, and Lavender Honey & Co. had become an extension of the farm. A two-is-better-than-one kind of concept or "all for one, and one for all," as Henri liked to quote from *The Three Musketeers*. Ben had also implemented all of her suggestions to grow Bee Hill's clientele and acquired a loan to turn the entire estate into a venue for destination weddings and events like the gala. They planned to include the farm's offerings as packages for purchase by couples, guests, and corporations.

"Brilliant, bloody brilliant, my darling girl. How'd I get so lucky?" Ben said, looking awed, when she presented the idea for consideration. For every snip Preston had sliced into Kate's confidence, the man she loved sowed a stitch to close the wound. Loving him was easy, and he returned the sentiment in both words and deed every day. Still, he seemed to have forgotten their previous conversation and neither Henri, Percival, nor the other farm mammals had suggested her single status would change anytime soon.

"Wow. You truly are breathtaking," Ben complimented in the accent that always made her go week in the knees no matter how many times she heard it. He stepped away from the vestibule where he'd been waiting. The man made her positively swoony in a tuxedo with tails, a real-life knight in shining armor, the dents and scratches he bore from the battles he'd won or lost through life making him the perfect match for her. Kate beamed as he took her hand and kissed the top of it before tucking it through his arm.

"So, about tonight—" he said, haltingly, causing her to look at him in alarm.

"Oh no, what's wrong? Is it the catering company? The florist left an hour ago, but the musicians should be warming up by now. It's okay," she said, rambling. "Whatever the problem is, I'm sure I can fix it." Ben held fast to her as she tried to veer off to the right in the direction of the wing containing the ballroom and recently renovated orangery.

"Nothing is wrong. In fact, everything is perfect," he reassured her as they walked the long hallway to the back of the house and onto the veranda overlooking the gardens, where Henri and Percival waited in matching off white bowties.

Kate's hands flew to her mouth in surprise as Ben dropped to his knee, a blue velvet box open in his hands. "Kate, I love you to the sun and back—"

"That's a lot," Henri interrupted as Percival barked in agreement.

She turned to look at the little boy dressed in a pint-size tuxedo and her heart melted, tears beginning to pinprick her eyes.

Ben cleared his throat to draw her attention back to himself. "I know spontaneity is highly overrated, but I was hoping you might do me the honor of becoming my wife."

"Please, please, pretty please, Kate," cajoled Henri, dropping to his knee beside his father.

"Darling, will you marry me…tonight?"

"Yes," she exclaimed, and Ben instantly swept her into his arms and swung her around in a circle, kissing her as they went.

"Whew!" said Henri as he swiped his brow. "Percy and I were worried there for a second. Weren't we, boy?" he asked his companion, receiving a bark in confirmation.

Kate and Ben laughed in unison while he slid a trinity ring

of yellow, white, and rose gold onto her finger, the diamonds nested within the thin bands winking in the candlelight. "It's not extravagant," he said, reaching for his bowtie.

"Three for friendship, faith, and fidelity. And for the three of us," piped Heri as he slipped his hand into Ben's.

"Aye, my brave boy."

"It's perfect," Kate whispered with awe, and it was. So long as he was at her side, it could be a key chain ring, and she would be deliriously happy. Cupping his jaw in her hand, she leaned in for another kiss, one of gratitude and unbridled joy.

"Eww, gross. Percival, I think that's our cue." The dog trotted after his boy toward the stairs leading onto the lawn.

"Actually, it's our cue as well," said Ben, leaning in to kiss her forehead before escorting her down the steps behind the other two scampering out into the garden.

"What do you mean? The guests for the gala will be arriving any moment now."

"The guests are already here and waiting for us at the abbey. You did hear the part where I asked you to marry me *tonight*?" Ben said nervously, stopping midstride. "We'll still hold the gala, but in the spring." He caressed her cheek. "Forgive me, but I couldn't wait another day to officially make you mine."

"But I planned...oh never mind what I had planned," she said, feeling witless with shock and excitement. "So, to be clear, the invites I sent out—"

"Never went out. Agnes swapped them out for wedding invites and your family has been in on the plan from the beginning," he explained, leading her through the gardens, their blooms heavy and pungent with the scent of delphinium, hollyhock, and peonies.

"Which explains my mother's overbearing involvement in the details."

"Sorry about that, but I needed her help, and she is a rather formidable woman," he grumbled, as if it hadn't been his idea to include her in the planning.

"Oh, you unfortunate soul. Did she run you over with lists and enthusiasm?"

"Only once or twice, but truth be told, I was hoping you'd feel a bit sorry for me," he replied with a wink.

She grinned all the way to her eyes, followed quickly by a frown. "Wait, don't the British traditionally get married in the morning or afternoon?"

"Aye, but this is more romantic, don't you think?" Ben said and kissed her cheek, handing her off to her father, who was waiting in front of the abbey entry, framed by wisteria. "Cal," he acknowledged, shaking the man's hand firmly.

"Ben."

"I'll be the one at the front, desperately hoping you don't change your mind in the next few minutes," he said and walked through the single existing door of the crumbling structure, giving Kate a moment with her father before the ceremony started.

"Hi, cow eyes. Don't you look as pretty as a fairytale princess."

"Hi Daddy, I'm so glad you're here." Of the three of them, Lon and Laura had always seemed to understand the gentle and quiet man standing before her best. Marrying Preston had only widened the gap between them—until now.

"Me too."

Kate looked down at the cobbled walkway someone had recently laid. The man she loved had been a busy bee, indeed. "I know my record isn't exactly stellar, but I picked a good one this time," she said, toeing the clover between the cobbles.

Cal Howard raised his daughter's chin gently with a finger until she met his gaze. "If I didn't think so, I wouldn't have said yes when Ben asked for your hand."

Delaying their flight to London and proving yet again how different he and Preston were, Ben had insisted they spend a few days with her parents, despite the time he'd already spent recovering from his wound. Kate sighed, weary of her ex's shadow. This should have been one of the happiest moments of her life, yet he'd still found a way to butt in on their special day.

"I can't say I'm sorry Preston is dead. I only wish I'd done a better job of protecting you to begin with. Can you ever forgive me?" said her father, his voice hollow with regret.

She knew how he felt. If she could go back and change the past she would, but all she could do now was live a new life born from the hard lessons she'd learned.

"Sometimes, you can't protect a person from themselves and it's not like you knew Preston would turn out to be a total loser."

"I knew enough."

"Promise you'll keep the porchlight on for me?" Kate asked, extending an olive branch in peace for a battle they'd both lost to a man who couldn't hurt anyone ever again.

"You can always come home," he said staunchly and pulled her in for a hug. "I love you, cow eyes."

"I love you too, Daddy," she whispered, hearing the click of closure on her former life as another door opened to her future. Tonight was the next chapter in a different book. One where she was more than a victim or a survivor. In this story, Kate was the leading lady of her life.

Her father caught a tear she failed to keep in check. "Now, let's get you hitched. I'm hungry and your momma's been talking about the reception for weeks," he said, handing her a bouquet of lavender, thistle, and roses.

Kate laughed knowingly.

Her father wound her arm through his, patting the top of her hand and walking her toward the future she'd hoped for on her darkest days. Being a hopeless romantic wasn't for the weak. It meant trusting herself enough to take a leap of faith, despite the possibility of failure. Kate knew Ben was the only one for her, but if for some reason it didn't work out, she knew she was strong enough to fight for another day. She would never again be someone's victim;

she was so much more than that and always had been.

She gasped as they crossed the threshold, the sound carrying through the space. Candelabras lined the aisle and lit the way forward to where Ben stood with Henri, Sam, and Felix at his side. The scent of fresh flowers and lavender hung in the night air and filled the sanctuary, while a thousand stars twinkled through the open ceiling. It was better than any fresco, and even more romantic than she'd imagined it would be.

Waiting opposite the gentlemen were Laura, Eliza, and Althea, each dressed in a floor-length gown of midnight blue. Leave it to Beth Howard to have every detail ironed out to perfection. Kate looked to the left to find her mother, dabbing discreetly at her eyes with a handkerchief, and mouthed, "Thank you."

Beth acknowledged her with a slight dip of her head, the navy feather in her fascinator bobbing with the movement. Laura and Eliza grinned mischievously from the front and blew Kate matching kisses as the string quartet started up with a song from Etta James.

Kate's eyes met Ben's as she walked toward the future. At last, she had found someone who loved her for everything she was and, more importantly, for who she wasn't.

Ben

Terror didn't begin to touch the feeling he'd had watching Kate walk away from him and out of sight with Preston so many months ago. Ben would have gladly taken a bullet to the chest to keep her safe and out of her ex-husband's hands, but he was thankful the vest had done its job. Aside from the scar he'd bear as a permanent reminder on his shoulder, he'd only been sore and bruised.

Though the other victims would never get their pound of flesh, the loss of Preston was hard for him to mourn, especially when the occasional nightmare still crept in to remind him of what the alternative could have been. Ben cast off the shadow of the dead man and turned his focus back to the present and his bride.

He planned to spend the rest of his life showering Kate with adoration and the sexy pillow talk he knew she liked. His darling girl might blush on the outside, but she was delightfully kinky beneath her classy veneer. He was more than happy to play out whatever fantasies she had and with no doubt as to how satisfied they would both be in the end.

Now all he had to do was get through the ceremony and stay an acceptable amount of time at the reception. He'd made reservations at a self-serve rental for the weekend before they left for a weeklong trip on the Isle of Skye. He intended to make the most of the privacy, count every single freckle on her body, and worship her until the only thing left on her lips was his name and complete surrender.

Kate handed her bouquet to Laura and placed her hands in his. Ben fell into her whisky eyes, content to drown there for the rest of his life. "I, Bennett Alexander Keats Galloway, take you, Kate Felicity Howard, to be my wife; to have and to hold from this day forward, for better, for worse, for richer, for poorer, in sickness and in health, to love and to cherish, till death us do part, according to God's holy law."

He looked at the minister who dipped his head in acknowledgment. The words he spoke next weren't part of the traditional vows, but rather an addition meant to convey a message to the woman he loved. "I promise to respect and honor you in body and word, to be your best friend, and your partner, to take your family as my own and to love them as I love you."

Kate smiled tenderly in understanding and repeated her own vows. As he escorted his wife down the aisle to applause, he caught a wink from Agnes beside his father, who wore the Galloway kilt in bright green and red. Some things never changed.

An hour later, Ben watched the friendly carnage unfold around him as the guests from his side proceeded to get smashed and dance awkwardly in the middle of the room, Henri spinning in circles with Percival at his heels. And was that Merlin under the cake table with a rat in his mouth? His new mother-in-law was going to have a conniption. He reached for his collar. The infernal thing was cutting off the supply of blood to his head.

His bride laughed, garnering his full attention. Ben smiled and turned toward Kate just in time for the piece of cake she shoved into his mouth.

"Here, you look hungry."

"If you ever tell your mother, I'll deny it, but she was right," he said around the mouthful she'd benevolently shared from her slices.

"About the cake?"

"Aye. Chocolate is far superior, regardless of tradition."

"I don't know, I kind of like the fruit cake."

"Liar."

"I didn't say it was my favorite."

"True."

"You know, I bet cake of any kind is better in bed," she said with a suggestive smirk.

"I like where your head is at."

"What do you say we take this with us and sneak out through the orangery?"

"Oh, my darling girl," he said as he entwined his fingers with hers. "Wait until you see what I can do with cake," he finished suggestively, causing her to shiver with anticipation.

"Does it involve your mouth?" she asked, breathless and starting to flush.

"The best things always do," Ben promised solemnly.

"Here," Kate said, thrusting the plate of cake into his hands and making him chuckle. "Let's make a run for it!

Picking up her skirts all the way to her knees, Ben admired her ability to run in heels and increased his own pace as he imagined her wearing nothing but them.

"All set for bed?" asked Ben, preparing to tuck his son in with a chapter or two. Though Henri tolerated fantasy for Kate's sake, he'd fallen head over heels for historical fiction. It was the best of both worlds for him.

"Ready Kate? Henri asked, reaching for her hand.

His wife's dimples peeked out in response to his obvious choice. Ben took no offense, knowing she did all the voices when narrating. He'd dallied by the door a time or two himself in order to hear her impressions of Blackbeard and Churchill.

"Don't take too long, darling," Ben whispered.

Kate gave him a coy smile in return. Construction on the cottage started Monday. They were adding a bedroom with an extra lavatory off the back of the house. His wife's only request had been enough space for a king-sized, four-poster bed and high-quality insulation within the walls. He liked where her head was at. And, if he'd included a tiny studio in the plans as a surprise for her renewed interest in drawing—where he fully intended to be her model—no fairy godmother would ever chide him. It was, after all, his personal mission to make all of her dreams come true.

She glanced back at him over her shoulder, as if she'd read his mind and he winked.

It felt like his heart might burst right out his chest with all of the emotion it held. When it miraculously stayed put, he set the needle to the gramophone, prodded the fire in the hearth to life, and poured a couple of drams as he waited for his wife to join him. He watched from the corner of his eye as Merlin slinked inside to find his own bed upstairs.

His entire world had turned upside down with one woman's appearance on his doorstep. Without Monique, he would have neither Henri nor the farm, and without Bee Hill, there would be no Kate. What he'd assumed had been the end of the story had, in fact, only been the beginning. Opening the book he'd started the previous night, he settled deeper into the couch as his eyelids grew heavy in the firelight casting shadows throughout the room.

Once upon a time, in a land filled with magic and lost heroes, an embattled princess arose from the ashes to become a powerful queen. Because, dear reader, a woman who recognizes her worth is a fearsome creature to behold. For in the end, it isn't how someone treats you that decides who you are, but rather what you do with it that reveals the truth.

As for the honorable lord our queen married and the child born under a full moon, they lived happily ever after—with one wizard, two knights of the round table, three Greek muses, the four horses of the apocalypse, and an errant black sheep. And no, we won't speak of the sultan and his harem, at least, not in polite company.

Epilogue

Aria opened her eyes to a gloomy winter sky, her arm flung over the other side of the bed and the covers wrestled beneath her. She wiped the drool from the corner of her mouth and cursed the noise that had pulled her from a dream she'd much rather be in.

THUD-THUD-THUD, resumed the sound of pounding on steel. Her brother was a dead man for coming by so early. Aria squinted in the direction of the alarm clock. Fine, ten-thirty wasn't early. Still, Nick and Laura needed to have another kid if he had the time to swing by on a Saturday morning when her kids were spending the weekend at Nonna's.

She swung her legs over the side of the bed and pushed up, the white button-down shirt soft from repeated washing falling to her knees with the motion.

THUD-THUD-THUD, pounded a fist against the door again.

"Coming," she yelled, her voice carrying through the tall ceilings of the loft.

She shivered, padding quickly across the freezing hardwood floors she'd paid a gazillion to refinish. The bank had passed her over for the vacant manager's position at her branch, in lieu of the president's nephew—shocker. Aria rolled her eyes yet again, giving nepotism the proverbial middle finger.

So, she kept doing what she did best: hustle. She could balance any set of books, and in half the time it would take her new manager. Her sisters called her a human calculator, but credits and debits made more sense than most people's decisions to her way of thinking. Of course, where the money came from or went to was something she never asked about. She only accepted cash for payment and ignored the fact that her clientele was shady, despite being married to a cop for thirteen years. A girl had to pay the bills somehow.

She checked the peephole, catching sight of broad shoulders and dark hair as she rubbed away an eye boogie and pulled her hair into a messy bun.

With a hard tug on the fire door her brothers had insisted on, she said, "Hold your horses, Nick—"

The words died on her tongue as she took in the man standing there with a coffee carrier, a white paper bag plopped haphazardly beside the cups. She closed the door in his face.

The loud, repetitive pounding resumed from a hand that had once touched her with such tenderness and deliberation she'd cried. Aria squeezed her eyes shut to erase the image.

"Aria, open the door," commanded a deep voice, making her melt like butter in a saucepan. She hated him all the more for it.

"Come on, songbird. Let me explain," he said more quietly, his nickname for her reverent upon his lips.

Forehead to the door, she sighed, weary, but eventually opened it wide enough to see a hard jaw covered in dark stubble. "What you do want, Sully?"

"You," he said, his gaze boring into hers.

"Well, you had your chance," she said, beginning to close the door in his face again.

"I brought croissants," he said with a lift of the carrier and confirming her earlier guess. "You eat; I'll talk."

"Fine," said Aria, snatching the bag from him and digging out a croissant filled with sweet almond paste—her favorite, regardless of who'd bought them.

"So, we're going to do this here, in the hallway?"

"I'm a fast eater; you should start talking."

"Songbird—"

Waving a croissant with one hand and jabbing her finger into the solid muscle of his chest, she said, "You lost the right to call me by that name when you disappeared without a trace three months ago."

"The dress shirt you're wearing might suggest otherwise," he replied too smugly for her liking, which only infuriated her further. It didn't matter if the shirt was his; it wasn't the reason she wore it, or so she told herself. Aria stuffed the last of the flaky goodness into her mouth, causing her cheek to puff out like a chipmunk's, and easily pulled the shirt over her head.

The momentary satisfaction she experienced as he hungrily took in every curve on display from head to toe disappeared in another flash of anger. "Here, you can have your shirt back," she said, balling the material and throwing it in his face.

He didn't drop the hot coffee, and part of her wished he had, but Sully had proven his ability to assess the real threat in any situation, including her temper.

"Aria," he pleaded, hoarsely. "I swear things are not what they appear to be."

"They never are with you." She sank her teeth into her lower lip to stop the tremble there.

She slammed the door again and marched into the bathroom. Ignoring the cost to her pocketbook, she turned the water on and let it run until the steam clouded her reflection in the mirror over the sink. The rainfall shower head had been worth the extra cost, and she raked the water painfully through her knotted tresses, refusing to acknowledge the taste of salt on her lips or the sobs shaking her frame.

She closed her eyes, the night before he'd left looping like a movie on repeat behind her eyelids.

"I have to leave for a few weeks…on assignment," he said into the quiet kitchen.

"What's the case?" she asked, chopping garlic at the center aisle Sully had helped her brothers install the month before.

When he didn't respond, she turned to find him leaning against the opposite counter.

"Let me guess, you can't tell me?"

"Sorry, songbird."

"I know," she sighed and gave him a shrug. "It comes with the job." She turned back to the garlic, determined not to ruin the evening with her worries. The kids would be home from school soon, and she didn't want to waste the time they had. "When do you leave?" she asked over her shoulder.

"Tomorrow."

"Oh. So soon?"

"I got word a couple of hours ago." Sully watched her solemnly, but didn't try to make her feel better. This was part of the dance they did. When Miles died, she swore she'd never fall for another first responder. But as the saying goes, *Want to make God laugh? Then tell him your plans.* Only she had gone and fallen for a commando instead. Well, a retired one who worked for the FBI, in any case.

"Call me when you get back?" she asked, trying to be nonchalant. After all, they were a distraction, not a couple, or so she told herself.

He nodded in the affirmative, tracking her movements in his typically intense way, and tugging on her apron until her back met his solid front. Sully wrapped his arms around her and nuzzled her neck, causing a giggle to escape, then hummed with the satisfaction of hearing it.

She had never been much of a giggler, but this man, who rarely smiled himself, knew exactly how to draw it out of her. In those hours spent with Sully, she wasn't only a single mother or someone's daughter or sister. With him, she was also a woman—desired, cherished, chosen.

After eating and tucking the kids in, they watched a movie, falling asleep together on the couch. He eased her off his chest and nimbly stood. Covering her with a plush throw and kissing her temple, he whispered, "Someday, I won't have to leave."

Whether it was for her benefit or his, she didn't know. Perhaps it had only been a dream, but she'd carried Sully's promise with her until he broke it, right along with whatever Miles had left of her heart when he died.

When Sully didn't call after three weeks, she excused it; the assignment had gone long. By the time week five came along, Aria was mad enough to swallow her pride and call him instead. The least he could do was to let her know he was still alive, even if he was no longer interested in whatever it was they'd been doing. But even that was a dead end; his voicemail was full, as though he hadn't used his phone in a while.

If the worst had happened, would anyone notify her? It's not like they were married. She'd never been to his place. They either went out or spent their time in the loft. She had no idea if Sully had friends or family, and he never talked about his work aside from letting her know when he'd be busy with it. He was a man of few words and private, but he'd seemed content to be an honorary member of the Kelly clan.

By the end of week eight, Nick asked a contact of his at the police department to check in with the FBI's White-Collar Crimes Division. But they had no record of Agent Tobias Sullivan—which was impossible because he'd been involved with the situation around Kate's ex-husband six months earlier.

It was as if Sully had vanished into thin air—that is, right up until she'd seen him standing outside the Ritz-Carlton near Manhattan's Central Park, dressed in a suit perfectly tailored to his powerful physique with a striking redhead hanging on his arm. The worst part, though, was she'd been so relieved to see him—alive— that for a split second she'd forgotten to be angry, sad, or a million other emotions she'd felt over the last three months.

Then he looked up, and the expression on his face said everything Aria needed to know. The man she knew, the one she'd fallen for despite her better judgment, that man no longer existed. Maybe he never had.

The End

Turn the page for a glimpse of Aria and Sully's story in

The Songbird Laundromat:

Coming Fall 2026

The Songbird Laudromat

Chapter 1

Nine months prior.

Aria

Buildings were funny things, thought Aria as she looked at the one in front of her. Constructed from concrete, wood, and glass, they sheltered dreams, housed hopes, and provided livelihoods. A witness to decisions, both good and bad, they were the literal foundation on which so many lives were built. On the other hand, they could also bury someone alive.

As far as she was concerned, the latter was exactly what the World Trade Center had done to her husband when he responded on 9/11. Not immediately, but in the end, the Towers claimed yet another life when Miles Wrenn died from a stroke at the early age of forty-two—not that they'd been able to prove it or receive any compensation from the government. Thirteen years with New York's police department, and not a single bullet wound or major injury—which, at the time she married him, had been her biggest fear. Life wasn't fair.

Aria swallowed the old bitterness. At least her younger brothers hadn't suffered the same fate as the other first responders in the family. Leo's cancer seemed to be responding well to chemo, and Nick was expecting his first child any day now. Maybe God had deigned to finally take mercy on her family.

She looked at the surrounding neighborhood and checked the address she'd written on a pink memo pad at the bank. Williamsburg was one of Brooklyn's recently gentrified neighborhoods, with art around every corner. Whether it was a sculpture, gallery, or mural splashed across large swaths of vertical surface area, everything about the area screamed creative beautification.

In contrast, the squatty, plain building before her stood out like a sore thumb, one that could easily be ignored if you weren't looking for it. The word LAUNDROMAT, outlined in black paint, was all the sign said against an otherwise dingy white background. She shaded her eyes with her hands and tried to see past the glare and old school shade drawn over the dusty window in the door.

The plastic sign read OPEN in neon orange, but someone

must have forgotten to turn the sign over the previous night at closing. Jiggling the door handle for a second time, Aria added some pressure and hoped it was only stuck the way old doors did sometimes. It didn't budge.

Her Uncle Guido had recommended the place. Okay, technically, he wasn't her uncle—more like a friend of her deceased Nonno, twice removed. But since her mother called him uncle, she and her siblings did too. Italian relations had as much to do with whoever had your back as they did blood, as far as her mother was concerned. And whatever Luna Ramono Kelly decided was the way it was. It would be easier to squeeze blood from a turnip than try to change her mother's mind—impossible and a waste of time.

Aria looked around again and then down at the ant piles forming in between the cracks of the sidewalk. She plucked a single dandelion from the many lining the nondescript, single-story building, closing her eyes and blowing on the fluff until the seeds scattered in every direction. She smiled tenderly. Miles used to tell her every seed counted as a wish, so whatever she wished for should be worthy of all those seeds.

Click went the lock on the other side of the door at the same time the shade rolled up with a muffled whir. Aria reached for the handle again and stepped into the whitewashed cinderblock space lined with stacked washers on one side and jumbo dryers on the other. There was barely room for a counter and register. One of the long fluorescent lights overhead flickered, drawing her attention to where it dangled precariously from a wire looped through a water-stained ceiling tile.

"What can I do ya for, gorgeous?" asked an older man wearing polyester brown slacks and a striped shirt with a wide collar, the top two buttons open to expose curly, grey chest hair. He removed his fedora and ran his hand over a thick mass of silver hair slick with pomade.

Aria blinked. "Um, Uncle Guido sent me," she said hesitantly.

"Luna's oldest girl, huh?" The man, who had yet to introduce himself, pushed off the wall and put his hat back on at the same time. Tucking a toothpick between his thin lips, he said, "Come on, then."

Come on where, Aria wondered. There wasn't anywhere to go. She followed him down a short, narrow hallway hidden behind the entry door she'd left open.

The first door they passed was labeled TOILET with one of those black and gold stickers affixed at an angle as if someone had done it without a level or ruler.

Amateurs.

The only other door was to the left of the bathroom, this one unlabeled. The older gentleman opened it, flipping on a light switch and illuminating what she presumed was the basement and any additional space not occupied behind the laundromat on the first floor. Aria gasped in surprise but followed him down the stairs, grabbing onto the banister when the structure seemed to sway beneath her with a loud groan.

"You get used to it," said her tour guide with a casual shrug.

A wood stage backed up to the far wall, littered with Edwardian-era dining chairs, their chintz fabric faded with dust and age. Against the left wall was a bar and a gilded mirror half covered by a flower-patterned bed sheet. Tables for craps and blackjack littered the rest of the space in the center.

"What was this place?"

"Originally, who knows, but in the twenties it was a bona fide speakeasy."

"During Prohibition?"

"Yeah. Bunch of junk, if you ask me, but Boss thinks it's nostalgic."

"Oh?" Aria asked absently as she continued to take in her surroundings.

"I'm not wearing this outfit for my health. Today is freaky Friday."

"Exactly what does that mean?"

"You'll see," he said, rapping a knuckle on the only door in the otherwise open space, another black and gold sticker slapped across the front to designate its status as an office.

"Come in," yelled a deep voice from the other side.

Mister No-name opened the door, gave a small tip of his hat, and strode off in the direction they'd come. Aria could hear running water coming from behind the partially closed door in the corner. The office was nothing to write home about, filled with the standard desk and a chair on wheels, along with several tall filing cabinets shoved into the area on the right. Behind the desk hung a large canvas painting similar to Monet's *Water Lilies*, only done in garish colors.

"Like it?" asked the deep voice she'd heard moments ago. "My wife thinks she's the next Jackson Pollock. Personally, I don't get the hype, but whatever keeps the little woman happy, you know?"

Aria spun around, finding herself face to face with a replica of John Travolta from *Staying Alive*, with the exception of a bulging middle, over which his white jumpsuit stretched tautly. She did a double-take at the long pipe wrench in his meaty hand. He held it up. "Pipe was leaking. Wanted to make sure it was fixed before you got started."

"Great," she squeaked, schooling her features and extending her hand in introduction. "Aria Kelly Wrenn."

"Tony," said the wrench-wielding man, shaking her hand and smiling broadly. "Welcome to the family business."

Jesus, Mary, and Joseph. Broke or not, this might be the dumbest thing she'd ever done.

"Books to balance are in the green cabinets," said Tony amiably. "Guido said to keep everything on the up and up, unless I want to face Aunt Luna's wrath."

Aria let out a huffed laugh. Of course, her mother had laid out the parameters on her behalf. Her father must be rolling over in his grave. Not that it mattered, because he wasn't here, and she needed the money—to finish the loft, to pay for Eleanor and Finn's school tuition, to give herself any breathing room until she made branch manager.

"Here are the keys. Remember, don't open the black one.

"Got it."

He grinned again and turned to leave.

"Wait! What about the laundromat?"

"What about it?"

"Is it…open?"

"You mean, is it a front?"

She bobbed her head up and down, not sure if she wanted the answer. The less she knew, the better for the sake of her…overall well-being.

Tony winked and merely said, "Everything has to get clean somehow."

The door shut behind him, and Aria reached for the desk to hold herself upright until it swung open again. Tony stuck his head back inside.

"I almost forgot, you get five sick days and a week's vacation every year. Sorry, no health insurance, the premiums are murder in this business."

"Makes sense."

"And no dress code except for Fridays."

"Oh?"

"Next week's theme is Rockin' Eighties, babe," he said, playing air guitar and tossing his head like he had long hair.

"Like, I can hardly wait, man," she replied, trying to be a good sport. It took all of her willpower.

Tony smiled and shut the door once more. Aria sighed, weary.

Hail Mary, full of grace. What the flip *have I gotten myself into?*

Author's Note

If you've experienced domestic violence or know someone who is currently experiencing it, please contact The National Domestic Violence Hotline for the US at 800-799-7233 (SAFE) or text BEGIN to 8878 or visit the website at www.thehotline.org. You are not alone, and advocates are waiting to help you.

If you have concerns or questions about your child's development, please contact your pediatrician, who can help you find the resources and support you may need. As a parent or guardian, you are your child's first and best advocate.

All stores mentioned by name were located in London as of 2024, with the exception of Sweet Bitter Bakes, Lavender Honey & Co., and Bee Hill, which only exist in my imagination.

I have long been a fan of historical romance novels and, with a nod to this, had a bit of fun coming up with a *nom de plume* using the letters of my own name. To my knowledge, Jinn Royce doesn't otherwise exist, and neither does her book *The Pirate and His Thief.*

A "bothie" is a simple shelter most often found in remote parts of the United Kingdom, especially in Scotland, Wales, and Northumberland. I took the liberty of adding one to Bee Hill for the purpose of the story and because I love how history constantly comes to life in a place like Britain. While they were once used by shepherds, they are now more often used to provide refuge for hillwalkers, climbers, and hunters during inclement weather. Please check with The Mountain Bothies Association at www.mountainbothies.org.uk for more information about use and approval.

A "brolly" is slang for an umbrella in the UK. Isn't it fun to say? Truth be told, I rarely use one myself. After living in the Pacific Northwest for over twenty years, I much prefer the practicality of Gore-Tex coats and a pair of boots (wellies) to a brolly with a more fashionable outfit. I'm certain Kate Howard would be properly horrified.

Lindores Abbey Distillery in Newburgh, Scotland was my inspiration for an abbey wedding. Not only do they host weddings on the grounds of the former abbey, but they also produce good Scotch whisky. Visit them at wwwlidoresabbeydistillery.com, or better yet, stop in for a dram and their history tour. *Slàinte mhath.*

Acknowledgments

Heavenly Father, thank You for everything, but most of all, for teaching me to define my worth through Your love. Here's to my wildest dreams and trusting you can make them happen, no matter which road I travel.

Michael, thank you for holding down the fort Stateside. Maybe someday you'll find the pieces of yourself within my stories. I hope they make you smile. Mama and Daddy, thank you for believing in me. I couldn't do any of this without your love and support.

Brianna Showalter, thank you for your steadfast friendship half a world away, and while I hope to see you regularly between now and then, I'll meet you at "the cottage" someday, friend. Cheers to the creative dream!

Arlyn Lawrence, editor extraordinaire. Thank you for your encouragement, direction, and teaching. I'll be sure to let you know when the film industry comes calling. Ha, ha, just doing some manifesting.

And finally, my readers. Thank you for reading *Bee Hill*. I hope you enjoyed Ben, Kate, and Henri's story. So far, this has been the hardest story for me to tell. I worried about doing justice to Kate's experience because I know not every Domestic Violence survivor has family or friends waiting in the wings, let alone a Cinderella story in the end. In the same vein, I'm aware that not every child who has autism spectrum disorder (ASD) is like Henri. Human beings are unique individuals, regardless of the labels we attach to them.

I'm certainly no J.R.R. Tolkien, but long before it was trending, he understood the importance of empathy and courage. One changes the lens we look through, and the other has the power to change someone's life. Be the light you want to see in the world; choose empathy, advocate where you can, but most of all, be who only *you* can be.

Appendix

....

Kate's "Cheater" Recipe for Popcorn with Chocolate Drizzle & Shredded Coconut

Ingredients:

2 bags of microwaveable popcorn

1/2 cup of white chocolate chips

1/2 cup of milk chocolate chips

Shredded coconut (sweetened)—enough to sprinkle over the top

Directions:

Pop one bag of popcorn at a time according to the manufacturer's directions and pour it into a large bowl.

Place your white and milk chocolate chips into separate microwave-safe bowls. Microwave one bowl at a time for 30 seconds. Stir and return to the microwave for another 15 seconds if needed. Repeat until the chocolate is melted.

Drizzle the chocolate over the popcorn and sprinkle with coconut to the desired coverage.

Bon Appetit!

Author's Playlist

Head Above Water by Avril Lavigne
Hang on Little Tomato by Pink Martini
Better By Myself by Jamie Miller
Classic by MKTO
Cherry Wine by grentperez
Nice to Meet Ya by Niall Horan
Christmas Sweater by Michael Bublé
Valentine by Laufey
One Too Many by Keith Urban & P!NK
One of Those Days by Kyle Hume
Good Day to Have a Great Day by Russell Dickerson
Optimist by Crash Adams
Troubled Waters by Alex Warren
Santa Tell Me (Live version) by Ariana Grande
Imagination by Laura Anglade
Lift Me Up by Blessing Offor
Slowly by Julianna Raye
Sweet Love by Myles Smith
Sunrise by Forrest Frank
Reckless by The Strike
I Hear a Symphony by Cody Fry
Turbulence by P!NK
Give You Love by Forest Blakk
At Last by Leftover Cuties

About the Author

 **Jaclyn Robinson** calls Washington State home, but was born in New Jersey and has lived in multiple places in between. She currently lives in Seoul, South Korea, with her husband, three children, and a cairn terrier named Mungo. Though she holds a B.S. in Exercise and Sport Science, she's been plotting stories in her head for as long as she can remember. Her reading habits are a bit compulsive, and while she has a penchant for romance, she'll read whatever is at hand. This tendency can sometimes make for interesting, if not downright, awkward conversation on her part. She drinks copious amounts of tea and adores sea salt caramels with her scotch. Neat and smooth, please. Ms. Robinson believes one can never have enough books in any form and, if given the choice, would spend eternity in an incredibly old and famous library.

www.jaclynerobinson.com